CREATIVITY IN BUSINESS

CREATIVITY IN BUSINESS

Michael Ray
Rochelle Myers

DOUBLEDAY
NEW YORK LONDON TORONTO SYDNEY AUCKLAND

A Main Street Book
PUBLISHED BY DOUBLEDAY
a division of Bantam Doubleday Dell Publishing Group, Inc.
1540 Broadway, New York, New York 10036

MAIN STREET BOOKS, DOUBLEDAY, and the portrayal of a
building with a tree are trademarks of Doubleday, a
division of Bantam Doubleday Dell Publishing Group, Inc.

Permissions are on page vi.

Library of Congress Cataloging-in-Publication Data
Ray, Michael L.
    Creativity in business/Michael Ray, Rochelle Myers.
        p. cm.
    Bibliography: p.
    Includes index
    1. Creative ability in business.   I. Myers, Rochelle.
II. Title.
HD53.R39   1989   88-18892
650.1—dc19   CIP
ISBN 0-385-24851-2 (pbk.)

Dedicated to
the Creative Resource
within everyone and
to those who enjoy
making life itself
a work of art.

Acknowledgment is made for permission to reprint excerpts from the following:

"Sweet Surrender" Words and Music by John Denver © 1974 by Walt Disney Music Company and Cherry Lane Music Company. Words Reprinted by Permission.

"The New Age Interview: Dr. Rupert Sheldrake" by Robert Anton Wilson, *New Age Journal,* February 1984. Copyright © Rising Star Associates, Ltd. Partnership.

I Am That, Third Edition, Revised, by Swami Muktananda. Published 1983 by SYDA Foundation. Copyright © 1978, Gurudev Siddha Peeth, Ganeshpuri, India. All rights reserved.

Siddha Yoga Correspondence Course. Published by SYDA Foundation. Copyright © 1983, Gurudev Siddah Peeth, Ganeshpuri, India. All rights reserved.

Hatha Yoga for Meditators. Published by SYDA Foundation. Copyright © 1981, Gurudev Siddha Peeth, Ganeshpuri, India. All rights reserved.

"The Kaleidoscopic Brain: Spontaneous Geometric Images May Be the Key to Creativity" by Roger N. Shepard, *Psychology Today,* June 1983. Copyright © American Psychological Association.

Siddha Path, November 1984, April 1983 and September 1984. Copyright © SYDA Foundation.

An Actor Prepares by Constantin Stanislavski. Used by permission of the publisher, Theater Arts Books. Copyright 1936 by Theater Arts, Inc. Copyright 1948 by Elizabeth R. Hapgood. All rights reserved.

The manuscript "Extended Perception Through Photography and Suggestion:" by Minor White courtesy The Minor White Archive, Princeton University. Copyright © 1986 by The Trustees of Princeton University.

"Knowing Your Other Mind" by Dudley Lynch, *American Way,* March 1982. Published by American Airlines. Copyright © 1982, Dudley Lynch.

Listening to the Body by Robert Masters and Jean Houston. Published by Dell, 1979. Copyright © Robert Masters and Jean Houston.

"Quotations from Chairman Bennis," *Humanistic Psychology Newsletter,* 1984. Published by the Association for Humanistic Psychology.

Personal Freedom by Arthur Deikman. Published by The Viking Press. Copyright © 1976, Arthur J. Deikman.

X-ray diffraction of Beryl by I.W. Bailey from *Structure in Art and in Science* edited by Gyorgy Kepes. Published by George Braziller, New York, 1965. Reprinted by permission of the publisher.

A flat representation of Gold (Element 79), from *Mandala* by José and Miriam Argüelles. Copyright © 1972 by José and Miriam Argüelles and by Shambala Publications, Inc. Reprinted by permission of the publisher, Shambala Publications, Inc.

Peanuts ® for March 10, 1985. Copyright © United Feature Syndicate, Inc.: by permission.

"Decisions Decisions," United Technologies advertisement. Copyright © United Technologies Inc.

"Intuition Is Good for Business" by James Bolen, *Psychic,* November/December 1974.

"Books and Ideas: Spreading the Word about Business" by Robert Lubar, *Fortune,* March 7, 1983. Copyright © 1983, Time Inc. All rights reserved.

"A Conversation with Jonas Salk" by Peter Stoler, *Psychology Today,* March 1983. Copyright © 1983, American Psychological Association.

"Little Gidding" in *Four Quartets* by T. S. Eliot, copyright 1943 by T. S. Eliot; renewed 1971 by Esme Valerie Eliot. Reprinted by permission of Harcourt Brace Jovanovich, Inc.

Story on Steven Jobs by Michael Rogers and Gerald C. Lubenow, *Newsweek,* September 23, 1985.

Yin/Yang illustrations from *The I Ching Workbook* by R. L. Wing. Published by Doubleday & Co., Inc. Copyright © 1979 by Immedia.

Lucid Dreaming: The Power of Being Awake and Aware in Your Dreams by Stephen LaBerge. Published by Jeremy P. Tarcher, Inc. Copyright © 1985 by Stephen LaBerge, Ph.D.

Mukteshwari, Volume 2, by Swami Muktananda. Published by SYDA Foundation. Copyright © 1973, Shree Gurudev Ashram, Ganeshpuri, India. All rights reserved.

Chapter Sixty-Six from Lao Tsu, *Tao Te Ching,* translated by Gia-fu Feng and Jane English. Published by Alfred A. Knopf, Inc. Copyright © 1972 by Gia-fu Feng and Jane English.

The Tao of Pooh by Benjamin Hoff. Published by E. P. Dutton, Inc. Copyright © 1982 by Benjamin Hoff.

ACKNOWLEDGMENTS

Appropriately enough this book on creativity has been nourished by many sources, including the creative example of family, friends, colleagues, co-workers, and business associates, as well as the creative professionalism of those involved in its production. To these people we give special thanks.

Our first experiences of creativity were provided beautifully and lovingly by our parents. Michael's father, Michael F. Ray, is still going strong and growing every day.

Michael's wife Sarah and daughter Sandy are evidence of the will, strength, and joy of creativity. Michael thanks Sarah in particular for absolutely changing his life, for giving him deep experiences of his own creativity, and for being a true friend. Our friend Annette Dell'Osso (Rochelle's administrative director) is an exemplification of the compassion we all must manifest to be creative in our lives. Rochelle especially thanks her for her genuine lovingkindness.

Dean Robert Jaedicke of Stanford's Graduate School of Business was an associate dean at the time he shepherded our course, Creativity in Business, through to its first offering. Associate deans Chuck Holloway and Gene Webb have been supportive through the years, sometimes by challenging our approaches. Michael's secretary Sylvia Lorton made her contributions look effortless. Betsy Friebel turned word processing into an art. And Lorna Catford started out as a research assistant, helped with editing, and finally became a full-fledged collaborator in our work at Stanford.

There is of course no way that we can fully thank our students. Perhaps the highest accolade we can give to them is that they became our teachers. Six of them have come back as speakers in their own right and many are quoted and named in this book. We wish we could name every single one of them, but specifically thank for their support and creativity Dan Lorimer, Tom Shannon, Bobby Toda, and Kelly Teevan. Dan was a partner and catalyst at the beginning of this project.

The first feature stories about our course were by Marcia Tanner, then a writer at Stanford, and by Eric Berg of the *New York Times*. Like many of our speakers, we didn't see that our work had any particular significance until someone outside saw it for us.

Once we left the confines of our course and Stanford, we were helped in many ways by a very wise and creative man: Michael's brother, Richard M. Ray. If there is a guiding force behind this book, it is surely Dick. He has been involved with every aspect of the book from initial concept all the way through to final boards for printing. His business partner, Bill Tomlinson, gave us his complete support also. And what wonderful people from the Catered Graphics firm worked with us: Jim Jenkins, Kathleen Parker, Linda Encinas, Janine M. Hunter, Miriam Boucher, Henry Dierkoph, Stewart Jenkins, and illustrator Roy Jones.

Paul Thackery routinely performed miracles in turning our manuscript into computer diskettes for publishing.

We can't imagine better or more complete editing than we have had on this book. Peggy Brandstrom Pavel brought her very considerable heart to the book. She is as precise as an engineer, as open as a blossoming bud. Peggy had support of her own from her husband Victor Pavel, who brought the experience of a substantial business career to bear on a careful reading of the manuscript.

While the Pavels helped us from Honolulu, Jonathan P. Latimer added his incisive editing from New York. Jon gave us encouragement as well. He saw both the potential and practicality of the book, and we thank him for that.

After the rest of us were finished having our cuts at the manuscript, we were most fortunate to have Les Pockell of Doubleday apply his sharp editorial sense on it. Les was ably assisted by Karen Johnston.

To all of them we say — in the manner of Siddha Yoga — with great love and respect: Thank you, thank you, and thank you.

CONTENTS

INTRODUCTION

One of the main problems in U.S. business today is that there are too many ideas, not too few. Dozens of solutions appear and disappear in chaotic piles of data, crowds of expert opinion, and a jumble of contradictory statistics and reports on every aspect of every issue. The pressure of limited time is increased by indecision and, beneath it all, the nagging suspicion that others will find your efforts insufficient and the results poor.

As we looked at this problem in the late seventies, it became clear that its solution lay in cutting through the chaos to reach the underlying answers. And the key to doing that lay in the creativity of the individual business person.

At about the same time, the media also saw the chaos. In 1980, *Time* ran a cover story that attributed inflation, low productivity, and failing international markets to management techniques and university MBA programs. *Business Week, Fortune, Dun's Review, Esquire, Atlantic Monthly,* and *Newsweek* quickly joined the attack. All made reasonably uniform criticisms: MBAs specifically, and American business generally, had become too analytical, too dependent on numbers, too conservative, unconcerned with people, shortsighted, and as a whole shamefully uncreative.

The worst of it was that their criticisms were valid. Some professionals even felt that nothing could be done about it. In a November 1980 issue, *Business Week* quoted an associate dean at the Wharton School of Business: "Is it true that we haven't been teaching creativity enough? Probably. [But] who knows how to do that? No one."

In recognition of this business-world turmoil, we launched a course called Creativity in Business for the Master of Business Administration program at Stanford.

A short time later, the media discovered a more positive trend in U.S. business. In February 1982 *Time* ran a cover story that heralded, "Striking it Rich . . . America's Risk Takers." The story featured four creative business leaders (who spoke to our classes and appear in this book): Steve Jobs of Apple Computer; Charles Schwab of Charles Schwab Discount Brokers; James Treybig of Tandem Computers; and Nolan Bushnell, video game innovator and founder of Atari, Pizza Time Theater, and Catalyst Technologies. The point of the *Time* article, and a number of others, was that through the general despair there emerged "a more cheerful phenomenon: the surprising surge in innovative businesses in America today, and the new generation of capitalists who are risking, and often winning, huge sums with their venturesome companies." One senior editor said, "It is the other, upbeat side of the economy."

About that time Harold J. Leavitt (another of our speakers) became big news in academic circles when he (one of the founders of managerial psychology) began to emphasize the nonanalytic aspects of management. James March promulgated his "garbage-can" model of organizational decision-making, and Henry Mintzburg applied split-brain research to business. James Adams — author of *Conceptual Blockbusting,* and another course speaker — compared this renaissance to the creativity of the fifties, when there was a flurry of interest in such idea-generating techniques as brainstorming, morphological analysis, and synectics. But, said he, the difference between the fifties and the eighties was a notable one; *now* these techniques were being related to the underlying human quality of intuition, and were supported by scientific findings.

Dun's Review ran a cover story called "Business Probes the Creative Spark," and many publications echoed this new business thrust: *MBA Magazine* with "Managerial Intuition"; *Fortune* with "Those Business Hunches Are More Than Blind Faith"; the *Wall Street Journal* with "How Do You Know When to Rely on Your Intuition?"

Even corporate advertising and promotion took notice. Motorola based a campaign on the Japanese challenge, Sperry on listening. Phillips Petroleum developed a film series called "The Search for Solutions." One Phillips ad headline was, "When curiosity flourishes, worlds can be changed." Standard Oil's television series, "Creativity with Bill Moyers" had several business-related segments.

As we developed our Stanford course, then, the prevailing business climate included an ongoing storm of concern over the failure of the scientific, analytic approach as well as a freshening wind of hope in the intuitive alternative. Both of us had worked in the creative area of business for decades: Myers as an artist and musician who had consulted with businesses through the Myers Institute for Creative Studies; Ray as a social psychologist and business professor who started bringing creativity into classes in the early sixties. We had each repeatedly observed that without the involvement of some very deep personal sources of creativity, idea-generating techniques used alone could produce confusion—or at best, short-term gains. As with the proverbial Chinese meal, an hour later and you're hungry again.

So we decided to try to create a course that would awaken students to their inner creative source, and that would show them how such creativity applied to their daily business lives. Such a course would depend very heavily on our own personal convictions that such a source exists. Initially, neither of us probably had much more sense of exalted certainty than the next guy, but we did have some very hopeful beliefs, plus firm threads of evidence running through our own individual lives.

Probably the most important aspect of our course and this book is that we go directly to what helps people bring out useful creativity in business. We don't try to solve the basic mystery of the physiological, cognitive, and social processes that underlie a creative act. Instead we simply note with excitement all the validations of the existence of a beneficial creative force coming from the research laboratories; we revel in each insight gained from spiritual works in both the Western and Eastern traditions; and most of all we glory in the steady, dynamic flow of confirmation and breakthroughs that come through our speakers as well as our students.

Who knows why our course works? But work it does. We—Myers and Ray—through teaching the course have gained the invaluable conviction that an ever-present creative source (in this book we call it Essence) is available to each one of us, and we have watched our students gain that same conviction as they prove it in their daily business lives.

Our wish is that this book brings the same conviction to you.

LAUGHTER, TEARS, AND APPLAUSE

A Thanks to Our Contributors

Over the past seven years at Stanford, we've had the privilege of hosting in our Creativity in Business class over sixty creative business leaders and creativity experts who realized that we were looking for more than just a recounting of their exploits. We knew about those already. What we wanted, and what our speakers were pleased to share with us, were their personal experiences.

We asked each to be "retrospectively introspective." Many said afterwards that speaking to our class was one of the most refreshing experiences they'd ever had because it was an opportunity to help others get to the most important aspect of life: the creative experience.

Each class is a celebration, a happening; students and speakers get absorbed in it immediately. Some speakers prepare extensively ahead of time. Others let the spirit of the moment grab them.

One who prepared was Tom Peters of *In Search of Excellence* fame. He said:

> *I really worked on this thing for today, which annoyed me when I realized—somewhere in the middle of last night—that I'd been had by a well-trained behavioral scientist. Ray invites me here, then he sort of casually hands me a list of the really famous people who have actually done things (who have spoken here before) and suggests that it's being taped. If one is either not famous or infamous, as the case may be, and wants to say things in private, that's a good incentive to get him to do something.*

Others were not so motivated to prepare before the class. Charles Schwab, founder of the discount brokerage, confessed:

> *I thought I'd just come down without knowing what I'm going to say, and just leap into conversation. It's all sequential. You don't know what I'm going to say, and I don't know either.*

The interaction between outstanding speakers and bright students produces unusually spirited interchanges, startling synergy. No group of working people, leaders, experts, and scholars has ever probed personal creativity *in business* in quite this way before.

The result was what you'd expect when creative energy is present. Lots of laughter. Some tears. And the kind of inside-outside applause that comes from the recognition of something great: the inner power we all possess but too seldom use.

The speakers came from a wide range of industries—from high-tech to smokestack, garbage collection to the arts, tableware to software, services to manufacturing—in both the private and public sectors. They also represented a wide range of jobs—consultants, line managers, entrepreneurs, scientists, marketers, organizational development specialists, human resources managers, finance and accounting officers. And they are responsible for an astonishing array of business and social phenomena, including: soft jazz mood music, creativity techniques in strategic planning, money market funds, rotoscope television commercials, video games, commercially applied radiation chemistry, multi-bank credit cards, sports performance videotapes, personal computers, fine stainless steel flatware, the marketing of Silicon Valley, discount brokerages, transformational management, major cures from genetic engineering, no-fault computers, wind energy farms, geodesic camping tents, consumer savings certificates of deposits, a deep slash (from fifty to twenty percent) in the capital gains tax, and the whole field of managerial psychology.

Even so, they convey the message that they are much like everyone else; they have their share of difficulties and anxieties, and in fact seem somewhat bemused by the attention they receive. One student expressed his admiration for Paul Cook's importance to Raychem, then asked: "What happens if you drop dead?"

Cook's reply: "If there isn't a strike, they'll probably bury me." The loud laughter was just as immediate as his reply.

Another student asked Bob Swanson of Genentech, "How do you feel about it being said that you have the opportunity to have a greater effect on the human race than any single person in this century?" [Laughter]

Swanson shot back with, "I guess I've always been a little more modest than that. [Laughter] Of course that's not a hard standard to meet."

Our students aren't in awe of the speakers, and the questions keep everybody modest. When sports psychologist and management consultant Joel Kirsch was talking about the bodily center the Japanese call *hara,* a student asked (to loud laughter), "That anything like the G-spot?"

"Oh, so this is what it's like to be back with students again," sighed Kirsch.

Hal Leavitt, who is an old hand at getting points across to students, was temporarily frustrated in trying to describe the devastating effects of socialization on creativity. Then he just let loose:

The reason I'm having trouble describing it is that it is such a pervasive problem that you can't say to someone, "Don't be socialized." We are just socialized as hell.

All of us go through the same environment. And all of us may learn the same skills. But there is some kind of distribution curve and way out there you can find somebody who says, "I got my Ph.D. in physics, but I still think it's horse shit!" (Laughter) *And them's the good guys!*

Some speakers question whether they have anything to say to a creativity class, because they don't really feel they have done anything particularly creative. Ted Nierenberg, founder and president of Dansk International Designs, Ltd., teary-eyed, his voice cracking with emotion, read a thank-you letter from his oldest daughter, Lisa. After reading it, he said:

> *That's what life is all about. When you are my age, and you get that kind of a letter from your kids, you've made it. To me that's the epitome of success—not just in business but in a total life. It's beyond all the self esteem, gratification, or gut feel you could imagine.*

We wish we could use this section as a repository for all of the gems that simply didn't fit into the rest of the book. Instead, we just thank our contributors and give you some idea of who they are.

* * *

Will Ackerman, founder and chairman of Windham Hill Records; guitarist

James Adams, professor of industrial and mechanical engineering; author of *Conceptual Blockbusting*

James F. Bandrowski, president of Strategic Action Associates; formerly director of planning, Di Giorgio Corporation

Tandy Beal, founder and director of the Tandy Beal Dance Company

James M. Benham, founder and chairman of the board, Capital Preservation Fund

Ron Berman, executive vice-president and executive creative director, Foote, Cone & Belding/Honig Advertising

Michael E. Bilich, managing director, F. A. Hoyt, Ltd.

Julius Brandstatter, physicist; consultant in behavioral decision-making

Nolan Bushnell, founder of Atari, Pizza Time Theater, Catalyst Technologies, and Sente

Lorna Catford, educational psychologist; writer; photographer

James C. Collins, management consultant; founder, Performance Sports Software, Inc.

Paul M. Cook, founder and president, Raychem Corporation

Gayle Delaney, psychologist; author of *Living Your Dreams*

Tom Dery, director of marketing, Ansett Airlines, Australia

Steve DeVore, founder and chairman, SyberVision Systems, Inc.

Jay Elliot, vice-president, human resources, Apple Computer

Joanne A. Ernst, triathelete; 1985 Female Triathelete of the Year

M. Scott Fitzgerald, formerly with Shell Oil and Fotomat; director, Confidential Consulting, Inc.

Ken Fox, hypnotherapist; director, Hypnosis Learning Institute for the Arts

Alissa Goldring, artist; photographer; consultant in dream work and dream analysis

Michael Gould, the founder and president of The Learning Tree Open University

Lewis Griggs, co-founder and director, Copeland-Griggs Productions; co-author, *Going International*

Victoria Hardy, director of William Carlos Williams Center and of the program in arts administration, Fairleigh Dickinson University

Willis Harman, professor of engineering and economic systems; futurist at SRI International; president, Institute of Noetic Sciences; Regent, University of California; author of *An Incomplete Guide to the Future* and *Higher Creativity*

Brian Hennessey, educational psychologist; president, Psykon, Inc.

Carol Hwoschinsky, psychologist; crisis counselor; expert on psychological aspects of money

Paul Hwoschinsky, venture capitalist and corporate director

Dale Ironson, psychologist; corporate human resources specialist

Steve Jobs, co-founder, Apple Computer; founder, Next, Inc.

Robert Kantor, psychologist; founder, The Pacific Graduate School

Joel Kirsch, psychologist; co-director, Kirsch Associates

Kenneth H. (Hap) Klopp, co-founder and CEO, The North Face, Inc.

Philip H. Knight, founder and CEO, NIKE, Inc.

Sandra L. Kurtzig, founder and chairman, ASK Computer Systems

Harold J. Leavitt, professor of organizational behavior; author of *Managerial Psychology* and *The Corporate Pathfinders*

Philip Lipetz, molecular biologist; chairman, General Molecular Applications; partner, Omnimax

Karen Malik, Northern California director, Monroe Institute

Robert Marcus, president and CEO, Alumax, Inc.

Regis McKenna, president, Regis McKenna, Inc.; author of *The Regis Touch*

Robert H. McKim, professor of mechanical engineering; partner, Onset, product development and financing; author of *Experiences in Visual Thinking*

Joseph H. McPherson, director of Innovation Programs, SRI International

Rene C. McPherson, former CEO, Dana Corporation

Robert W. Medearis, real-estate developer; corporate director; chairman, Silicon Valley Bank

Susan Miller, computer systems manager, Crocker Bank

William C. Miller, senior management consultant, Managing Change and Innovation Program, SRI International; author, *The Creative Edge*.

Robert A. Moog, founder and president, University Games, Inc.

Ted Nierenberg, founder, Dansk International Designs, Ltd.

Ken Oshman, co-founder and CEO, ROLM Corporation; vice-president, IBM Corporation

Howard W. Palefsky, president and CEO, Collagen Corporation

Helen Palmer, psychologist; director, Center for the Investigation and Training of Intuition

Thomas J. Peters, founder, The Tom Peters Group; co-author of *In Search of Excellence* and *A Passion for Excellence*

Michael Phillips, banking innovator; author of *The Seven Laws of Money* and *Honest Business*

Lisa Pickar, psychologist; meditation teacher; executive recruiter

Don Prentice, computer engineer; organization development specialist; founder, Perspectives

Lama Sogyal Rinpoche, founder, director of the worldwide Rigpa Centers

Anne Robinson, president, Windham Hill Records

Thomas Robinson, organizational development specialist and researcher

Heidi Roizen, co-founder and president, T/Maker Corporation

Claude N. Rosenberg, Jr., senior partner, Rosenberg Capital Mgmt.

Charles R. Schwab, founder and CEO, Charles Schwab & Co., Inc. discount brokers; director, Bank of America; author of *How To Be Your Own Stockbroker*

Marc Steuer, director of field support systems, Syntex Corporation

Vice-Admiral James B. Stockdale, America's most decorated naval hero; co-author of *In Love and War*

Peter Stroh, senior partner, Innovation Associates, Inc.

Robert A. Swanson, founder and president, Genentech, Inc.

James G. Treybig, founder and CEO, Tandem Computers, Inc.

Wayne Van Dyck, venture capitalist and founder, Windfarms, Ltd.

Jonathan Visbal, manager of market development, Pacific Telesis International

John Waldroup, real estate developer; educational innovator; owner, The Barnyard shopping complex

Stephen Westley, Northern California chairman, Democratic Party; program manager, GTE Sprint

Lee Wood, restaurateur; yoga instructor

Edwin V. Zschau, U.S. congressman, founder and formerly CEO of Systems Industries Inc.; former business professor at Stanford and Harvard

Brian R. Zwilling, formerly director of new products, Spalding Sports Worldwide; vice-president and general manager, Sporting Goods Division, Dielectric Industries

ESSENCE

1

BUSINESS AS ART

The uncreative life isn't worth living.

> Ted Nierenberg
> Founder
> Dansk International Designs, Ltd.

Creativity is within everyone. That is a really wild statement. But I really think it's true.

> Rene McPherson
> Former CEO
> Dana Industries

Imagination is more important than knowledge.
> Albert Einstein

Business is my art.

> Robert Marcus
> CEO, Alumax, Inc.

For most people, the word creativity is more easily applicable to art than to business. You expect the Picassos of the world to experience creative breakthroughs, but are less convinced that business people have anything to be creative about.

But a wise man has said, "Art is basically the production of order out of chaos," and isn't chaos the natural environment of business?

In speaking to our class, Wayne Van Dyck, founder of Windfarms, Ltd. and several other enterprises, had this to say:

The highest art form is really business. It is an extremely creative form, and can be more creative than all the things we classically think of as creative. In business, the tools with which you're working are dynamic: capital and people and markets and ideas. (These tools) all have lives of their own. So to take those things and to work with them and reorganize them in new and different ways turns out to be a very creative process.

Dozens of course speakers and hundreds of MBA and Sloan Management students and workshop participants have confirmed over and over again that successful business people approach their problems creatively. They might not verbalize in terms of art, but they express in myriad ways the same approach that artists do: They become totally immersed in expressing their inner visions, knowing that their chief challenge is to organize familiar materials in a fresh way. They are curious, adventurous, experimental, willing to take risks, and they are absorbed in meeting the challenges of their working day.

But even if the regeneration and sustenance of American business has been due to such creative individuals throughout its history, how does this relate to you now? The answer is that you too can contribute creatively, and by developing your own inherent creativity, you can lead a completely fulfilling and valuable life, both in and outside of business. You can live your life as a work of art.

The Heuristic Approach

The value of developing your inner resources becomes apparent as you look more deeply into the nature of creativity. Theresa Amabile provides this scientific definition in her book *The Social Psychology of Creativity:*

A response will be judged as creative to the extent that (a) it is both a novel and appropriate, useful, correct, or valuable response to the task at hand and (b) the task is heuristic rather than algorithmic.

The (a) of Amabile's definition is easy: What you do is creative if it is new, different, and helpful. Thus, if during a drive or walk or business meeting you do anything the least bit unusual that is "appropriate, useful, correct, or valuable," you are being creative. Even routine activities are likely to elicit something new: new perceptions, a new mood, a new need of the moment, a new decision or response.

Part (b) requires further definitions, however. A *heuristic* is an incomplete guideline or rule of thumb that can lead to learning or discovery. An *algorithm* is a complete mechanical rule for solving a problem or dealing with a situation.

Thus, according to Amabile, if a task is algorithmic, it imposes its own tried-and-true solution. If a task is heuristic, it offers no such clear path. You must create one.

But when is a situation in business totally algorithmic? Isn't it possible that a task becomes algorithmic only when you approach it algorithmically?

It is the premise of this book that a heuristic response to problems is the open-sesame to personal creativity in business.

Each of the following chapter titles are heuristics, and each chapter provides explanations, actual business experiences, and exercises for living with these credos or heuristics. Since heuristics are rules of thumb or guidelines for discovery, they relate to exploring your creativity as a road map relates to exploring a new area. Just like a road map, our heuristics don't tell you exactly what to do on your trip, when to leave, what vehicle to use, what route to take, or how far to go in what time period. They allow your own creativity to determine its own path. One student discovered:

Creativity isn't a destination, it's a journey.

With this heuristic approach to business, you can see that creative behavior is integral to business, because such behavior is useful, resourceful, correct, valuable, and self-expressive—not different for the sake of difference.

Creativity in business is a way of life. It is an ongoing process, not a series of isolated aberrations. It is a productive attitude developed by individuals throughout their business lifetimes, not a random good idea that happens to work.

Creativity thrives at all levels and in all phases of business. Beginning clerks, corporation heads and everyone in-between can be creative. This includes data analysts as well as the idea men and women in marketing and advertising.

Our approach also implies that creativity is more individual than organizational. Some people live creatively in smokestack industries in the American Midwest. Others stagnate in Silicon Valley. It's easier to be creative in a company whose policies invite it, of course, but corporate policy is not a requirement for individual creative expression.

Your Creative Experiences

The word "heuristic" has the same Greek root as the exclamation "Eureka!" so often accompanied in comic strips with the flashing light bulb of a new idea. The Eureka! phenomenon has been a part of discussions on creativity ever since the day Archimedes reportedly ran naked through the streets shouting "Eureka!" (I have found it)—having discovered, as he sat in a bath, his principle for identifying a metal's composition by the water it displaces.

Have you had any Eureka! experiences lately?

If we ask our students on the first day of class to rate themselves on a creativity scale, many put themselves below average. For that reason, we confront them with the task of recalling a time when they had a great idea, one that solved an important problem for them. By merely contemplating their own past experience and hearing the experiences of others, they recognize the presence of their own creativity.

You can do the same thing with the following exercise. As with all the exercises in this book, just reading the directions and the sample experiences can give you a sense of what the outcome will be for you if you complete the exercise. In this case, it may be enough for you to just quickly remember a time when you solved a problem. Or you might try doing this in a meditative way, as follows:

Sit comfortably, with your back straight and your hands in your lap. Close your eyes and breathe deeply into your belly. Notice your stomach rising and falling as you breathe from your center, doing easy abdominal breathing. Now think of a time when you had a great idea—one that solved a problem or dealt neatly with a situation. It doesn't have to be a business idea. If it was briefly important to you, that's enough.

With your eyes closed, breathing from your center, remember how it felt to have that idea. What was the specific problem? How long did you struggle, and against what? What emotions did you feel? How did your rational processes go? What was the Eureka! moment like? What were the surrounding conditions? What happened to you and your idea next? Was it actually used? How did that come about?

Enjoy the memory for as long as you like. When you open your eyes, consider taking the time for further exploration. You might write down the details, your feelings, and the upshot of this creative experience.

Over the past twenty years or so, thousands of people from all sorts of academic and business settings have done this exercise with us. No matter how uncreative someone believes himself to be, he soon recalls a past idea, and he eventually recalls many. These episodes are evidence of the inherent creativity in each individual.

Many of the great ideas, like the following two, are business-related.

Bill Camplisson, now director of marketing plans and programs at Ford-Europe, tells of a time when design engineers couldn't find a cost-effective way to produce, for a new sports car, bucket seats that would automatically adjust to body contours. Months of work seemed wasted on exorbitantly expensive mechanical models. One night Camplisson sat back, exhausted, in one of these seats and started daydreaming of playing on the seashore as a child. A big guy stepped on his beach ball, crumpling it. Camplisson (the child) started to cry. His father came running and pushed in the edges of the ball. Eureka! The ball popped out, as round and firm as new.

The dream beach ball exploded in Camplisson's mind. Through its dynamics, the engineers created a cost-effective design for bucket seats that responded to body contours.

A second example of a great idea comes from Mary Lou Shockley, now chief financial officer of the Spectrum Services division of Pacific Telesis. She relates that she had presented to her company, at that time Pacific Telephone, an analysis of their poor performance in the timely installation of data services. She was flying back to Los Angeles with her boss, Doug Fagg, having an end-of-the-day drink, when:

It dawned on me that the responsibility for the installation of the service was in the hands of only fifteen people in a department of sixteen hundred. Why not set up a club that would meet every two weeks over lunch to discuss the roadblocks to service installation?

Implementation of this idea required additional ideas and much hard work, but in six months Southern California's data service went from the worst to the best in the Bell System.

Many of the great ideas involve career changes. It seems that creativity blossoms for many people when they are doing something new, something that is forcing them to grow in all parts of their life. Like a new love or the renewal of an old one, a career change forces one to look at things in fresh ways.

Some great ideas are very personal and perhaps trivial to the outside world, but they are examples of creativity nonetheless. They give validation to each person's inner creativity.

One man, for instance, was extremely depressed after business and social failures and deaths in his family. His great idea recollection went back to childhood—when he was six years old and was sent with another boy to the principal's office to be disciplined for fighting. By telling the principal they were friends (having formed an uneasy alliance in the hall enroute), they avoided punishment. He applied that childhood success to his adult depression by making friends with himself. As with Camplisson's bucket-seat breakthrough, the solution came through a daydream. It led to his getting on with his life in a very positive way.

Your Inner Creative Resource

Reviewing your great ideas and those of others gives you impressions of the creative process. It seems that creativity starts with some problem or need and moves in various ways through a series of stages, consisting of information-gathering, digestion of the material, incubation or forgetting the problem, sudden inspiration (when the conditions are idiosyncratically right), and, finally, implementation.

But the creative process can be distinctive for every person and every idea. More important than striving to pin down the process is getting some experience and practice in living with your enormous, almost unfathomable, inner creative resource.

Jim Benham, founder of Capital Preservation Fund as well as of a performing jazz band, says this about his own creative process:

I really do get a lot of good ideas when I play my horn. This type of meditation I'm describing is a very creative process. When I practice my horn, I don't look at music. I don't read a note. I simply play, I play melodies that come into mind. I play scales. I play slow exercises. I'll be playing my horn and all of a sudden some business thought pops into my head. I'll go write it down. I don't know how to explain it, but that's just what happens.

Where *do* ideas come from? Benham is not alone in his puzzlement; the source of creativity has been a mystery throughout the ages. When you have an idea or when you have an experience of your own potential, what is it that you are experiencing? What can you expect if you were to fully realize your potential?

In some sense you can't describe your inner creative resource in words. It is the very fact that it is beyond words that makes it so potentially powerful in your life. So we emphasize experiences in this book—experiences of creative people in business and experiences you can have. But let's give you a starter description of your true potential.

Your inner resource is so immediate and yet timeless, so basic and overarching, so individual and also universal that we have chosen the word ''Essence'' to describe it. Our speakers and students, many philosophical traditions and even principles of great art cry out with what this creative resource can mean in business and life.

First, your inner creative Essence provides the quality of *intuition*: a direct knowing without conscious reasoning. Intuition has always been a powerful mainstay of great business, but until fairly recently it has been denied as a business tool in the era of overdependence on analysis. This is no longer true. Business people now speak of intuition with pride. It is considered a mark of management ability.

Artists would relate intuition to the art principle of design. And the word ''design'' describes perfectly what you are doing when you use your intuition. You see instantly with clarity the design of a solution, a design for your life.

But intuition alone is not enough either to describe your Essence or to sustain a creative life. A second quality, *will*, begins to fill in the picture. It is the part of you that can take responsibility. It is the ground of your creative actions. People who are creative in business have a compelling vision or mission, and this exemplifies will. It is most directly related to the art principle of unity, and it does have that characteristic of unifying, giving you a singular purpose to integrate all your creative breakthroughs.

The third quality of Essence is *joy*. This book could have been called *The Joy of Business* because, for all the work and frequent difficulty that creativity entails, it always brings a sense of joy. When you get a hint of your own creativity or potential, you always feel this bright, shimmering quality of joy. It is best related to the art quality of balance. When you have balance within yourself and between all parts of your life, you experience the joy of the flow of creativity.

We often talk about creativity in terms of breakthrough. And to break through a wall of fear and criticism that might stop you, you need a fourth quality, *strength*. Creative business people take appropriate risks. Their strength allows them to do that without even seeing risks as risky. This inner strength overcomes fear. This Essence quality is most closely related to the art principle of contrast. Just as an artist—a painter or a photographer or a choreographer or a composer—relies on contrast to make a strong point, the creative businessman has the strength to be new and different when new and different is exactly right. You have this strength within you, waiting to be tapped.

Finally you can draw on a fifth quality of Essence, *compassion*, to completely bring your creativity into the world. This compassion isn't the mushiness of do-gooders. Instead it is loving kindness, first for yourself and then for others. When you operate from this compassion you nurture your own ability, recognizing your own creativity and that of others. It causes you to experience the ultimate Eureka! feeling of "I Am." Creative business people can implement their creativity so well because they have that confidence in their own creativity and bring it out in others too. Compassion of this sort is best related to the art principle of harmony, and you can see how it can create harmony, not only among all the qualities of Essence but also in your business life.

Intuition, will, joy, strength, and compassion—these qualities of Essence form your creative base. Consider what your life would be like if you lived every moment with what you can have at your beck and call.

Philosophical and psychological traditions often emphasize the enormity of Essence by characterizing these qualities in totalities: infinite intuition (design), complete will (unity), absolute shimmering joy (balance), overwhelming strength (contrast), and boundless compassion (harmony).

This vision of creativity is far wider and deeper than mastery of problem-solving techniques. It is also far more personal, but at the same time impersonal. We look within to find our own individual and universal source. That source has been called the inner self, the Self, the hidden mind, the divine spark, the Divine Ego, the Great I Am, God, and Essence. Some say that the very purpose of human existence is to get acquainted with your own essential qualities and express them in your daily activities. Whether it is the purpose of life or not, it is a fine definition of personal creativity: living every moment from your Essence.

Bringing Art into Your Business Life

A question that has occurred to many thoughtful people might be coming to your mind now. If you have this inherent creativity within you, this Essence with its five magnificent qualities, why hasn't it appeared more often? Why haven't you been more naturally and consistently creative?

The answer is that your creativity has been inhibited by fear, negative personal judgment, and the chattering of your mind. Your creative Essence is often blocked by what is called the false personality, the ego or the external self.

And the key to personal creativity in business is in eliminating the conflict between false personality and Essence. The creativity techniques from the 1950s, such as brainstorming, do little to deal with this basic conflict—a conflict that keeps you from being consistently creative. Trying to destroy the false personality also has problems, because you can damage or submerge aspects of your persona that are truly valuable to developing your full potential. Your best approach is to awaken your own Essence by experiencing it strongly; then you can intelligently overcome your own false personality as your true self manifests itself more and more in your life.

This strategy builds on the kind of experience we have all had; a deep, personal love for someone. Such love is an experience of Essence. We know that when we're in love we are not very much affected by fear, negative internal judgments, or the endless chatter of a broken-record mind.

Of course it is not possible to fall deeply into love every day before we go to work. At least it's not possible for most of us. But it is clear that outstanding business people are successful because they deeply love what they do; they seem to live directly from Essence, without static from a false personality.

Only a few people naturally find this kind of love for their work and art in their life. For the rest of us, the Stanford course and this book offer ways to repeatedly experience personal creativity. With practice it becomes natural to replace confusion with will, fear with strength, negative judgment with intuition, and the ceaseless mental chattering with joy and compassion.

The heuristics will help you to find your way. In the next four chapters they are used, along with exercises and experiences, to give you four essential tools—almost super-heuristics—that you need to develop in order to manifest your creativity fully. These tools are: faith in your own creativity, absence of negative judgment, precise observation, and penetrating questioning. In fact you had and used these abilities as a child. The next four chapters—the section called Preparation—will help you rediscover them.

Of course you can't have creativity without a problem or issue in your life. When we ask business people what is bothering them, the answers fall almost entirely into five categories: career or purpose in life, time and stress, balancing personal and professional life, issues of money and self-worth, and bringing personal creativity into the business organization. Do they sound familiar to you? They are so pervasive that we now call them the five challenges. They must be met in order for you to have a fully creative life in business. The last five chapters of the book—in the section called Inspiration and Implementation—each concentrate on one of these five challenges.

We trust that as you live with the heuristics, develop the essential tools and apply them to the challenges in your life, your true creative potential will manifest more and more in business. You will become an artist in the largest possible sense.

PREPARATION

2

IF AT FIRST YOU DON'T SUCCEED, SURRENDER

Whenever I have heavy problems I simply introduce the question to my mind, what the problem is, and, in time, I always get an answer. The answer is always there on time. I think I have spiritual friends. I believe they will have me pick up a book or a magazine or read something somewhere, or have someone say something to me to give me input to help me with questions that I have to deal with. It doesn't always feel like they're going to be on time. But they usually are. That's how strange it is with me.

> James M. Benham
> Founder and Chairman
> Capital Preservation Fund

Let go . . . let it happen.

> W. Timothy Gallwey
> *The Inner Game of Tennis*

There's a spirit that guides me, a light that shines for me.
My life is worth livin', I don't need to see the end.
> *Sweet, sweet surrender...*
> *Live, live without a care*
> *Like a fish in the water*
> *Like a bird in the air...*

> John Denver,
> Songwriter and Singer
> "Sweet Surrender" ©

Do you have as much confidence in your creative ability as James Benham does? As much faith in each day's outcome as Gallwey and Denver? If you live by the credo of this chapter, you soon will. Starting today, and for at least a week, put yourself into the shoes of an MBA student with this class assignment: Apply the heuristic "If at first you don't succeed, surrender," to your daily living.

Impossible? Goes against every grain of your being? You're among friends; we've all been taught that determination is a virtue. Well, have faith. We'll ease into it. Start by surrendering to the message of this chapter.

Passive submission is no part of this kind of surrendering, except insofar as you give up striving. Simply work with absorption, surrendering to the task at hand, not to someone else or to striving. Consider this: If at first you don't succeed, something is blocking your way. Is that block your own anxious striving in one of its overly frequent manifestations?

Webster defines "strive" as "To make efforts; to endeavor with earnestness; to try; to contend; to vie." Harmless enough; praiseworthy, even. But in the language of this book, we find insidious thought processes attaching themselves to "contend" and "vie." This includes the concern for self-image, the need to outdo others, the wish to impress; anxiety about living up to the expectations of bosses, spouse, old teachers, or even the newspaper boy. In this kind of striving, each act is a competitive one, an accumulation of false superiority. Thoughts focus on past and future triumphs or failures, and energies dissipate in a long ricochet of emotions.

You can recognize this kind of striving by its beguiling cloud of self-centered questions: How am I doing? Is anyone noticing? Did I just show them or did I just show them? Has so-and-so noticed how well I did? (Or how poorly I did?) How can I find the chance to say what I didn't say in that devastating, tongue-tied moment?

Not you? Not the kind of thought that has ever whirled about in your mind? Of course not. You already know the difference between submitting to a false ego and surrendering to your own creativity. You're like business-man Stephen Portis. In a class paper, Portis says:

> *What does surrender mean? To me, surrender doesn't mean to quit or give up, but rather to let go of any emotional attachment to the final outcome.*
>
> *To whom do I surrender? For lack of a better word, I would say I surrender to God. God provides a feeling of hope and goodness that I cannot always find within my own intellect.*
>
> *The feeling that accompanies the action of surrender is one of relief. When I stop trying, it means I can also stop worrying. Suddenly a big weight is taken off my shoulders. My mind is set free and a feeling of expansion prevails. In fact, the experience of surrendering is so wonderful that I think the best way to live my life would be the following: Don't try, just surrender!*

"IN GOD WE TRUST"

Portis talks about God, "for lack of a better word." James Benham, in the opening quotes, talks about spiritual guides. We think they're doing the same thing: giving a name, within their own contexts, to experiences many people have had in their business and personal lives.

Plato was speaking in his own context when he said there were three ways of knowing. The first two—through the physical senses and through reason—are familiar to each of us. The third way, divine madness, refers to a spiritual or a divine way of knowing that seemed to rise uncontrollably in an individual. Today we find this idea discomforting. Divinity is something few people talk about at business lunches or on the commuter train or in the check-out line at the local supermarket. Divine madness (or Essence or God) is nonetheless an inner creative quality to which we would do well to surrender if we want to be creatively efficient in business.

Managerial psychologist Harold J. Leavitt has studied this kind of knowing. He talks about *pathfinding*. He describes three ways of defining your own life's voice, or mission. You can be *proactive*—aggressively seek, air, and pursue your problems and goals. You can be *reactive*—passively adjust to whatever life thrusts upon you. Or you can be *enactive*—work on a specific problem until you find the right path or solution, trusting that problem and solution constitute a personal dialogue, an exercise in communication between your inner and outer selves.

Leavitt talks about this by referring to a book, *Creative Vision*, by psychologists J. W. Getzels and Mihalyi Csikszentmihalyi:

It is a study of problem-finding in the arts. Let me just say a few words about it, because it's simple-minded but good. They worked with students at the Chicago Art Institute. They were interested in the conditions under which students produce creative paintings as judged by external experts. They ended up taking students one at a time into a room in which there were two tables. This is a highly analytic study about creative problem-solving. One table holds a lot of objects—a trumpet, a toaster, a spoon, a plant. Thirty or forty objects. You tell the students, "Look, take any items you want off that table. Put them on the other table, and do a painting." You say, "Try to do it in a couple of hours."

Then you do three things. You film the process. You interview the students afterwards. You have the paintings judged independently.

The questions are: What's the process by which the paintings that are judged more creative are created? And: What's the process by which the ones that are judged less creative are created?

The answer is that those that are less creative are the ones, characteristically, that were planned. That is, if the kid brings the stuff over to the table, sets it up, says, "This is OK," paints the painting, hands it in—those paintings are not judged as creative.

The creative ones are apt to be changed seventeen times in the process. If you ask the student if he's through, he's never through, and he'll say, "Yeah, well, it's better than it was before, but I'm not sure that I'm finished." There's a hell a lot of shifting, changing, erasing, painting over, modifying, approaching some degree of satisfaction.

And this kind of muddling-through process—not knowing at the be-ginning what you're going to be doing, not being able to say what you are doing, trying a variety of things, and finding that some are closer to what you want than are others—this is kind of what I'm trying to get at with enactive. That doesn't mean it's a random process. The fact that these kids are changing things, and modifying things, and doing things differ-ently than they did five minutes before does not mean it's random, or that they don't know what the hell they are doing. It's got to be, I think, that they are carrying around some kind of standards, but they can't really verbalize them or even visualize them clearly enough to say what things ought to be.

We would say that these creative artists were surrendering to the better painting within.

Steve DeVore, founder and CEO of SyberVision Systems, Inc., speaks of his company's study on high achievers:

One of the spiritual characteristics of the high achiever that we have identified is what we call "the sense of higher self." High achievers have a sense of almost believing in themselves as possessing godlike abilities, that nothing is impossible. They believe that almost to the point of having control over their environment. They believe that just by being present they can control their environment and their circumstances themselves. It could be construed as having a big ego perhaps. But in a very healthy sense. Saying, "Nothing is impossible for me—I possess the intelligence of a god."

Paul Hwoschinsky—venture capitalist, corporate director, and hobby photographer—shares this experience:

I'm somewhat embarrassed to tell about this, but I had been photograph-ing the creek outside our house in the Tahoe area for about twelve years, a single hundred yards of this creek—as a discipline so I could train myself to "see." Suddenly, this one time, a voice said, "Go down there and turn left and there's a picture." I thought to myself, "That's screwy." So I didn't do it. But the voice kept coming back. Finally I looked around and no one was watching: I was alone. And so I thought, "What the heck, I'll do that!" And I did. It was an extraordinary photograph.

You don't have to hear voices in the woods to feel that there's some sort of guidance in your life. Psychologist Albert Bandura has made a study of chance occurrences, finds them to be crucial in people's lives, and men-tions several turning points of his own. Of course, these "chance" occur-rences aren't really chance at all. They're the welling up of an internal self that is beyond rational thinking.

Rene McPherson, who brought Toledo's Dana Corporation to multibil-lion dollar sales, calls his inner guide "luck." He links success with "being dumb enough'' to barge into a situation—as when he switched jobs among personnel in a Canadian division to shake up traditional job concepts. ''It worked.'' And when the newly assigned, totally inexperienced, marketing vice-president raised prices, that worked too. ''He didn't know he shouldn't do that. We were lucky.'' McPherson likes to talk about luck as a way of business:

I think you have to plan on it. It doesn't mean you get to be a slobby dog. You have to work like crazy, but you also have to have that magic ingredient. Who anoints you? I don't know.

Howard Palefsky, president and CEO of Collagen Corporation (a medical products company), reports a similar experience. His company was having trouble marketing Zyderm, an implant material used in plastic surgery. The vice-president of marketing, fairly new to the pharmaceutical drug field, didn't know that it wasn't considered proper (or even practical; Zyderm, like prescription drugs, is available only through doctors) to advertise to consumers (potential patients). She did—and it worked. She created public awareness and consequently a market.

This confidence, this surrender to our inner creative ability, this ''dumb luck'' is a force SyberVision's DeVore understands when he talks in one moment about inner faith and in the next about electromagnetic energy:

I'm not preaching religion here, but we now have (with findings about electromagnetic energy) a definition of what religions call faith. Jesus, for instance, said that if you believe or you have faith you can move a mountain. He must have understood the laws of electromagneticism, because that mountain is composed, in its most sublime form, of electromagnetic energy. If we have faith, as he called it, or sensing, as I call it, if we can sense that mountain moving with enough intensity, we will produce enough energy to affect the electromagnetism of the mountain. This is what Zen Buddhists and virtually all the religions of the world have talked about for thousands of years.

In business you don't have to move physical mountains, but you can accomplish amazing feats by simply believing in your ability to do what is yours to do: the job you see in front of you. Time after time when the speakers in our class are asked how they made their enormous breakthroughs, they seem surprised at the question, not acknowledging that they ever did anything outstanding.

Take the case of Steve Jobs, a founder (with Steve Wozniak) and former chairman of the board of Apple Computer. A multimillionaire whose personal net worth increased over a quarter of a *billion* dollars during one eleven-month period, Jobs watched Apple move into the Fortune 500 faster than any company in history. He was the youngest board chairman on that list. It might be argued that he is not one of the inventors of the personal computer, but he is certainly as responsible as anybody for making it an integral part of American life. Yet he did all this and continues to make big strides simply by surrendering to his vision. Here's how he tells it:

Like most great ideas that people I've known have thought of, it came from something that was right in front of us. We designed this computer because we couldn't afford to buy one. There were a few kits on the market, and they cost about five hundred bucks. We didn't have five hundred bucks. So we liberated some parts from Atari and Hewlett-Packard and designed this computer, and built one, and all of our friends saw it. Of course we designed it to what we wanted. So we were the initial market. We discovered that our secondary market was all our friends.

It took about forty hours to build one of these things and forty hours to troubleshoot it. We were spending every spare moment building computers for our friends, because they couldn't build them. This got very tiring. So we decided to make what's called a printed circuit board, which saves approximately sixty of the eighty hours. I sold my VW bus, and Steve sold his calculator. And we got this pc board laid out, and we were going to sell pc boards for double the price that we could make them for (about fifty dollars; we could make them for twenty-five). We figured we could sell maybe a hundred and make twenty-five hundred bucks. And that was great. So I was out trying to peddle boards one day, before we made them, because we wanted to presell them. I walked into one of the early byte shops and showed them the prototype and explained the plan, and he said that he'd take fifty. I saw dollar signs, because that was half of our run. But he had a new twist: He wanted them fully assembled.

And so again the next step of getting into business was something right in front of us. And it just proceeded that way. We built the hundred, fully built. We sold fifty. We went down to the electronics distributors because we didn't have any money to buy parts. The byte shop was going to pay us in cash, but we didn't have a cent. So we just went down there and out of sheer enthusiasm convinced them to give us ten thousand dollars worth of parts on thirty days thin-air credit. We built the boards, shipped fifty of them, got paid cash and paid the distributor off in twenty-nine days. And that's how we got started. We got started with nothing, just nothing!

Until you intentionally live by the surrender credo you might not know you're doing it. John Waldroup, real estate and educational innovations developer, at one point wanted to convince the student manager of a bookstore at the University of North Carolina (Waldroup's alma mater) to carry and display a book on meditation. This was the Bible belt; Eastern meditation was unusual, to say the least. As the manager resisted, Waldroup received an inner message that he had other connections with the young man, whose last name was Baker. (Name changed here.)

"Do you come from Mitchell county?" The manager did, and Waldroup remembered, "Why, you can't throw a rock up in Mitchell without having it come down on a Baker. Any relation to Langhorne Baker?"

Langhorne Baker was the manager's father and a friend of Waldroup. The young man took one hundred books and supported them with a strong display.

Luck? PR tactics? Fate? Essence erupting?

Psychologist Helen Palmer, director of the Center for the Investigation and Training of Intuition, analyzes the mechanics of surrendering this way:

Usually you come to the edge of your intellectual conclusions. Then you have to presuppose, you have to use some function that is already contained within you. You don't go blank, and you don't go to sleep at the wheel. But you have to inspect the particular piece of goods, the decision that has to be made, with some part of the self that is not "thought." And at that moment an inspiration of how to proceed, a direction that might cut corners, a new way to solve the problem, is possible.

When Sandra Kurtzig, founder and CEO of ASK Computer Systems, looks within, she finds unfailing confidence in her own ability:

I never gave it [failure] any thought. I just seemed to say, "This is what I'm going to do." And you know, I just mapped out the way to get there, and just did it. I think I've always had that sureness. I know that when I was in high school and I wanted to make best salesperson in a certain department, I just did it. I never thought that I couldn't do it.

Actually, I think if you can just be yourself in any company, you should do well. I think the thing that separates people who have been successful in business from others is that they have enough self-esteem so they can just do their own thing and not worry about what their image is.

Kurtzig has come a long way on that confidence. Her MRP (Material Requirements Planning) package was one basis of her hundred-million-dollar company, listed in *Inc.* magazine's 1982 rating as the eighth-fastest-growing company in the U.S. When she was an employee at GE, and her bosses asked her to consult with manufacturing clients, she was "the least likely to know anything about manufacturing."

But the MRP package was conceived because she listened—to the experts and to her own Essence.

IN SCIENCE WE TRUST

As you see from the foregoing experiences, you need have no fear that we expect you to submit to any outside force or person. Instead we urge you to surrender to your own creative ability. We consider "surrender" an active verb, involving much more mental motion than "accept" or even "have faith." It is a matter of knowing as fact what is true about your own nature.

Few business people question the wisdom, honesty, or appropriateness of the declaration "In God We Trust" on the nation's money. At the same time, most businessmen and women take pride in being complete realists, putting their faith in the evidence of their senses plus common sense. Like the Chinese who worship their ancestors "just in case," their credo might go something like, "In God we don't mind hoping, but in science we certainly trust."

Strangely enough, the science they are trusting in is about three hundred years behind the times. If their science conforms with what their senses tell them, they are subscribing to Newtonian views developed during the seventeenth century. This mechanistic science leads us to view humans as machines that respond to internal and external stimuli, each living in a separate corner of a larger machine: the physical universe. Such a view leads us to believe that we are completely separate, self-animating beings. Our bodies house brains, but our thoughts are only side products of our physical machines; consciousness, free will, divine purpose, and Essence are superfluous at best. The mechanistic view has led us to try to predict and control nature rather than to harmonize with it. We strive rather than surrender.

Let's catch up with the twentieth century.

The New Physics

An increasing body of scientific evidence contradicts the mechanistic view. Sir Isaac Newton, hero of the scientific revolution, became (at least to sarcastic doctoral candidates in philosophy of science programs) "poor bumbling Newton" after Albert Einstein's revisions came on the scene. Einstein's theory of relativity led to a system of quantum physics proving Newton's predictions to be only approximations, holding true only in such large-scale events as the movement of planets. In the world of the very small or the very fast, Newtonian mechanics are totally wrong.

The world of mechanistic science consisted of large solid objects with empty space between them. The world that the new science sees is primarily made up of vibrations and energy waves. What appears to be solid matter is what a physicist might call an energy knot. The revolutionary implication of Einstein's simple equation, $E=mc^2$, is that there is no true distinction between energy and matter.

Let's force ourselves to look at the discoveries of modern physics and to consider their implications. We use the word "force" advisedly. These discoveries are so at odds with our typical thinking that we have not yet begun to absorb them, much less apply them to ourselves.

Quantum Physics

We start with the modern physicist's ongoing search for the smallest particle of matter. (Quantum physics gets its name from this search; a quantum is an elemental unit such as a photon.)

In Newtonian physics the atom was supposed to be the smallest particle of matter, with the word "atom" meaning "that which is indivisible." It is not hard to see why seventeenth-century physicists made that assumption since a hundred million atoms placed side by side would make a row only this long _____ (one centimeter).

Today's scientists know that these atoms constantly move at relatively great distances apart, and that each atom contains a tremendous amount of empty space plus countless particles so tiny that a million of them, side by side, would barely reach across a single atom. The nucleus of each atom consists of protons and neutrons, with electrons spinning around this nucleus. The nucleus accounts for almost all of the atom's solidity, yet occupies only one-million-millionth of its total volume. The rest is empty space.

Like the atom, our bodies are also made up almost entirely of empty space—space so empty that if the solid material from every human body on earth were lumped together, the resulting object would be no bigger than a pea. The solid matter from the entire physical world would fit inside any major football stadium.

Does this give you a feeling of insecurity? It shouldn't, because matter is energy. The cells of our body vibrate at about a thousand times per second; molecules, a million; atoms, a quadrillion. It is this movement that gives our bodies and the world around us the *appearance* of solidity. Physicists have, so far, identified more than two hundred types of elementary particles, each with the ability to vibrate and oscillate at even greater speeds. Each sets up electronic fields, and it is the resulting cohesion and adhesion that gives us the *feeling* of solidity.

How can we be so wrong about our own substance? For one thing, our eyesight is not sensitive to the levels of light that come through the vibrating particles. That's what X-rays are all about; they give us the ability to see through these vibrations.

For another, not everyone has been that wrong. The ancient Indian philosophy of Kashmir Shaivism (to name just one) states that universal consciousness performs five functions: creation, maintenance, destruction, concealment, and revelation. These same five functions seem to be going on constantly within every atom of the universe. Photons collide with electrons to form a new type of particle at another level of existence. Then a new photon emerges and a new electron bounces back to another state, with no intervening steps.

The new physicists' picture of reality is very much like that of many Eastern mystics and Western sages. They now agree that each individual has the potential for performing the godlike functions found at the level of universal consciousness and in the minute world of quantum mechanics. They validate the inner creative potential that seems so incredible to everyday, nonscientific, nonspiritual thinking.

What does this mean to your daily and business life? That your very thoughts have the potential for creation. Psychologists have long acknowledged that attitudes can affect perceptions, and that perceptions in turn affect behavior. You can have faith in your inner creative power. You can depend on it.

Bell's Theorem

The new physics not only tells us that the world is composed of vibrations; it also tells us that these vibrations affect each other. Even Einstein originally doubted one of the implications of his own theory. In an article published in 1935 he and his co-authors suggested that one prediction of quantum theory—that an effect on one quantum would transfer immediately through space to another quantum—couldn't possibly be true.

In 1964 physicist J. S. Bell proposed a mathematical theorem stating that two particles, originally united but eventually separated, could and would affect each other, immediately and from afar. His theorem was confirmed experimentally in 1972 and has been reconfirmed by a series of experiments since then.

Specifically this means: If you break up a molecule so that the electrons fly apart, and then change the spin of one electron, the spin of the other electrons originally joined to it will immediately correspond, no matter how far apart they now are.

This kind of scientific theorizing and evidence gives support to such people as entrepreneur Steve DeVore, who feels that visualization can actually move mountains. Bell's theorem reaffirms that there is a connection between you and everything and everybody in the world. Your effort, your surrender to the task in front of you, however small, will produce the "chance" events that make up a creative person's life. Just like the spinning electrons of Bell's theorem, your efforts will create a world for you and affect others.

Left and Right-Brain Hemispheres

Since the last century doctors have recognized that damage to the left side of the brain produces very different results from damage to the right. In the early 1960s Roger Sperry and his colleagues did a number of experiments with split-brain patients—individuals whose connection between brain hemispheres had been severed to decrease the effects of epilepsy.

Sperry's studies confirmed that the two sides of the brain perform different functions. The left side (which controls the right side of the body) appears to deal mainly with language, logic, and time; the right side mainly with vision, intuition, and spatial orientation.

In one experiment, a split-brain patient held a pencil in his right hand, where he could not see it. Because the right hand is connected to the left hemisphere, he could describe it. When he held the pencil in his left hand, he could not identify it by speech, but he could identify it by pointing to a picture—thereby demonstrating the visual capacity of the right hemisphere.

Many such experiments, some with nonsplit-brain subjects, confirm these findings, and in 1983 Sperry won a Nobel Prize for this work.

Throughout history much profound speculation has confirmed the dual nature of our being. Ancient Chinese philosophers delved into Yin (right hemisphere) and Yang (left hemisphere). Plato's divine madness could well be considered a right-hemisphere function, his concepts of the senses and reason a left. Neither Freud nor Jung had heard of such a thing as split-brain research. But Freud developed concepts of the conscious (left) and unconscious (right) minds, with the ego (left) and the id (right). And Jung proposed four functions of the mind: thinking and sensing (left); feeling and intuition (right).

Following Sperry's discoveries there have been a number of attempts to locate the source of creativity in the right hemisphere of the brain. However, given the nonsolid, energetic nature of the universe, it seems unlikely that such a small part of human anatomy could house all creative ability, and little psychological or physiological research supports this belief of a specific location for creativity.

Most researchers feel there is a much broader creativity or Essence than that attributed to the right half of the brain. Psychologists have found that functions of various types can exist in either half of the brain, and some subprocessing mechanisms exist in both halves. The split-brain research gives scientific respectability to the notion that *everyone* has a creative side to his nature. This is what you can surrender to and depend on. But science goes far beyond the right brain in describing the inner creative resource.

The Triune Brain

Visualize the brain: Its hemispheres constitute the neocortex—its very top. Underneath lies the top of the limbic system. Much older than the neocortex, it is called the old mammalian brain because we share it with such lower mammals as rats, rabbits, kangaroos, and horses. The brain stem just below, known as the reptilian brain, we share with such reptiles as crocodiles and snakes.

Researchers know that these three parts of the brain (neocortex, limbic system, brain stem) are very different from each other in structure and chemistry, as the Golgi method of staining brain tissues proves. And studies with animals prove that each of these magnificent computers has its own functions.

Psychobiologist Paul D. MacLean's theory of the triune brain posits that emotional and motivating behaviors come from the two lower levels. The limbic system, the human mammalian brain, seems to have some intelligence of feeling; when it is stimulated either experimentally or naturally it triggers sudden jolts of positive or negative emotions as well as Eureka! experiences. Some experts speculate that the lower brain contains our basic knowledge, what psychologist Jung called the collective unconscious and what others might call the basis of creative ability. Some even surmise that when we surrender to dreaming, deep sleep, or meditation we travel to these lower brain centers.

At base, MacLean shows that creative ability lives not only in the right hemisphere of the neocortex but also in the lower parts of the brain. Other evidence indicates that we are maximally creative when there is an integration between right and left brain, the neocortex, as well as the two lower centers. Imagine the inner creative resource housed in this ancient remnant of the prehistoric lower brain: the feeling, motivation, and ancestral lore of the species.

But that's not all. Today's scientists see a further integration.

The Holographic Brain

Karl Pribram was a student of psychobiologist Karl Lashley, who for thirty years searched for the engram—the physical location of the memory trace. Lashley trained monkeys at simple learning tasks, and then damaged certain portions of their brains to determine where the memory trace for particular activities resided. He was unsuccessful. Even when he destroyed large brain portions the animals could still carry out their learned activities, albeit at a somewhat impaired level.

The experience of writing up Lashley's research left Pribram with a burning question: How could specific learning be distributed throughout the brain? The beginning of an answer fell into his lap. In the mid-1960s he came across an article on holograms—the three-dimensional, laser-generated "pictures" that can be viewed from all angles, as if they were three-dimensional objects. Pribram's inspiration came from the correspondence between the physical and mathematical bases of holograms.

If, he reasoned, the brain operates as a holographic plate, any part reconstructs the full three-dimensional image. Thus, interference patterns throughout the brain operate like holograms to represent memory traces and interaction with the environment—and that would explain the lack of memory loss in the monkeys' damaged brains.

Others had suggested a connection between holography and consciousness, but Pribram had the evidence of research with approximately two thousand monkeys to support it. In them he had observed interference patterns between memory and incoming visual information similar to those in holography. And experiments have shown that responses of human subjects can be duplicated by using Fourier mathematics, the basis of holographic images.

Pribram's theories have expanded since his first paper on the subject in 1966. In the early 1970s he began to ask a more sophisticated question: If the brain puts together the internal memory frequencies with new external experiential frequencies, who is interpreting the resulting holograms? This is the age-old philosophic question: Who experiences our experiences? It underlies the sometimes jolting and mystical nature of the creative process and specifically rises here as "Who am I surrendering to?"

Sociologist and science writer Marilyn Ferguson tells this story in her book, *The Aquarian Conspiracy*: Pribram was lecturing one night in a symposium in Minnesota and considering this philosophical question about the genesis of our ideas. Suddenly he blurted out, "Maybe the world is a hologram!"

Pribram's physicist son put him in touch with the work of a leader in his field, David Bohm, who was actually making explicit the idea of nature as a hologram. On reading Bohm's papers, Pribram realized that Bohm was describing a holographic universe.

The new physics gives scientific evidence of each person's potential power and connections to the world. Split-brain research and the triune brain findings established that everyone has an inner creative resource with great breadth and depth. Pribram and others provide an integrated scientific justification for believing in your own experience of creativity. If the world is a hologram, that means your perceptions form your world; that your thoughts (in the form of holograms) can have an effect on what you actually experience as the world; and that what exists inside you is what is manifested as the entire world. If the universe is holographic, its concreteness is an illusion created by your own mental construction.

Truly, as the sages say, "The world is as you see it," and your inner creative ability is powerful indeed.

Bohm's Holomovement

David Bohm, protegé of Albert Einstein, is one of today's foremost theoretical physicists. His book on quantum mechanics is a standard text in universities throughout the world.

Bohm proposes exactly what Pribram suspected: that the whole world has holographic properties and that each individual is one fragment. Since any piece of a holographic image can project the entire three-dimensional system, their work is a scientific representation of two main currents of spiritual truth: the Western "The kingdom of God is within you," and the Eastern "As above, so below."

At one point Bohm says, "Mind and matter are two parallel streams of development arising from a common ground beyond both." And what is that common ground? Bohm echoes the findings of the new physics and then goes beyond them, saying, "There is an implicate order and there is an infinite sea of energy, and this unfolds to form space, time, and matter." He goes on to speak of an underlying realm of "infinite dimensionality."

He illustrates this realm by telling us to visualize two video cameras focusing on a fish bowl from two angles. The fish swims in three-dimensional space but the video screens project it onto two two-dimensional screens, each screen showing a different view. Like the two particles of Bell's theorem, the two screens are correlated events; a movement on one links to a movement on the other. But we happen to know that the underlying cause is the three-dimensional event of the fish in the aquarium. In the same way, Bohm says, the godlike implicate realm projects itself into the four-dimensional (three dimensions of space and one of time) world we know.

In Bohm's work we see a convergence of the in-God-we-trust and in-science-we-trust justifications for individual surrendering to internal creativity. His implicate order is something that you can look at physically and also feel internally as consciousness, or Essence. "Thought," he says, "does not merely reflect things; it is something in and of itself. It is a real factor in the world."

Sheldrake's Morphogenic Fields

Biologist Rupert Sheldrake, in taking the ideas of physics into the biological and psychological realms, offers a strong case for considering seemingly random chance events as dependable creative manifestations.

The new physics indicates that tremendous energy resources lie within each of us and that we are united with energy patterns in the universe. Sheldrake proposes that there are morphogenic fields, or "invisible organizing structures that mold or shape things like crystals, plants, and animals, and [that] also have an organizing effect on behavior." He posits that these fields contain influences from all of history and evolution. As such, they begin to explain the "lucky coincidences" that sometimes solve our problems.

Sheldrake would say that when you surrender to your own inner creative source you are simply tuning in to morphic resonance—the communication across space and time via morphogenic fields between similar biological structures or thoughts. Putting it in terms of common experience, he compares people to television sets that pick up invisible information from a nonlocal source: the transmissions from the television station. Like these sets, our function is to tune in to the vibrations that are always available.

He sounds mystical, but his conclusions are based on experimentation and are undergoing verification in several fields of science. His ideas first came from his analysis of William McDougall's rat experiments at Harvard in the 1920s. Sheldrake says:

McDougall first began to test learning in rats by running them through a water maze. Twenty-two generations of rats later, he found that even rats descended from parents that were selected for being generally slow learners were finding the solution to the maze almost ten times faster than the first generation had. There is no explanation for this within existing biology. My hypothesis is that the information was carried to the later-

generation rats by the morphogenic fields, invisible pattern-making structures in nature.

Incidentally, McDougall's experiments were later repeated in Scotland and Australia, and then even the first generation of rats mastered the same maze as quickly as McDougall's fastest learners. You can see that such data badly need an explanation: information is getting transmitted across time and space that seems to affect all rats; it cannot be transmitted by genes, so I am suggesting a field that can serve as a transmitting agent.

Further support comes from the finding that crystal growth at one location regularly proceeds more easily and quickly than identical growth occurring earlier at another location. One study showed that non-Japanese children and adults memorize age-old Japanese nursery rhymes more quickly than they do contemporary Japanese poetry or gibberish in Japanese. Hidden-faces problems—some of which had been exposed on television—were presented to people who had no possibility of seeing them previously. The problems that had been on television and seen by many other people were solved more quickly than problems not previously exposed.

Alternative explanations of these phenomena exist, but Sheldrake's does the best job. Though the final proof is not yet in, mounting interlocking evidence suggests that rational and biological processes are only part of your mental environment. When you experience creative breakthroughs, you might well be contacting larger morphogenic fields.

No matter the terminology, scientific evidence confirms that everyone has free access to the accumulated wisdom, knowledge, and creativity from all of the world and from all of the ages.

Prigogine's Theory of Dissipative Structures

The old mechanistic physics included Newton's second law of thermodynamics, with a concept called entropy. It states that it is the nature of the world to continually run down. If this is true (and it is for a wide range of life's processes), how can creativity—which takes things to a higher level—occur with any frequency? Can you depend on it occurring if you surrender?

The scientific answer is a decided "Yes" according to Belgian physical chemist Ilya Prigogine. His theory of dissipative structures (for which he won the 1977 Nobel prize in chemistry) suggests that people are open systems, or dissipative structures. We use energy and are complex in the sense that we have within us many connections and energy flows. This means that in scientific terms we are far from a state of equilibrium.

It is this very instability that leads to your creative responses. Anything that increases the stress on the system leads to a jump to a higher state of being. Instead of breaking down physically you jump through a creative Eureka! experience into a higher state of mind.

Experimental evidence supporting Prigogine's theory in chemistry includes molecules cooperating in vast patterns in reaction to a new situation; bacteria that, when placed in a medium that would normally kill them, develop a new interaction that enables them to survive at a higher level; the Belousov-Zhabotinsky reaction, in which beautiful scroll-like forms unfold in a chemical solution in a laboratory dish while the colors of the solution oscillate; and complex patterns occurring in a sudden and nonlinear fashion on the surface of oils when they are heated.

Prigogine's work in chemistry expands to include humans. His findings imply that there is a scientific basis for the creativity in your life. Just as you see ideas ignite in an instant, so should you know that this is a process that amounts to a law of life.

IN OUR CREATIVE ESSENCE WE TRUST

To feel confident in surrendering as a way of life you have to trust—as fact—that change, transformation, and the creative response is possible from within. Most of humankind's spiritual leaders speak in terms of awakening to an internal reality that transcends understanding. Many people call that understanding ''faith'' and are as likely to view it with awe (or alarm) as to pursue it for themselves.

But as you have just seen, many of today's scientific breakthroughs are also revelations in a profound spiritual sense. In implying that each individual contains an invisible creative source, involving more than a conscious brain, science too makes the demand for awakening and transformation.

Countless spiritual leaders make this clear in their writing and in the process agree with modern science. Swami Muktananda says:

Man goes to great trouble to acquire knowledge of the material world. He learns all branches of mundane science. He explores the earth, and even travels to the moon. But he never tries to find out what exists within himself. Because he is unaware of the enormous power hidden within him, he looks for support in the outer world. Because he does not know the boundless happiness that lies inside his heart, he looks for satisfaction in mundane activities and pleasures. Because he does not experience the inner love, he looks for love from others.

The truth is that the inner Self of every human being is supremely great and supremely lovable. Everything is contained in the Self. The creative power of this entire universe lies inside every one of us. The divine principle that creates and sustains this world pulsates within us as our own Self. It scintillates in the heart and shines through all our senses. If, instead of pursuing knowledge of the outer world, we were to pursue inner knowledge, we would discover that effulgence very soon.

But how? How do we tap into the creative reality? How do we open the channels for its free flow into our lives?

A large proportion of the business people who used this chapter's heuristic found that the easiest way to surrender is simply to do the work that is in front of them. Recall that you surrender to your own inner Essence and at the same time surrender striving. This means that you would actually work quite hard. And the best way to do this is to direct your attention without striving to what you consider the most important thing to do.

Through our work at Stanford we have evolved four general pathways to surrendering: 1) Drop mental striving; 2) Apply yourself to a task; 3) Maintain a spirit of inquiry; and 4) Acknowledge that you don't know how it's going to turn out.

Drop Mental Striving

Learn to recognize in yourself the kind of anxious striving that is the opposite to surrendering: apprehension, anxiety, tension, competition, anticipation. Clearly it would be a great relief to surrender all of this garbage.

The next step is to replace that false picture of yourself with a better one. Think about your Essence, with full intuition, will, strength, joy, and compassion. Those characteristics are yours, and you have within you boundless energy to bring them into play.

You might try confirming and prolonging such beliefs through meditation. Sit quietly and comfortably. Close your eyes and breathe naturally from your bodily center just below the navel. If thoughts come let them go, or observe them as clouds going by. Don't get involved with them. Pay attention to your breath.

You will probably be surprised at the calming results of even a few minutes of such discipline. Know, as you do it, exactly what you are doing: turning off the faucet of ego, and turning on the flow of Essence.

This can affect the most mundane daily events. Student Robin Simpson tells of the day when, two-thirds of her way home, she remembered she'd left critical material at the office:

I was furious with myself and became very agitated at the thought of the hour's delay caused by my forgetfulness. Then I thought, "Okay, use something from Creativity to help this situation. How about the surrender heuristic?" So then I tried a related exercise. Instantly I felt grounded and calm. It was nice to be driving my car on a sunny day, listening to a favorite tape. Who cared about the delay? It's still astonishing to think about that lightning change of mood, and how it made the rest of my afternoon happy, relaxed, and easy.

Lao Tsu in his *Tao Te Ching* shares an invaluable piece of wisdom: "The world is ruled by letting things take their course. It cannot be ruled by interfering."

Apply Yourself to a Task

The successfully creative business leaders who speak to our classes don't strive. They apply themselves to a task for the sheer joy of doing it. It is in this sort of effort that you, too, can experience your inner creativity.

In our Stanford classes, we recommend this: Get to work on something (almost anything) productive, with the simple (even foolish) confidence that the work that's in front of you is part of your answer.

Lawyer and businessman Davis Goodman, dealing with a problem of time, stress, and tremendous work load, had this experience:

I tried and tried to think through how best to assault this mountain of individual tasks; and then, failing to figure out which to do first, how long to spend on each one, I surrendered and just started. I don't even know how or why I picked which task to start on, but once I had begun, the pieces fell into place. One task simply followed another, and the time spent on each seemed just right. I find it very difficult to accept how easily it all worked even as I say this, for I feel that I did not use my mind to find the solution. It was as if I did not plan or control it. I hope I can continue to surrender, but it is a constant struggle.

Later Goodman had to come up with an idea for an especially difficult legal issue. He says:

Again, before I could start, I racked my brain with various lines of reasoning, with solutions that might or might not follow these lines of reasoning I had not yet developed, and with worry over whether I would be able to proceed. In addition, there was an approaching deadline for the first draft, and I could not decide where to begin. This time, I quickly decided to use the surrender heuristic—and I have begun, and I know which direction to pursue. I just gave in and started with a section of the legal brief that involved less thought and creativity and assumed the rest would follow. The ideas I needed did appear.

Another MBA student reported that he had been putting off an academic paper. Finally:

To get to the point, I pulled an all-nighter. I hadn't done that since my junior year in college. The surrender to a single task was perhaps the fundamental thing that I can comment on. I felt wonderful. There was a great sense of accomplishment. I still feel it when I recall the endeavor. Mentally, sensations started as resentment at having so much work to do, coupled with doubt of ability to complete it. After surrendering to the task at hand, however, intensity and concentration built to the point that I sat at a computer terminal typing from 11 p.m. to 5:30 a.m. without a break. Other thoughts were suppressed, and physical sensations of hunger, fatigue, or thirst did not manifest themselves.

What did surrender feel like? It was euphoric. I finished up at 6 a.m. and was on campus for class at 8 a.m. I was tired but at the same time very alert and didn't want to go to sleep (partly for fear of sleeping through my deadline). So I took a bicycle ride around campus, observing and listening and feeling in super touch with my surroundings. The sun was up, and many birds were about, and I spent quite a bit of time observing these things. Having gone through the experience of physical and mental focus and sacrifice, I was in touch with myself and the elation that comes from the simplest tasks and the least looked-forward-to situations. This raised the week from one that would have drifted away on the tide of forgotten memories to one that comes crashing back in a flood of vivid images and sensations.

Why does it work? Our present theory is that devotion to a task at hand puts us into harmony with our creative source. We dedicate ourselves to the work itself, not to a false personality.

Maintain a Spirit of Inquiry

Do as the scientists do: Objectively and openly observe your actions, reactions, emotions, motivations—and constantly question their validity in terms of your growing understanding of creative thought processes. As you do this, you will build up confidence in surrendering through the things that start happening to and through you.

One student who applied the surrender heuristic to personal problems stood off from himself, almost as a scientist, witnessing his own striving:

I have been taught to play the one-upmanship game rather effectively, so I had an empty feeling, as if I were missing out by ceasing to play this game. The frustration, however, turned into a calm, relaxed sensation as I practiced the surrender credo. I began to substitute fights with meditating—by sensing my arms and legs, relaxing, and listening. Slowly I began to get more balance in my life.

Another student applied self-inquiry and surrendering to a career change:

I've had a tough week. I spent much of it agonizing over my two basic options: Stay at Hewlett-Packard and let them lead me through a long process under general management, or cut bait and go to Trammell Crow Company and become a real-estate leasing agent for the next two years with the goal of development in mind.

Somehow I was reminded that I always land on my feet; that my gut has always been right and would continue to be. My gut is saying: that I'm wrong in giving weight to the professional over the personal; that the really most important thing in my life is people—my good friends and new people I haven't even met yet. My gut is saying I don't know yet what I want to be when I grow up. So big deal.

So my surrender this week is to my gut—to trust it and know that it will be right. I'll go to the Trammell Crow office next week and spend time with the people there and my gut will tell me if it's right or not. My job decision will depend entirely on a feeling—if I'm happy there or not, and that will be just fine. I just want to have fun, everything else results from that. If my gut says it's fun, then I like it, people like me, I'm good at it, I'm successful, I'm happy—what more could I ask for?

Surrendering to my gut. I'm a little scared, but probably more relieved than scared. I do trust it. Why should I second-guess it? I still want to know when it will tell me what to do, so I guess I'm a little anxious but basically comforted by a sense of trusting.

We asked our students to observe water as a way of understanding the power of surrendering. (See the water exercise later in this chapter.) One student described his experience in this way:

I begin to wonder what's so captivating about water. I can sit for hours looking at the ocean, a creek, lake, or fountain, and feel totally absorbed as well as soothed. I wonder why. A breeze comes up and fractures the lake's placid surface into a wild pattern of dancing ripples. Several thoughts about water come to mind. Water is dynamic, always different and never the same; water is flexible with a fluid adaptability, yet it has a collective force that's awesome; water is without color of its own—it reflects beautifully the color and lights of its surroundings; water is. Water is? Sure, it never pretends to be something else. This is the essence of its being, its natural intelligence.

One business student described learning to surrender as "maintaining a kind of subconscious urgency about the situation, but avoiding beating your conscious mind to death thinking about it."

Acknowledge that You Don't Know How It's Going to Turn Out

Instead of worrying over the many possibilities in any situation, just let go. You really surrender when you drop attachment to a particular outcome.

But to let go of anxious striving—to stop masterminding the results—can seem a fearsome thing. Most see it this way: A man falls off a cliff. On the way down he manages to grab a branch. Hanging on for dear life, he appeals to the heavens, "Help me, please! I'll do anything you ask!"

Almost immediately a booming voice from above intones, "Yes, I can help you. Will you do anything?"

"Anything, anything. Please help me. I'll do anything!"

"All right. Let go of the branch."

"Are you crazy?"

One of our students recalled how water led her to surrender, with surprising results. At twenty-two she didn't know how to swim, primarily because she was afraid of water. Then she found herself in Greece, on the Mediterranean.

I slid off the rocks into the sea. My toes sought to touch bottom, but found nothing. My mind experienced the dreaded moment of panic. Then I felt the water's calmness and warmth, and allowed it to calm me. I chose not to fight the natural sensation of buoyancy. I let my limbs move freely and instinctively. That moment of surrender was exhilarating, for I felt a sense of relief and accomplishment. I had thought that I would never learn to swim for fear of having to submit (drown). Surrender was so freeing. Why had I fought so hard against it?

Davis Goodman, the lawyer-businessman who earlier recounted his success with surrendering, adds this thought:

I still mistrust letting go and surrendering because I'm not sure what, if anything, will appear. What if nothing does? I feel that I've been lucky—something always has appeared, and it's beginning to look as if letting go is the way to make something appear, but I'm still not sure. Letting go and surrendering without worrying about this is still the hardest thing for me to do, but eventually I forget to worry and something appears. (But what if it doesn't?!)

Yes, indeed—what if it doesn't? The surprising thing is that so often it does. And the point is that you haven't really surrendered until you let go of your outline of the outcome.
One student said:

My approach has always been to hammer away at a problem until I find a solution or, failing that, I usually give up. This brute-force approach does produce results but at the cost of great stress and unhappiness at not finding a solution. With surrendering I felt much more at peace with myself, and I actually attacked problems with greater confidence.

Bart Littlefield tried surrendering while playing tennis. Here he tells us what happened:

I hadn't played the game for maybe four months, so I didn't know how it would go against this opponent who usually thrashes me completely. I expected the worst, but I thought about the surrender credo as I stepped onto the court. I thought to myself, "Just don't try so hard." We started warming up by hitting ground strokes. I was hitting them solidly, and they were the kind of shots that went skimming over the top of the net, landing just inches inside his baseline. The kind you dream about. Well, I thought, this isn't that unusual, because I usually warm up strong, and fade once the game starts, when it becomes more important to win points than to merely smack the ball back.

Finally I went back to serve, looked over the net to my target, tossed the ball, and thought about nothing but hitting the ball cleanly. The serve went in. The next few went in, solidly enough so that my opponent had to struggle to get them back. And each time I had to get to the ball, I thought merely about the ball and not about the mechanics of what it takes to make the perfect shot. Sometimes I thought about where I wanted the ball to go, and that worked well too, as long as I didn't want it to go somewhere too badly. In that case I found my striving counterproductive, and I would botch the shot. When I was in the receiving court, I would watch the ball only, as he tossed it up, hit it, and it came into my court. Then I would typically hit a good return, deep and low.

Before I knew it, I was on top in the first set 4-3 and was serving. I'd usually have already lost the set 6-0 to this guy. He was as surprised as I was. Well, this was the first time I really thought about what the score was, and then winning each point became important to me, and I started trying, perhaps too hard. I lost my serve, and three of the next four games to lose 7-5. The next set went the same way—I stayed on serve or up a game until about 5 all, at which point I began trying to win. And then I lost. But for about three-quarters of the time I was playing tennis last Tuesday, I was playing close to the best tennis I have ever played.

Had he been trying to mastermind the results, he probably would have said something like "Let me be the winner," or "Let this one clobber him." But he wasn't trying to win or to clobber; he was surrendering. And while he was surrendering to his own inner ability and the rhythm of the game, something beyond him took over.

As Timothy Gallwey says in *The Inner Game of Tennis* (which Littlefield had not read), "Let go . . . let it happen."

STEPS TOWARD SURRENDERING

Relax. You don't have to let go of *your* branch right now. You can take advantage of the small handholds represented by the exercises in this section. Instead of just reading and thinking about surrendering, you can *do* something.

It is unlikely that you will find all or even the majority of the following exercises useful immediately. You can read through them now, try one or two, and remember to use them as you bring the ideas of this book into your life.

Letting Go

To have an immediate experience of letting go you can always stand up and stretch as much as you can and then relax. You've done that thousands of times in your life, and it almost always provides an instant burst of good feeling, clarity, and energy. The following two exercises are expansions of the same idea. One of them emphasizes letting go physically, the other, mentally.

Physically. Sit a in chair with your hands on your legs. Tense your legs and keep them tense as you successively and steadily tense your pelvis, rib cage, shoulders, neck, and jaw. Hold all of that tense for a moment. Now relax. You have just let go. How did it feel? Observe.

Mentally. Imagine that something you mentally carry around with you—a strong opinion, belief, or thought that blocks your way—is actually represented by something you are wearing. It can be a shoe, watch, ring, bracelet, scarf, or tie. Strongly imagine that this blocking mental set exists totally in that article you are wearing. Then: Take it off!

How does it feel to let go in this way?

Dream Work

Sleeping is probably the most common form of surrender in a normal lifetime. All the blocks to your creativity that occur during striving—judgment, ego, false personality, fear, and the chattering of the mind—are obliterated by sleep. True deep sleep produces a void that is completely refreshing and allows you to operate more easily from Essence. But during every night of sleep you also go through a dream period. It is important to realize that these dreams come from within. You are the producer, director, all the actors, and even the scenery; your hidden mind presents the whole production. Since you have totally surrendered, your own innate wisdom treats you to a movie about the issues you must deal with in real life.

How can you bring this dream-manifested wisdom out into the waking parts of your life? The following steps should help.

Ask a clear question about a key issue before you go to sleep. Remember that you are attempting to maintain a spirit of inquiry. State the question in a way that will give you further insight into the problem. You might try writing the question down—even drawing it. Repeat it to yourself as if it were a mantra. Put a great deal of effort behind it. Even if you don't remember your dreams, you could get an answer in the morning.

As you go to sleep, either keep repeating the question to yourself mentally or meditate. Decide before you go to sleep that you will fully carry out the dream even if it involves aspects that in everyday life would be frightening. If you tend not to remember dreams, you might want to set your alarm clock for forty-five minutes earlier than usual—so you'll wake up during a dreaming period rather than long after one. Make sure you have a paper and pencil right next to you or, better yet, a tape recorder to record your dream immediately upon waking.

When you wake up, lie perfectly still. Try to prolong the calm and peace of sleep; then immediately record your dream with a minimum of movement. (If you move too fast or too much, your mental and physical processes might wipe the dream out.)

Now ask yourself a series of questions about the dream, such as: What is the answer the dream is giving to me? What is it trying to tell me about the people, places, and activities related to key issues in my life? If I consider myself to be the key actor or aspect of the dream, what does this tell me about its meaning?

Draw a picture that comes from the dream. What does this tell you? Read or listen to your dream description and then ask yourself the meaning of it before going into a short two or three-minute meditation.

Water Power

When you are surrendering your false ego, you are tapping into a natural resource—the flow of your creativity. Even though you feel far from this power source now, you can learn to recognize it in nature, and by so doing begin to go beyond your mind.

Perhaps the best way to characterize water is that it operates on the basis of a natural intelligence. The contemplation of water is a strong meditation in itself. As you practice appreciating water (and other natural phenomena), know that you can operate from the same kind of intelligence by surrendering to your source. Here's a start:

Water is all around us in many different forms. See it in the shower or bathtub and notice how it conforms to the shape of your body with a very soothing feeling. Observe the effects of water, the way it looks and the way it sounds when you are, perhaps, running water to wash dishes. Observe it in fountains of many different types. Watch it coming down in a rainstorm, forming rivulets in the ground and moving along the side of the street. While you wash your car, watch the splashes bounce off the surface, the drips run down the smooth painted metal, and see the little streams the water forms. Or ride in your car as it goes through a car wash, and notice how the water surrenders to the pressure, pushes the dirt off, and soaks into the rags.

Look at a pond or small lake and see what happens when a wind whips up the surface, or when somebody throws a stone into the pond, or when the sunlight and shadow cause various patterns and affect your ability to see through the water to the various forms in the bottom.

Or go to the seashore and see the effects of the tides. Observe waves breaking on the shore. See the shapes that they have cut into the sand and into the rocks.

Look at a waterfall or a stream. See the slow and fast parts. Notice the turbulence and the calm, and how water affects and is affected by everything around it.

Get right into it. You can experience being a part of it. And you can imagine what it would be like to live a life the way the water does, having tremendous power along with patience and a true harmony with its environment.

Getting in Touch with Your Inner Guide

This exercise is designed for those who take a dim view of passive surrendering, and want a bit of animation along the way. (Remember James Benham, in the chapter's opening quote?) It is a guided meditation, which means you should either tape it or have someone read it to you—slowly, to allow enough time for you to experience each part of it.

In this exercise you meet your wisdom-keeper or spirit guide—an inner person who can be with you in life, someone to whom you can turn for guidance.

You can choose someone from history, perhaps based on Buddha, Jesus, Moses, Socrates—someone considered wise. Or choose someone of rare brilliance and accomplishment, like Einstein, or a mythical figure, or someone you have never heard of or seen before—a man with a long white beard sitting on a cloud, or a wise older woman, or a science-fiction space figure. Or choose someone you know or have known, like a wise and inspiring grandparent or parent or friend.

It might take a couple of tries before you begin to build up confidence in this inner guidance. Then, in the course of your everyday activities, you can begin to depend on your own inner guidance, just as do many of our Stanford speakers. Those who have diligently used this exercise eventually don't even conjure up an inner guide; their surrender to their inner resources comes as quickly and naturally as a well-practiced move in sports.

Ready to go visiting? Here we go.

Sit comfortably in a chair with your back straight, your hands in your lap and your feet flat on the floor. Relax and breathe from center. You might want to pay attention to your in and out breaths. Close your eyes gently, listen, and experience the following:

Begin to notice an ease settling into your body. You're feeling very easy. Let go of all the activities of this day. Begin to sense yourself sitting in the chair. Feel your body and its contact with the chair and notice the sense of peace settling in. And now notice a deeper sense of relaxation settling in. Now go deeper into still another level of spaciousness, peacefulness, nothingness.

Now surround your body with a white light. Bring up a white light and let it glow. And feel the comfort around you.

Now imagine that you're walking into some kind of situation or favorite place—a house or a mountain top or a boat or a room. You're walking into this place. Picture all the details of it. What does it look like? What does it feel like? What does it smell like? What sounds can you hear?

And now your inner guide comes to meet you here. Focus on this figure as it walks toward you. Look at the face. What do you see in the face? Notice your own reactions.

And now say, inside, to this wisdom figure, "Be my guide. Introduce me to new ideas. Help me make wise decisions. Lead me to the source of my creativity."

And now have your guide answer. You might have a brief dialogue: exchange names, discuss a specific problem, elaborate on details. Make it as real as possible. Allow twenty to thirty seconds for this dialogue to occur inside.

And now bring the conversation to a close. And have your guide say to you, ''Call on me whenever you need me. I will always be here for you.'' And feel yourself trusting that.

When you're ready, open your eyes but don't put aside the knowledge that you have this inner guidance that you have seen and experienced in this guided imagery.

IF AT FIRST YOU CAN'T SURRENDER, DON'T WORRY

We hope you will actively attempt each heuristic in this book, but we know it might not come easily. Have fun; discouragement and tension are counterproductive. Use the exercises to help you relax. Even if you notice that you are not surrendering, that is enough. Observe as a scientist observes: with curiosity, focus, and interest, while drawing no conclusions and forming no judgments.

Remember that our students are often surprised when they write down their experiences with each chapter's credo. You might try the same thing each week. The discipline of analyzing your experiences brings new light.

Don't think that you have to develop a perfect relationship with your own creativity only on the basis of reading this chapter and applying it for a short time. If you continue to live with this chapter's heuristic and the others, you will notice that your relationship to them will change. You will experience them in different ways and with deeper levels of understanding. Notice positive experiences when you have them, and keep on observing and experiencing, without heavy intellectualizing. Remember the bit of Zen wisdom, ''Water is harder than stone,'' and have confidence in your inner Essence.

3

DESTROY JUDGMENT, CREATE CURIOSITY

We were struggling for a year and a half to find a perfect model to use in our videotape program, "SyberVision Muscle Memory Program for Golf." Then I thought of Al Geiberger, who is recognized by golfers as having perfect golf form. He also set the record—59—on the PGA Tour for the lowest eighteen-hole score, in Memphis in 1978. But almost as soon as I thought of him, I thought, "Well heck, I'm not really qualified to call somebody like him." Then Golf Digest *did a three-month special series on Al Geiberger, which I read. I thought, "I would really like to call him and invite him to be a model, but he doesn't know who I am. He'd probably hang up on me, or, you know, I'm insignificant." Then I said to myself, "Come on!" And I kicked myself in the rear end. I said, "I am significant, and I know from my past experience that all I have to do is create a mental blueprint of whom I want to choose and the events out there will make that happen." So I called him.*

Steve DeVore
Founder and CEO
SyberVision Systems, Incorporated

The pattern of events preceding Steve DeVore's phone call occurs millions of times each business day. You are concerned about something, you work hard on it, you drop the problem, and an idea appears. Ideas flow easily but too often hit a snag—the negative thoughts we call "fear, judgment, and the chattering of the mind." What's worse, you get many ideas every day that never come into your conscious awareness, because your own judgment so quickly and almost automatically knocks them down and out.

But a few people, like our Stanford speakers, not only get ideas but also follow through on them. Any bit of internal judgment (as in Steve DeVore's experience) yields quickly to a recognition of Essence. This process works so swiftly and automatically for the creative people who talk in this book that they very often forget about the negative or judgment-laden stage.

If you had trouble surrendering to your creative Essence in the last chapter, you were probably listening to your own mind judging you incapable. If you have trouble taking risks, or knowing when to take a risk, you are probably afraid of stumbling over the blocks thrown up by your own mind. If you lack the confidence to create, you are undoubtedly tuned in to the Voice of Judgment that all of us have within. You might think that the inhibiting pronouncements come from your associates, or the mores of your business environment, or society as a whole, but if you allow them to stop you, it's your own internal broadcast you are listening to.

That Voice of Judgment is so pervasive that our students have nicknamed it VOJ. In this chapter you'll begin to see how destructive it is to creativity; you'll also learn how to silence it.

Even a slight decrease in judgment increases your ability to respond creatively to situations. It has been estimated that a normal individual uses only five percent of his total capability. We blame that on the VOJ. If, by silencing the VOJ even a bit, you reclaim only an additional five percent of your total mental capacity, you will *double* your present efficiency and creativity.

Small wonder, then, that people who follow the practices we suggest have amazing immediate results. The very recognition that they are harboring a false accuser does much to unblock the channel. The less judgment the more curiosity, and the more curiosity the more creativity.

So let us begin the adventure of living with this chapter's heuristic: "Destroy judgment, create curiosity." The first step is to recognize the power of your own thoughts by exploring your inner terrain.

An Experience of the Inner Terrain

Nothing can affect you unless you let it affect you. As meditation teacher Ram Butler says in the *Siddha Yoga Correspondence Course:*

Amazing as it seems to the average individual, all the problems, fears and anxieties that plague him in life originate from the mind and exist only in the mind. The conditions and experiences of our daily life are simply reflections of our mental state. We tend to blame the obstacles and pressures of life on circumstances or other people. However, this is our basic delusion. The truth is: everything we experience in life, and all the conditions that affect us, are due to our own mind.

Consider any group picture of people from a magazine. What do you know about them? From surface details—clothes, facial expression, mannerisms, posture—you might congratulate yourself that you could, in a few minutes of face-to-face conversation, place each rather solidly in the American scene. But each has an invisible and rich inner world that determines the character of his life. Maurice Nicholl says in his book, *Living Time:*

We can all see another person's body directly. We see the lips moving, the eyes opening and shutting, the lines of the mouth and face changing, and the body expressing itself as a whole in action. But the person himself is invisible. All our thoughts, emotions, feelings, imaginations, reveries,

dreams, fantasies are invisible. All that belongs to our scheming, plan-
ning, secrets, our affections, speculations, ponderings, valuities, un-
certainties, all our desires, longings, appetites, sensations, our likes,
dislikes, aversions, attractions, loves and hates—all are themselves
invisible. They constitute oneself.

Obvious as it seems, this is an extremely difficult thing to grasp: that the
internal world, that which is invisible, is the *entire* source of what we
experience and how we navigate through our external world.

One thing is easy to grasp: Our inner terrain has none of the limits of the
outer terrain. In our minds we can move through time and space, and we can
exercise our senses, faculties, emotions, and imagination far more freely
than in the outer world, no matter how advanced its technology.

To experience this for yourself, try the following exercise.

Sit comfortably, breathing from center. In turn, read each of the sentences below, then close your eyes to follow the instructions. (Elaborate on
them if you wish.) Stay with each experience until you feel that you've
finished with it.

Move through time. Think back to approximately a year ago today.
What were you thinking? What were you doing? How did you feel about
your life? Bring back some of the details: the people, your routine, your
clothes, your mood.

Move through space. Mentally go to your grandmother's house. Then
go to the place in the U.S. you like best. Move on to your favorite European
city, whether you've been there or not. While your suitcase is packed, go to
the planet of your choice, or to some star or other solar system. Revel in the
details of each stopover. What do you wish you'd brought with you?

Experience colors. See red, then yellow, blue, green, orange, purple.
Put them together in combinations, or move them around in swirls. What
does each color say? How does each make you feel?

Materialize objects. Conjure up a fork, your telephone, your favorite
childhood toy, the house you'd like to live in. Do something appropriate
with each. Then do something inappropriate.

Feel sensations. Imagine you're on a roller-coaster ride, grinding up-
wards then dashing down, looping, twisting, turning. Feel the wind on your
face, and the grip of your muscles. See the skyline, then the people below.
Where's your stomach? Where's your comb?

Taste things. Cut open a lemon. Squeeze a drop of it on your tongue.
Roll it around. Then open your eyes and close them again. Bite into a piece
of chocolate fudge. Let it slide across your tongue. If it's studded with nuts
or marshmallows, enjoy the texture contrast.

Hear sound. Listen to a wave lapping, a whisper, a motor starting, the
growl of a dog, a snore, a thunderstorm, a scream, then—all the way
through—the *Star-Spangled Banner*. Notice all the background noises too.

Feel emotions. Pre-live a great loss—the death of someone you love very much, or the dashing of an ideal. Then recall a happy surprise. Dwell on the details of the event, and on your own physical reaction.

Do the forbidden. Sass a parent, disobey a boss, throw your hand at a bridge partner—anything you've always wanted to do. Luxuriate in the emotional aftermath, then pick up the pieces.

Give birth to an idea. Remember an idea that's come to you lately. Shoot it down with judgmental and negative thoughts; resurrect it with cool, clear logic. Repeat the performance with a brand new idea.

Easy, wasn't it? If you're like most people, you felt at home in your inner terrain, and found many familiar rewards there. Your own logic should tell you something: In this exercise, you knowingly programmed yourself to have certain kinds of experiences. In everyday life, you might unknowingly be at the mercy of your false self, with all its destructive judgments.

The VOJ: A Wolf in Sheep's Clothing

Your implicit understanding is probably that judgment can keep you on the right track. Webster attaches to it good sense, discernment, understanding, and wraps it up with ''the ability of judging fairly, wisely, skillfully.''

That's how it comes to us first: as a quality we want in our lives. As we learn to live in the world, we learn that we're a part of a family, a neighborhood, a community, a nation, and for judgment to be good it must also be unselfish, fit the wishes of others—parents, relatives, teachers.

But most of us also learn—late in junior high school, or early in high school; whenever our first serious social aspirations come into bloom—that unselfishness is a synonym for conformity. We discover within ourselves a great longing to be like, and be liked by, everyone else in our peer group. So we submit ourselves to the kind of judgment that has conformity as its goal. This judgment condemns, criticizes, attaches blame, makes fun of, puts down, assigns guilt, passes sentence on, punishes, and buries anything that's the least bit unlike a mythical norm.

Brian Zwilling, director of new products at Spalding Sports Worldwide, says it this way:

Let's say that your total creative potential is represented by a broad gray line.

If you put a microscope over that line you would see individual flecks or dots. Assume that this line is a linear representation of your total personality. You spread from one side to another. That's you. That's every one of your traits: introvert-extrovert, laid back-not laid back, whatever. That is the total representation of your total personality. From the time you're born you are compressed: "Sit up!" "Don't eat your soup with a fork!" At home. In school. "No, I want you to answer the question this way!" and so on. Society, home, school, peer group, what-

have-you, takes you and compresses you so that you don't use very much of your real self. You might say that of your total personality you use only a little space that is between two vertical lines on the broad gray line.

This happens because you begin to think, "I want to be normal. I'm only going to manifest personality traits that are accepted. I'm only going to let the world see this small part of me." Compressed. And most of us exist only in that small vertical area of ourselves. If you allow the effects of living to make you operate only from a smaller area, you're allowing the part of you that hasn't been touched to be broader. It is from the parts of you that are pushed away by society—the part that is still pure, that is uniquely you, that has not been suppressed, repressed, changed, modified—that creativity comes.

You might think that the VOJ plays a very small part in your business life, that self-criticism is good because it keeps you on track. That's a reasonable position, but that thought actually comes from your VOJ. Remember that the VOJ can destroy fresh ideas before they even reach you. So suspend your judgment for a moment while we look at the VOJ's nature and effects.

There are four levels of the negative kind of judgment: self-judgment, judgment from others, collective judgment, and judgment judging the judgment. Let's examine them more closely.

Self-judgment. At this level, the VOJ speaks from within. Why can't you be honest? Serious? Obedient? Perfect? Happy? It's a voice from your past: a parent, a teacher, a store-keeper, a traffic cop. Freudian psychology tells us that at about age four we begin to develop a superego—the culture's concept of correct and responsible behavior. We learn to distinguish right from wrong as children, and then carry these values into adulthood—unchallenged. They often include our childlike inefficiencies, irrelevant emotions, and distorted impressions of our own capabilities. These values also include—because they come from many sources and stages—conflicting demands. These values become the standard for our VOJ.

Businessman Peter Broer analyzes his own VOJ:

The moral code is imposed from outside when one is too young to discern oneself . . . but then, unfortunately, these rules are dragged around through life when one has far outgrown them. Like training wheels on a bicycle, they support us when we are young and clumsy . . . but then get in the way when we have mastered the complex principles.

Judgment from others. The second level of judgment enters when someone you know labels you as you might label yourself. Because it sounds so much like your own VOJ, you hear the label as a confirming truth.

For example, a wife says to a husband, "My god, you're a lazy slob. Just look at your messy closet!" The husband feels angry and hurt, but basically agrees; his own VOJ has already attacked him with the same opinion. But does that make the two opinions truth? No. No person is something called lazy. Laziness is a symptom that something is incomplete, unresolved, uncomfortable. That which is left incomplete and therefore uncomfortable signals a block—usually fear. Who's afraid of a messy closet? The child within.

This kind of external judgment, as you see, gets its power from your confirming internal judgment. Less obviously, it also gets its original impetus from your own VOJ: You send out signals, and someone else picks them up and speaks them aloud as facts.

This pattern is especially prevalent in the business world. There it is important to separate blame, criticism, and negative judgment from clear, rational assessment. Assessment and objective intelligence are cool and constructive; negative judgment is hot and destructive. The trick is to know the difference.

James F. Bandrowski, former director of planning at the billion-dollar Di Giorgio Corporation, is as responsible as anyone in American business for bringing creativity into strategic planning. He says:

> *Most managers are used to being very judgmental, very cruelly judgmental. So you see some great ideas, whether your own or someone else's, just getting a "That's no good" or "That's ridiculous" response without a fair hearing. The typical knee-jerk reaction is a put-down rather than real curiosity and consideration.*

Such observations are supported by scientific research. Theresa Amabile, in *The Social Psychology of Creativity*, says:

> *Intrinsic motivation is conducive to creativity, but extrinsic motivation is detrimental. It appears that when people are primarily motivated to do some creative activity by their own interest and enjoyment of that activity, they may be more creative than when they are primarily motivated by some goal imposed upon them by others.*

In a series of well-controlled and designed experiments she found that the expectation of evaluation can undermine creativity for both adults and children, and for both artistic and verbal creativity. Furthermore, she found that even positive evaluation can undermine future creative performance, apparently because it leads to expectations of future evaluations.

Ron Berman—who was responsible for a television commercial that at one time had the highest recall scores in television history—like virtually everyone who spoke to us at Stanford mentioned the need for organizations to foster creativity by stopping organizational judgment and criticism and by making mistakes more acceptable.

> *If someone asked me what all the businesses need that they don't have now, I'd point to this: freedom to fail. Everybody's hearing footsteps. (Like the wide receiver going out to catch the ball and then dropping it*

because he hears the defender behind him.) People are afraid of making a mistake, because they won't get their promotion, they won't get their raise, or they might not even keep their job—and that happens up the ladder, all the way up the ladder, maybe to the chairman of the board who is afraid of the stockholders. And then the stockholders go back and they're afraid of somebody in their own company.

Collective judgment. The third level of judgment is not one particular voice but a set of collective voices. Fashion establishes hemlines, nationality establishes food and beverage patterns, social class establishes decorative taste, etiquette establishes which fork to use. These invisible voices also operate in your life as a source of judgment; you are likely to conform to their dictates blindly or feel guilty if you don't.

Your defense is not necessarily to ignore or disobey these voices. Many such "rules" offer handy guidance and eliminate constant fussing. But it is necessary to recognize each collective voice for exactly what it is: an external standard of behavior. It is also necessary to know that a collective voice is only a pretender to power. You still have the freedom to govern your own behavior.

Another word for this phenomenon is "socialization." Discussions of creativity in business often expose this conflict: Creativity demands independence; organizations demand conformity, or socialization. Such socialization is intended to provide a structure that allows individual creativity. But you can be personally creative only if you recognize the judgmental aspect of an organization and do not let it interact with the other three levels of judgment.

Judgment judging the judgment. The fourth level of judgment depends for its impact on the existence of the other three levels. It comes into effect when the others have started working on you. The first level, your self-judgment, says, "So you're thinking of changing your job. You haven't even been there for a year. You're thirty-five years old. Other people your age have it all together, and you still don't know what you want to be when you grow up."

As a result of this inner attack, you become depressed; depression is usually anger turned toward the self. In no time at all the second level, judgment of others, comes at you. You meet someone who says, "You look awful. What's the matter?"

That's when the third level, collective judgment, zaps you: You've broken a social rule; you should always look happy and prosperous. Enter the fourth level. You feel bad. It's bad to feel bad. You are bad. The judgment judges the judgment, and lays the blame on you.

Sound familiar? You're not alone. Consider these experiences from two business people:

I also saw myself being very concerned about how I perceived others were judging me based on my job selection.

And . . .

*It seems that there is a momentum effect when I start to judge that I am
"bad" for some perceived failure. This judging starts a process in which
I feel even worse about me as time proceeds, and there seems to be a
self-fulfilling prophecy. If I think that I am worthless, I act in a manner
that confirms this feeling to me. For large periods of time I don't
accomplish anywhere near the amount that I am capable of accomplishing. But time isn't the problem. My ability to accomplish what's required
isn't the problem either. The problem is my attitude. I put myself down
and actually prevent myself from being what I want to be. I find that I
often accept others' opinions of me and internalize these opinions and
say, "See, they were right. You are screwed up."*

Thus we see that the VOJ, pretending to be your own thinking, comes
from many sources: from parents, teachers, friends, business associates,
and society as a whole. The louder your VOJ, the muddier your perceptions
and the less appropriate your actions.

Before we talk about ways to silence your own VOJ, let's share some
time with arts administrator Vicky Hardy, who has already silenced hers.

MANAGING WITHOUT THE VOJ

At the time she spoke to us Hardy was director of public events at
Stanford University. The success of her revolutionary direction of the
Lively Arts at Stanford series was all the more surprising because it had to
compete with a tremendous number of cultural and entertainment events
around the San Francisco Bay area. Such university arts programs usually
lose money heavily. Vicky Hardy created a program that not only featured
top artists, drew large audiences, and fulfilled the University's cultural
goals, but also broke even financially. Later she achieved the same kind of
turnaround at the William Carlos Williams Center in New Jersey and at
Fairleigh Dickinson University where she developed an arts administration
program.

Vicky Hardy creatively balances everything: her personal and professional life; the mundane aspects of organization and the excitement of
performing arts; financial constraints and cultural goals. Constantly curious, clear of negative judgments, she apparently finds her creative resource
readily available.

But she faced an avalanche of outside judgment as she moved through
college.

*My first encounter with the gender issue was in college. I wanted to be a
doctor. I spent five years—eighth, ninth, tenth, eleventh, and twelfth
grades—in special National Science Foundation programs every summer. I have a lot of math. I have lots of science.*

When I got into college, a small state university, and I wanted to continue my interest in science, I hit an absolute stone wall. The first time in my life I'd ever done that. They said, "You can't be a doctor and live a normal life." By normal they meant get married, have children, be a woman, all those sorts of things. "You ought to go into research. You're very bright. You should go into research." "I don't want to go into research," I told them. "I want to be a doctor."

So after arguing with them for two years and working in the labs and all that sort of stuff, I finally decided well, that was their problem. If they weren't going to encourage me, I wasn't going to stay in it. So I changed majors, and I went into English and theater and speech and drama and all those things that I'd always done as an avocation. Loved it and have never left it. But gender has not been an issue for me since then.

One of the ways to tell whether you're being judgmental toward yourself is to see how judgmental you're being with other people. When Hardy was asked how she looked at others, she said:

I see people in a variety of ways. I see people as either creative or non-creative, gifted or not gifted, intelligent or average. I think part of it is the ability to see people, accept them for what they are, and operate with them within the system in the way they function best.

I think I have a lot of tolerance, and I don't know whether the creativity allows that or whether that's just my personal value system and my ethics. I'll tolerate almost anything. There are a few things I don't tolerate. I don't tolerate dishonesty or lying when I know someone's deliberately lied. In this particular business you get a lot of that.

Judgment is really fear, and fear creates judgment. Asked if she was ever afraid of anything, she said:

I went through a period three years ago at Stanford when I really thought I was going to lose my job, because I was making some major changes, and some of them weren't very well liked. And I sat down, and I went through a process. I remember the weekend I did it. And I said, "So what's the worst thing they can do to you? Are they going to take you out to White Plaza at high noon and strip you of your arts management degree? No. Well, what's the worst thing they can do? They could fire me! Well what would happen then? Well, I could sell everything I own and take that money and travel around the world. Go live in Mendocino for a year and paint. Go to Mexico, go to China."

All of a sudden all of these alternatives sounded like just absolutely wonderful things to do, and I lost my fear. Once I got to that point where I said, "God, the worst thing they could do to me is fire me, which could be the best thing they could do for me," my fear in that situation vanished."

Is it possible for the rest of us to destroy judgment and create curiosity? If that question occurs to you, it isn't the real you speaking. It's only your own

VOJ trying to dissuade you from destroying it. So let's ignore that kind of thinking and get into the fun, adventure, and struggle of destroying the VOJ.

HOW TO DESTROY JUDGMENT

The VOJ must be destroyed before your own creative voice can come through. Picasso put it this way:

Every act of creation is first of all an act of destruction.

One interesting version of this need for destruction in the creative process appears in an ancient eastern text *The Pratyabhijnahrdayam,* or "The Secret of Self-Recognition." This philosophy says that each of us carries out the five functions of God, or universal consciousness—manifesting, maintaining, destroying, concealing, and revealing—on our ordinary plane of existence. Interestingly, the commentary on the text by the tenth-century yoga master, Kshemaraj, implies that our everyday creativity occurs during the destroying or withdrawal function. We have a "sudden flash of delight" when we destroy the surface mind chatter (including the VOJ) by turning within and momentarily recognizing our inner creative Essence.

In *The Courage to Create*, Rollo May also underlines the destruction of judgment as essential to both artistic and everyday creativity. He uses the words courage, rage, fight, and rebellion to describe what is necessary to create in the artistic sense. He says:

The creative artist and poet and saint must fight the actual *(as contrasted to the ideal) gods of our society—the god of conformism as well as the gods of apathy, material success, and exploitative power.*

May identifies part of what we are calling the VOJ as a type of guilt:

The guilt that is present when this breakthrough occurred has its source in the fact that the insight must destroy something. My insight destroyed my other hypothesis and would destroy what a number of my professors believed, a fact that caused me some concern.

But fleeting guilt is a small price to pay for the destruction of judgment and the subsequent creation of joy. As May puts it:

What the artist or creative scientist feels is not anxiety or fear; it is joy. I use the word in contrast to happiness or pleasure. The artist, at the moment of creating, does not experience gratification or satisfaction (though this may be the case later, after he or she has a highball or a pipe in the evening). Rather, it is joy, joy defined as the emotion that goes with heightened consciousness, the mood that accompanies the experience of actualizing one's own potentialities.

Believe it or not, the judgment that can be so destructive in your life is itself relatively simple to destroy, although you must work at it consistently over a long period of time. We suggest seven approaches to destroying judgment. Use them singly or jointly, depending on what is most effective for you personally.

Pay Attention to Your Thoughts

The first step is to become aware of the VOJ. People who have lived with this chapter's credo are amazed at the number of negative and judgmental statements they make throughout a day. One student counted eighty-seven negative judgmental thoughts on a particular Saturday and a hundred on Sunday. Usually the ratio of negative to positive thoughts is quite high—four to one, even eight to one. Several of our students used the metaphor of rodents to describe these thoughts, calling them mice, rats, or weasels.

So start noticing that the judgment is present. Tally your judgmental thoughts when that is feasible: during meetings and conversations, while driving, or when you are part of an audience and not really participating. Be especially alert to the VOJ's presence when you have difficulty, feel fear, or feel depressed. Look to your body for clues; it will tell you when judgment is lurking in the shadows waiting to pounce. You might feel a heaviness in your chest or an overall body tension. You might develop an upset stomach or a headache. Or you might feel blue.

Once you are aware that the Voice of Judgment is present, identify precisely what it is saying. You will have to listen carefully. Sometimes it's ice cold: "No one is going to have anything to do with you anymore." Sometimes it sounds disinterested: "Well, do whatever you want, you're the loser." Sometimes it rages furiously: "You really blew it. You'll never get another job, you stupid ass."

Although it involves a little work, you might want to keep a Judgment Journal. To prime your pump ask yourself the following questions at the end of a day of observing judgment:

When do I notice the Voice of Judgment most? Is it more active in my personal or professional life?

About how many times a day do I judge myself for something? How many times do I find myself judging others? About how many times a day do I allow others to judge me?

What did the VOJ prevent me from doing in the past? What did it prevent me from doing recently? What does it say about some of my future plans?

When I'm in a group (meeting, work discussion, a party) how much time can elapse before the VOJ appears? When I hear it speaking, how do I handle it? Where do I notice it least?

Am I presently aware of a relationship between my VOJ and depression?

After a period of this kind of observation, whether or not you keep a journal, you can move into what meditation masters call witness-consciousness, or the observing self. This is recognizing that you are not your thoughts, or your ego, or false personality. Instead, you are the inner self or Essence. You are beyond the trivial chattering of the mind and the VOJ. One businesswoman visualized her inner creative Essence acting like a large, languid cat watching indifferently as mice ran by carrying little day-glo cards flashing judgments. Every once in a while the cat would swat away a mouse and kill it.

Another example of witness-consciousness is provided by restaurateur Lee Wood. He tells the following story:

> *Once Buddha had a young man as a follower or disciple, and the young man's father hated the fact that his son was wasting his time following this guru. The more the man thought of it, the more enraged he became, until finally he went to Buddha and began to yell and scream at him, telling Buddha how terrible and wicked he was and calling him every foul thing. The man went on for a very long time, but Buddha just sat very quietly not saying anything. Finally the man became quiet and Buddha asked him, "Have you finished?" And the man replied, "Yes." Then Buddha said, "Well then, I would like to ask you only one question." The man said okay. Then Buddha asked, "What happens to the food when you prepare a feast for someone and he doesn't come?" The man thought for a moment and replied, "Well, you wind up eating the food yourself." Then Buddha said, "You have just prepared a feast for me, and I don't intend to eat it."*

Attack the Judgment

Once you've identified what your VOJ is saying, turn to it and yell. Keep the message short. A classic one is "Get the hell out of my life!" At this point, if the VOJ feels threatened, it might come back with a rational-sounding statement such as, "Yes, but you do know that jobs are hard to find." This is simply a more subtle form of judgment at work. It pretends to be reality; it's judgment in disguise. Yell at it, too—out loud if necessary.

When you first start attacking the VOJ, you'll find your timing is slow. Your judgment of another person might blur your perception and affect your reaction before you even think of attacking. Or your judgment of your own abilities might curtail your efficiency before you even notice it. Don't worry about that. Instead, realize that the ensuing self-rebuke is just another judgment from the VOJ, trying to head off your attack. So attack it anyway. Each time you attack you will improve your ability to recognize and attack it sooner next time.

The important thing is to stand your ground. Be firm. Don't let judgment have its say. Yell at it and keep yelling at it until you finally shut it up.

Remember that the VOJ is devious, and has habit on its side. It will try to tell you that you don't know what you're doing, or that it is hopeless to try. Defend yourself by knowing that even a slight decrease in judgment can double your creativity. Know also that consistent attack can have a cumulative effect; it is possible to destroy your VOJ with an extended period of concentrated effort.

But expect results even from sporadic effort. Don't let your VOJ put you down just because you are not keeping track of it every minute.

Make the Judgment Look Ridiculous

Some people find that it is effective to take an especially bothersome statement of judgment and blow it up like a balloon until it bursts.

To do this, shut your eyes and imagine that you can hear and see a VOJ statement—maybe, "People don't like me"—in its normal tone. Then begin to intensify and enlarge it, making it more and more strident, perhaps flashing in brilliant neon lights. Then make the voice scream out in a tremendous echo chamber, with mile-high letters in view of thousands of people.

If this works for you, you will find your own creative ways to intensify, enlarge, amplify, and explode the judgment. And you are likely to laugh out loud as you realize how insignificant and puny the VOJ really is—or would be without your attention to support it.

Once you begin to realize how ridiculous the VOJ is, you will remember that you really are the Essence, or inner self, and as the new physics tells us, you have tremendous power and connection to universal consciousness.

Another way to undermine the ridiculous VOJ is to review some historical bloopers. Like these:

In Columbus's time, the advisory committee to Ferdinand and Isabella of Spain wrote, "So many centuries after the Creation, it is unlikely that anyone could find hitherto unknown lands of any value."

In 1878 Western Union rejected the rights to the telephone with the statement, "What use could the company make of an electrical toy?"

In 1902 an article in *Harper's Weekly* proclaimed, "The actual building of roads devoted to motor cars is not for the near future in spite of many rumors to that effect."

A letter to Paul Klee dated November 21, 1910, gently complained, "Your works have been on show at our gallery since November 15. We are obliged to note, however, that the great majority of visitors expressed very unfavorable opinions about your works, and several well-known, respected personalities asked us to stop displaying them."

In 1945 Vannevar Bush, a presidential advisor, warned, "The bomb will never go off, and I speak as an expert in explosives."

In 1958 British astronomer Dr. R. Woolsey pronounced, "Space travel is utter bilge."

Hindsight tells you that such utterances from the VOJ were as silly then as they are now. Your inner creativity can tell you the same thing on a day-to-day basis, once you silence your own ridiculous VOJ and let curiosity move in.

CREATE CURIOSITY

When you were a child, the world was new and you looked at it with curiosity and wonder. Gradually habit dimmed your eyes, and so did the labels given to you by others in the form of judgment.

Can you remember the surprise of your first bite of watermelon? The original wonder of holding a kitten? The awe of watching a balloon escape into the huge sky above? Surprise, wonder, and awe are all elements of curiosity—and that's what your Essence gave you originally, before the VOJ moved in.

Businessman Eric Patel relates:

Toward the end of the week, I found myself putting judgment aside, at least part of the time, by telling myself to concentrate on what people were saying, or to focus on what I'm looking at, hearing, or feeling underfoot. At such times, a feeling of wonder did begin to enter my thoughts. I found this worked best while walking outdoors. The rhythm seemed to bring on a semimeditative mental state, and there's so much outdoors to wonder at.

John C. Gonzalez gets curious about his own curiosity in this analysis:

When I replaced judgment with curiosity, I found an interesting thing. It allowed me to focus on the source of the very real thoughts I was having, the very positive judgment I wanted to make. In asking, "Why is that person so tense?" instead of saying, "God, what a bitch!" I often saw much more than I otherwise would have. My exploration stops when I declare that the person is a bitch instead of either reacting to her discomfort in a supportive manner, or placing myself in a position to be more comfortable with the manifestations of that discomfort.

Another businessman who lived with the credo tells us:

I have been going to dance performances for quite some time now, and I have noticed that I take a very different attitude to these performances. Not schooled in the art myself, I long ago decided not to sit in judgment of the performances as they were happening, or even afterwards to any great extent. Rather, I just let the performance unfold and flow over me. I don't get drawn into critical discussions, and I enjoy everything I see because I look at each performance as a statement. I try to understand what is being communicated instead of viewing them as performances that I have the ability or need to evaluate. I suspect that I enjoy even "bad" performances more than many people enjoy "good" ones.

When you catch yourself labeling something as good or bad—a performance, a plan, a person, a people—stop and look at it hard. Flex your objective intelligence. Is that goodness or badness actually in evidence to your own clear perception? Or is judgment shrouding what actually is there—something far more interesting or complex or challenging or rewarding?

Remember that the VOJ is a criticism. Its function is to close the door on further investigation or even curiosity; like a flashbulb, it reveals its all in one brief burst. Your essence gives you the tools— curiosity and objective intelligence—for a critique. The function of a critique is to illuminate; like a strong flashlight, it sheds light on the corners and thus widens your path.

Let's look closer. Imagine you are thinking of spending two thousand dollars on a trip you've always wanted but don't really need. The VOJ might say:

You're crazy. You can't afford it. How can you leave everything at a time like this and go off and spend money you don't even have? You sound like an irresponsible child. You should feel guilty for even considering it.

Now let's assume that you've learned enough about your VOJ to resist such bullying.

Well, let's see. Give me the facts. Is it true that I can't afford the trip at this time? Let's make sure. Bring out the financial statements and look them over. Okay. I see now that it would be pretty tight, but maybe there is something I would be willing to give up for several months, something that might be worked out differently so that I might go. If I can, maybe it's a good idea to do it now and enjoy it. If I can't, maybe I can budget it for next year.

The character of the VOJ is to put you down and keep you there; the character of your own objective intelligence and curiosity is to open you up to new experiences and satisfaction.

The contrast is obvious in the experience of a businessman who left a company and returned to school. His VOJ told him "You were a quitter when you left the company." His curiosity led him to ask, "What did I find so uncomfortable there?"

Later his VOJ nagged, "So now that you're out of business school, you should be able to save the company—why don't you?" His curiosity led him to examine the whole situation with such questions as "Do I have to? Do I want to save the company to redeem myself, or to battle my partner and ex-friend? Is it worth it?"

If you doubt the value of following your own innate curiosity, take it from some creative business leaders who mentioned it as one key to their success. Paul Cook, founder and president of Raychem Corporation, said:

When I grew up I had a tremendous technical curiosity. I went through the things that most technical kids do; I built my own telescope, and I had my own chemical laboratory in the cellar. I was insatiable with trying to learn and understand. And I'm sure that was very important. We find at

Raychem that the people who come up with the best answers, the most creative answers, are those who have an innate curiosity that you just can't extinguish.

When Robert Marcus, president and CEO of Alumax, was asked what in his background led to the sort of creativity he exhibited, he said:

Well, very early in life I got to love knowledge. And fortunately in my work I've been able to travel and meet a lot of people, and I continue to read a lot. Whether you develop curiosity formally or informally I don't know.

When Thomas Edison was intent upon creating incandescent light, he went through more than nine thousand experiments in an attempt to produce the bulb. Finally one of his associates walked up to him and asked, "Why do you persist in this folly? You have failed more than nine thousand times." Edison looked at him incredulously and said, "I haven't even failed once; nine thousand times I've learned what doesn't work."

Do Dharanas, or Concentration Techniques

Dharanas are short, yogic concentration techniques that you can use to focus your mind on the inner self or Essence. The word "yoga" means union, and the practice of yoga is designed to reunite you with your inner creative resource.

The following two dharanas are adapted from an ancient text known as the *Vijnanabhairava or Divine Consciousness,* which contains over a hundred dharanas for experiencing the self or Essence. (Many of these concentration techniques appear throughout this book.) They are especially effective because they come from an ancient tradition, but you can develop your own concentration techniques that fit each particular credo—such as contemplating the big languid cat swatting the scurrying mice of judgment.

To do the first dharana—which helps to destroy judgment—sit comfortably with your back straight, close your eyes, and breathe from center. Now begin to sense the skin on your body. Notice how the skin covers every part of your body, that it is a complete covering for your body in every detail. Then imagine that there is nothing inside of the skin—that your skin is just a membrane that has covered your whole body, but with nothing inside of it now. You are completely empty. There is nothing inside of your skin; it is a membrane covering what was formerly your body. Experience the emptiness that is inside that membrane. Just keep experiencing that openness and emptiness within the membrane for one or two minutes more.

The second dharana can build on the first by creating curiosity. Again, sit comfortably with your back straight, close your eyes, and breathe easily from center. Allow thoughts to come into your mind as they will. But know that wherever the mind goes, whether toward the exterior or toward the interior, everywhere there is a state of universal consciousness or Essence. Since God or universal consciousness is omnipresent, where can the mind go to avoid it? Don't be perturbed if you are unable to concentrate on some mysterious universal reality or creativity. Don't worry if you seem to be thinking about things that seem like judgments or blame or criticism. Whatever attracts the mind—whether it is something external like the color blue or yellow; or something internal like an emotion or thought—take it as universal consciousness or Essence. Accept it with full conviction and make it an object of meditation.

Any thought that you have now is a thought of the highest reality. It is totally pure. Anything you think of is composed of unlimited intuition, solid will, full joy, amazing strength, and abiding compassion. Anything you think of now is fused with your concept of God, universal consciousness, or the divine presence. Your mind might be chattering away, moving from place to place, thinking or feeling or judging or imagining—but you know in your heart that wherever it goes it is simply contacting the highest reality. Not only is there nothing wrong with any thought you might have, but every thought is permeated with the highest truth. So continue meditating and understanding the nature of every thought drifting through your mind now for at least a minute more.

Exercise to Remove Judgment

When you feel depressed, you are probably turning anger on yourself. Scientific research indicates that aerobic exercise, which accelerates the heart rate and breathing and increases oxygen levels in the blood, is helpful in fighting depression. In their article, "Influence of Aerobic Exercise on Depression," I. Lisa McCann and David S. Holmes reported in the May 1984 *Journal of Personality and Social Psychology* that "The subjects in the aerobic exercise condition evidenced reliably greater decreases in depression than did subjects in the placebo condition or subjects in the no-treatment condition." Although the authors reviewed a number of other studies that showed that aerobic exercise decreased depression (and therefore in our opinion decreased inner judgment or VOJ), theirs is the first study that had full appropriate experimental control concerning the effects of strenuous exercise on depression.

Many business people who used this chapter's credo say that exercise seems to break the lock of judgment. One reports:

I found that when I am running, swimming, or cycling, only rarely do I find myself passing judgment on either myself or others. I now realize that the quitting of my judgmental mind chatter is one of the reasons I exercise. I previously exercised just for the sake of quiet concentration, but now I know that I must do it to silence my judgmental mind.

In one of the exercises at the end of this chapter we describe a hatha yoga movement that produces an aerobic effect. You can combine it with a mantra or measured breathing. But even with a combined approach, exercise alone will not fully destroy judgment and create curiosity. Use it as a supplement, not a distraction.

Reap Your Rewards

People who don't understand where creatively successful individuals get their confidence and risk-taking ability don't know what you know about the devastating VOJ. Judgment creates fear and destroys confidence. Judgment shows any alternative to be fraught with risk. Judgment says no to experimentation, discovery, trail-blazing. Judgment says "Stay right where you are and like it."

Nor do they know what you now know about curiosity. Curiosity eliminates fear and creates confidence. Curiosity sheds light on the unknown. Curiosity says "What if I considered such-and-such?" and "What can I lose by trying?" Curiosity shows you the facts and then says, "What now?" as it leads you onward and upward on a joyful quest.

EXERCISES

Salutations to the Sun *(Surya Namaskar)*

This hatha yoga exercise, like aerobics, can decrease judgment. It also provides the ancient movements of yoga that prepare the body for union with the inner creative resource. If you wish you can accompany it with a mantra or pay attention to your breathing while you do the exercise. The text for the following exercise has been excerpted, with permission, from the book, *Hatha Yoga for Meditators,* published by SYDA Foundation, 1981.

This is a graceful series of movements that traditionally was performed in the early morning, facing the rising sun, as a form of worship. Today, it remains as an extremely effective way to activate and loosen every part of the body, and to develop breathing capacity. It is very helpful in preparing you for the practice of more difficult and complicated *asanas* (physical postures) by making the spine flexible and strong. The various movements stimulate the entire body, including all of the systems (endocrine, circulatory, respiratory, digestive, etc.), and greatly assist in loosening the joints and muscles of legs. The synchronization of the movements and the rhythm of the breath develop coordination and breath control.

Upon arising in the morning, you can do it rapidly to energize and stimulate the body and mind. In his Ganeshpuri Ashram, Swami Muktananda taught it to the young boys, and encouraged them to practice it very rapidly, without sacrificing the precision of each movement. Many of his students perform Surya Namaskar 100 times (50 rounds) each morning before meditation. This takes about 20 minutes and has an aerobic effect on the cardiovascular system, similar to that of running. At other times of the day you can perform slowly and gracefully to release tension in the muscles and remove fatigue.

Surya Namaskar should always be followed by Shavasana (described following this exercise) for a few minutes, allowing the heartbeat and respiration to gradually return to normal, and relaxing the body completely. Once breathing is back to normal, begin to do the Full Yogic Breath (breathing from center).

Initially, you should perform the various movements slowly and carefully, perfecting each individual posture. Then coordinate breathing with the movements, always inhaling when the chest is expanded, exhaling when bending forward. Once the sequence comes easily, allow your own breathing rhythm to guide the speed with which you practice the movements.

Position 1

- stand with feet slightly apart, feet parallel
- straighten spine
- hold palms together at chest in namaskar (prayer) position
- exhale slowly

Position 2

- raise arms above head
- inhale, stretch up and slightly back
- keep buttocks tight and tucked under

If you have a weak lower back, you should avoid sticking the buttocks out, thereby arching the lower back, creating pressure on the lumbar vertebrae and aggravating existing back problems. Instead, loosen the knees slightly, tuck the buttocks under, and stretch up without arching backwards.

Position 3

- keep back straight
- bend from hips, reach forward as far as possible
- exhaling, bend forward
- bring head toward knees
- if you can easily touch floor with fingers, do so, placing hands next to feet, aligning tips of fingers with toes
- relax in forward bend position, keeping knees straight

Avoid bending from the waist, which creates tremendous pressure on the spinal discs and can lead to injury. Consider the hip sockets as hinges and bend forward keeping the back as straight as possible. This movement will stretch the hamstring muscles at the back of the legs. Generally, it is the tightness of these muscles that prevents us from being able to touch our toes easily, and once the hamstrings are loosened, our flexibility increases enormously.

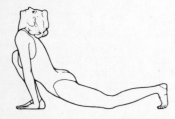

Position 4

- place palms on floor, fingers in line with toes. (If necessary, bend the knees.)
- step back with left foot, place knee on ground, curl toes under
- inhaling, press hips down
- arch back, look up, expand chest

Position 5

- exhaling, bring right foot back beside left foot
- raise buttocks to form apex of a triangle
- keep arms and legs straight
- push with arms and extend spine
- lower heels toward floor

This position gives an intense stretch to the hamstring muscles and is an excellent warm-up for runners.

Position 6

- hold breath out, drop knees to floor
- lower chest to floor between hands
  The chin should touch the floor, while the abdomen and hips remain as the apex of a smaller triangle.

Position 7

- inhaling, lower hips to floor
- slide trunk forward
- arch head and chest backwards
- straighten arms

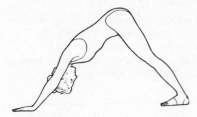

Position 8

- exhaling, lift buttocks high, as in Position 5
- push up from hands to extend spine as much as possible

Position 9

- inhaling, bring left foot between hands, line up toes and fingers
- place right knee on floor
- press hips down
- arch back, look up, as in Position 4

Position 10

- bring right foot forward in line with left foot, keeping feet slightly apart for balance
- straighten knees, hang from hips, as in Position 3
- exhaling, draw head toward knees
- keep palms on floor, knees straight

Position 11
- keep back straight, extend arms
- raise upper body, using hips as a hinge
- inhale fully, raise arms above head
- gently stretch up and back, as in Position 2

Position 12
- exhaling, lower arms to chest in namaskar position, relax body
- center your attention inward
- observe the sensations of change taking place within your body

Positions 1 through 12 constitute half of a full round of Surya Namaskar. For the second half of the round, repeat the same movements, with a variation in Positions 4 and 9. In Position 4, the right leg should go to the back, and in Position 9, the left leg should go to the back.

Two halves complete one full round of Surya Namaskar. Once the leg changes are learned, counting the number of rounds becomes easy. When the left leg is back you know you are on the first half of the round; when you swing your right leg back, you know you are on the second half.

When beginning, start with two or three rounds a day, and add one round each successive day. Advanced students can do as many rounds daily as they wish. When Swami Muktananda was asked how many times one should do Surya Namaskar, he usually replied, "The King of Oundh in Maharashtra State popularized the practice of Surya Namaskar many years ago. He did it 1,000 times.* It takes three hours, but if you do it that many times then it's not necessary to do any other asanas. However, anybody can do up to 100."

* 500 rounds.

Shavasana (*Shava*, corpse; corpse pose)

This is the posture recommended for complete mental and physical relaxation. Initially, the position may seem uncomfortable and you might feel inclined to move your hands, or place a pillow under your head, but with practice, your body will naturally begin to adjust, and you will fully experience the state of relaxation.

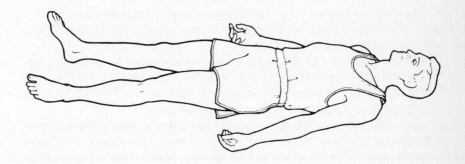

Instructions
Lie on your back

- slightly separate legs, allow feet to fall apart
- place arms slightly away from body, palms facing up
- relax entire body
- focus on the breath, or repeat a mantra

Illustrations on pages 57-61 are by Roy Jones

Stated Goal

This technique works best when you have a goal that you just don't seem to be able to reach. When that condition exists, some judgment is blocking the way. That judgment causes fear and stops you from doing what you really want to do. This exercise forces you to recognize, state, and write down the exact VOJ blocks to realizing your present goal.

The last two pages of this chapter contain two forms for doing the Stated Goal exercise, one of which has been filled out as an example. Let's go over it.

When you are doing this exercise with a friend, first write his name in the circle at the bottom of the form.

Next, ask your friend to state a goal that he would really like to attain, something he wants to do or change in his life. Ask him to write that goal as clearly and concisely as possible in the large circle on the top of the form.

Then ask your friend what is getting in the way of reaching that goal. The answers should be similar to the ones on the example; that is, they should always start with the word "But."

It might take some probing to get eleven reasons, but it's worth it. Each answer is likely to reveal deeper and more meaningful blocks to action. One of the reasons it is best to do this exercise with someone else is that it takes two to really probe and get at deep reasons. So probe.

Once you have written down the eleven reasons, give the sheet to your partner and ask him to look at it as if it came from someone other than himself. Ask what he would say about this person. This is important in revealing what is really going on.

Once in a while the test-taker discovers that his goal is not a true goal at all—just a grass-might-be-greener daydream external to his real desires. (And it doesn't hurt to know that.)

But most people find that their goal is really a deep and sincere longing, blocked by a series of excuses that come from judgment and fear. And the techniques in this chapter provide the tools to destroy that judgment and fear.

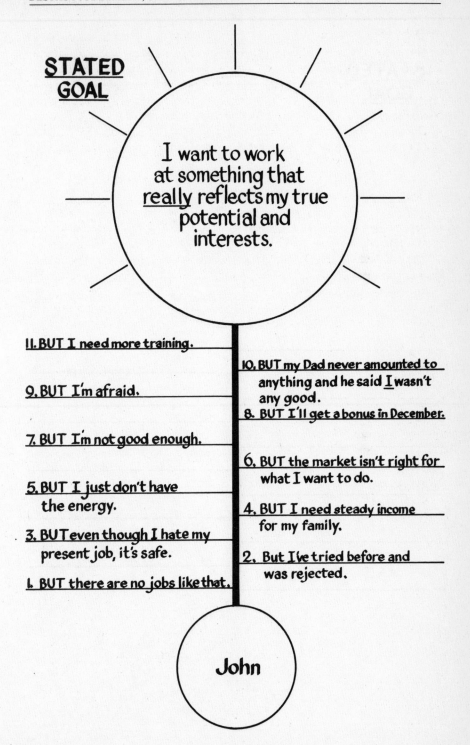

STATED
GOAL

I want to work
at something that
really reflects my true
potential and
interests.

11. BUT I need more training.

10. BUT my Dad never amounted to
anything and he said I wasn't
any good.

8. BUT I'll get a bonus in December.

9. BUT I'm afraid.

7. BUT I'm not good enough.

6. BUT the market isn't right for
what I want to do.

5. BUT I just don't have
the energy.

4. BUT I need steady income
for my family.

3. BUT even though I hate my
present job, it's safe.

2. But I've tried before and
was rejected.

1. BUT there are no jobs like that.

John

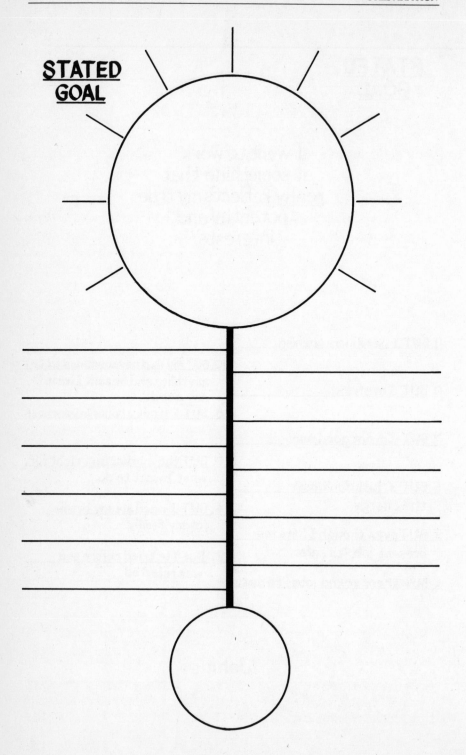

STATED GOAL

4

PAY ATTENTION

The obscure we see eventually, the completely apparent takes longer.

> Edward R. Murrow
> Broadcaster

The mere act of observing something changes the nature of the thing observed.

> Werner K. Heisenberg
> (Heisenberg Uncertainty Principle)

First we see the hills in the painting, then we see the painting in the hills.

> Li Li Weng

I asked a very successful friend at our twenty-fifth alumni reunion of the Harvard Business School for his measure of success. He said, "I learned to smell the roses."

> Robert Medearis
> Chairman
> Silicon Valley Bank

To know is not to prove, nor to explain. It is to accede to vision. But if we are to have vision, we must learn to participate in the object of vision. The apprenticeship is hard.

> Antoine de Saint Exupéry
> *Flight to Arras*

If you see in any given situation only what everybody else can see, you can be said to be so much a representative of your culture that you are a victim of it.

> S. I. Hayakawa
> Semanticist and former senator

A Western businessman heard that a Zen master living on a faraway mountain knew the three basic secrets of life. Anyone who could obtain these secrets would know everything he needed to live a happy, fulfilling life. The businessman, whose life felt empty, reflected at length on what these three secrets might be. What possible words would answer all of life's problems and guarantee constant feelings of well being? Determined to find out, he finally sold his business and began his travels in search of the master. Two years later he arrived at the top of the right mountain and at the right zendo. There sat the Zen master.

The man approached the sage and said, "Oh, master, I have traveled far and wide to hear the three secrets that I need to know in order to live a full and rich life. Would you tell me those secrets?"

The master bowed in return and said, "Yes, I will tell you. The first secret is pay attention. The second secret is pay attention, and the third secret is pay attention."

You are in good company if your first response is something like "Is that all? I was hoping for something profound." But let it sink in, and you might wonder "What does it really mean to *pay attention*?" It took us several years to see how truly meaningful the message is. Now each time we hear it, we gain fresh insight and deeper appreciation of its importance.

Pay attention to what? For starters: to what you are feeling, what you are sensing, and what you are thinking; to the sounds around you, the opening bud, the color of the autumn leaf; to the wind, the shrug of a shoulder, the taste and texture of your food. This kind of paying attention immerses you in life in a new way.

If you pay attention at every moment, you form a new relationship to time. Your own absorption slows you down internally. That slowing down feeds your sense of deep appreciation and at the same time produces more energy. In some magical way, by slowing down you become more efficient, productive, and energetic, focusing without distraction directly on the task in front of you. Not only do you become immersed in that moment; you *become* that moment.

Start Right Now!

This kind of attention-paying is thoughtfulness without thinking. The Buddhists call it "mindfulness." It is attention without thinking, without memories, without associations, without feelings. Most of us lose the knack for it in childhood. But you have already reawakened some of your abilities through reading the last two chapters—by surrendering to your Essence and by attacking the VOJ.

This chapter will develop your third tool for creative living: penetrating observation. Within you, fogged in by the VOJ, abides your Objective Intelligence, the part of you that clearly senses and perceives every situation. It is your inner voice of assessment, objectivity, appraisal, and impartiality (in contrast with the VOJ's blame, criticism, shame, and scolding) that leads you to observe as a scientist observes, without the pollution of stray emotions and nattering judgment.

You can learn to hear the inner voice of your Objective Intelligence just the way you learned to recognize the VOJ. With the VOJ, you go on a search-and-destroy mission; with your Objective Intelligence you're on a homeward trek, because it's a path toward manifesting your full potential.

Now hear this:

"I noticed that."

"Let's take a look."

"There's something here to see."

"I wonder what the truth is in this situation?"

"I'm curious about what the choices really are."

When you are thinking like that, you know that you are out of judgment and into curiosity; you are beginning to respond to your Objective Intelligence.

There is a real art to attending to the world of each moment in this way. At first you are confused. "Are we supposed to attend to everything?" *Yes!* "But aren't we supposed to focus? To keep an eye on the ball?" *Yes!* "So which is it: everything or focus?"

In *aikido,* a soft martial art, there is a powerful concept of "soft eyes" (see page 204). In it your eyes are open but not focused. Even so, everything in your largest possible visual field is available to you.

Professional baseball players tell Joel Kirsch, a management and sports psychologist who uses aikido, that they perform outstandingly when they are in a fog—probably a soft-eyes form of keeping their eyes on the ball. Basketball star Bill Russell, in his book *Second Wind,* described such moments of paying attention in this way:

> *The game would move so quickly that every fake, cut, and pass would be surprising and yet nothing could surprise me. It was almost as if we were playing in slow motion. During those spells I could almost sense how the next play would develop and where the next shot would be taken. Even before the other team brought the ball in bounds, I could feel it so keenly that I'd want to shout to my teammates, "It's coming there!"—except that I knew everything would change if I did. My premonitions would be consistently correct . . .*

If we can truly pay attention—without mind chatter, the VOJ, or habitual responses—our Essence takes over and directs our attention and responses in an efficient and resourceful way.

Michael Bilich, general manager of the F. A. Hoyt leasing firm, puts it in a larger context:

> *Einstein's equation $E = MC^2$ (that is, energy is equal to mass times the speed of light squared) is nothing more than the relationship between mass and energy. A very small amount of mass can be converted into a tremendous amount of energy. To me, this means that we all have the equivalent of an atomic bomb within us if we could somehow recognize how to cross over from mass to energy. We are all mass, and we have to*

somehow create this energy within us. Now how do you go about this? What I have come to realize is that the difference between consciousness and habit is crucial.

To me consciousness, as opposed to habit, is nothing more than literally being conscious of everything around you at every moment of your existence. Habit is just an unconscious state. When you do something by habit you are not conscious that you are doing it; you are simply doing it because you have done it many times before.

Well, I suppose there might be room for a few habits, but what I work on continually is to rid myself of all habits and to recognize that I am a conscious being; I'm conscious day and night. I'm even working on it while I sleep (although I've been unsuccessful so far). It's like learning to be a carpenter, I guess. If I hit nails hard enough, enough times, I'm going to start putting them in straight. Same thing with this. Habits are simply things we create. If you've created something, you can uncreate it. But it takes work, and it takes practice, practice, practice.

Most of us walk around most of the time as if we were dreaming, paying little attention to what is going on. We need to wake up and hear the birdies sing, keep our eyes on the ball, smell the flowers.

Set an hourly alarm if you must to wake yourself up to your daily daytime world. Remind yourself constantly to pay attention fully. Bilich suggests further:

One thing that really has helped me, and I very highly recommend it to you, is to pick any day you want and be conscious of being conscious that entire day. Every single thing you do, recognize not only that you're doing it but also the purpose for which you are doing it. And all of a sudden you'll start to see things opening up all over the place.

As you practice the pay-attention credo, you begin to realize that both the pleasure you feel and the beauty you begin to appreciate come from within, from your own creative resource. By sharply focusing and truly perceiving, you allow your own Objective Intelligence to take over and present the world in a far more intriguing way than does the VOJ.

UNCOMMON SENSE IN BUSINESS

While most of us pride ourselves on using common sense, a minority of very successful people use uncommon sense; that is, they really know how to pay attention.

James Treybig of Tandem got the idea of his no-fault computers (which never stop working unexpectedly) because he noticed and paid attention to the tremendous problems caused to insurance companies, reservation agents, banks, research facilities, hospitals, military operations, and manufacturing operations when computers went down. At the time virtually no one would support him with capital. Experts and friends thought that both Treybig and his idea were literally crazy.

Ted Nierenberg, founder of Dansk International Designs, calls his kind of paying attention "pattern recognition," an ability to see the exceptions. He elaborates:

When we are professional about something, we really develop added recognition. You can watch a tennis match that goes to five sets, and you can talk to someone like Bjorn Borg afterwards. And you can say, "Where did you win or lose that match?" and he says, "In the third set, second game, the score was 40 to 30 and that was the decisive point." Or you talk to somebody like Jack Nicklaus, and he can tell you it was on the thirteenth hole, coming out of the low rough. I often wonder, "Do these guys have incredible memories? Do they remember every single shot at their fingertips?" And the answer is, "No, they don't, but they remember the exceptions."

In the mid-fifties, when Nierenberg was out of a job, he and his wife Martha went to Europe on a shoestring to distance themselves from their problem of lack of steady income. At an industrial fair in Hanover, Germany, they were impressed by the many booths showing stainless steel flatware. At that time in America, stainless steel tableware was still in army mess halls, school cafeterias, and picnic baskets. But Nierenberg—a man of uncommon sense—smelled another possibility. He visited factories in Germany, checking equipment and costs. Then he visited young designers in Scandinavia to see if they were making anything that would appeal to American tastes. That was the beginning of the enormously successful Dansk, and of a new style in American tableware: elegant stainless steel.

Much is said about the power of visualization, imaging, and positive thinking—all techniques that can help in achieving goals. But where do the goals come from? In a creative life they come from paying attention. Openness to what exists in each moment begins to build a relationship with the creative essence that leads to the kind of vision Ted Nierenberg and our other speakers manifest.

Visualization is especially effective in sports. Evidence indicates that if athletes visualize a certain quality of performance they are more likely to achieve that quality. This seems to be true in business also. If you have to make an important presentation, it helps to visualize an image of poise, power, and clarity.

Both Steve DeVore and Stanford psychologist Roger Shepard have found that a strong sensory orientation, particularly visual imaging, is related to creativity and achievement. For Shepard a visualization led to a creative breakthrough that he describes in *Mental Images and Their Transformations*, a book coauthored with Lynn A. Cooper. He reports that his original visual experience occurred between sleeping and waking on November 16, 1968, as follows:

Just before 6:00 a.m. on that morning and in the absence of any noticeable precursors, [I] experienced a spontaneous kinetic image of three-dimensional structures majestically turning in space. Within moments and before full emergence from sleep, the basic design of the first of the chronometric experiments on "mental rotation of three-dimensional objects," as it later appeared in the journal Science ... *took essentially complete—although as yet completely unverbalized—shape.*

The work that Shepard and his coworkers did following that initial visualization was so pathbreaking that his depictions of it have appeared on the covers of major science publications and at least one cognitive psychology textbook. He says further: "I like to caricature perception as *externally guided hallucination*, and dreaming and hallucination as internally simulated perception."

Shepard's internal imagery, sparked by external attention-paying, is so strong that it even helps him deal with the judgment of others. Skeptics criticized his drawings as too vivid for such a dream state, speculating that he added richness and structure after he woke up. But in the June 1983 *Psychology Today* Shepard says:

On the night of August 29, 1971, I in fact had a dream concerning this very issue. I dreamed that I had awakened and was thinking about the dream I had just had. I went on to dream that I got up, dressed, and was driving down the street on an exceptionally brilliant day. As I drove along, I took special note of the blueness of the sky, the various shades of green of the leaves of the trees along the sides of the road, and, especially, the crisp rich articulation of the leaves and branches of the trees, and of the sidewalks and buildings behind the trees as these flowed past the car. I also noted my own hands on the steering wheel immediately in front of me. At this point I exclaimed to myself in the dream, "Yes, the skeptics are right; no dream could ever approach the perceptual richness of waking experience such as I'm having right now!"

And then I woke up.

Shepard's work clearly suggests that we should pay attention not only to the external world but to our inner world of images and dreams, and that the interaction between the outside stimulus and our inner creativity leads to breakthroughs in all sorts of fields. You can get an idea of the breadth of the potential effect of the pay-attention credo from this excerpt from his October 1984 *Psychological Review* article:

It was apparently through such dream simulations that Jack Nicklaus changed his golf grip and subsequently improved his waking golf game by 10 points; Taffy Pergament, the 1963 national novice figure-skating title winner, originated her new jump, the "Taffy"; a gynecologist discovered how to tie a surgical knot deep in the pelvis with one hand;

Elias Howe had the crucial insight necessary for his perfection of the sewing machine; Louis Agassiz found a way to extract a fossil, undamaged, from a slab of stone; James Watt came up with a simpler method of manufacturing lead shot; H. V. Hilprecht realized how to fit certain archaeological fragments together, enabling him subsequently to decipher their cuneiform inscriptions; Friedrich Kekulé solved the outstanding problem of the molecular structure of benzine; Otto Loewi devised the experiment that led to his 1936 Nobel Prize for the discovery of the chemical basis of neural transmission; and (in the related hypnopompic state) I myself conceived of the experimental study of mental rotation.... And every waking day, by thought alone, physicists, stereochemists, mechanical engineers, inventors, architects, carpenters, interior decorators, and just plain folks successfully anticipate the consequences of carrying out complex physical manipulations and rearrangements of objects in the three-dimensional world.

Unfortunately, as do most scientists doing research related to creativity, Shepard neglects to mention creativity in business. But that consideration is covered quite well by Steve DeVore in the work he did to develop his learning program, "The Neuropsychology of Achievement." His findings are similar to Shepard's although DeVore's purpose is more applied and less scientific. His conclusion:

The main characteristic of historical as well as contemporary high achievers is what we call "sensory orientation." Creative high achievers practice a positive sensory orientation. If you ask them to explain to you their goals, their hopes, their aspirations, they would be able to do this in three-dimensional sensory detail. They would be able to paint a picture for you with their words of what their hopes, aspirations, and goals were. If you ask them to explain to you their failures in life, all of a sudden it becomes one-dimensional. The words become more abstract. They become devoid of meaning.

But, continues DeVore, the high achiever pays attention to his or her failures:

The high achievers can tell you in three-dimensional terms what they learn from their failures and how they applied that. They view their failures not as failures but as learning experiences to be applied, and they can explain this to you in three-dimensional, sensory-rich words. They can paint a picture for you about that.

Now the underachievers have a negative sensory orientation. If you ask them to explain to you their hopes, goals and aspirations, their explanation is one-dimensional. "I want to be happy." "I want to be fulfilled." "I want a big house." "I want a college education." If you ask them to go beyond that explanation and explain the sensory detail, they can't. It becomes a collage of words that have no meaning. But if you ask them to relate to you their failures and their fears, all of a sudden they can create a holographic three-dimensional image of what their fears are, because they have already experienced their fears. It is much easier for these people to experience the consequence of their fears coming to pass, and they can do it in sensory detail. They can explain for you their failures because they live with them every day. They replay them every day.

Did you just put yourself in one of the boxes—positive or negative sensory orientation—that DeVore described? It's a natural thing to do. We are always trying to find out more about ourselves. But pay attention! You don't have to go into a box—especially a negative one. If you pay attention to everything in each moment, your Essence will direct you to the main event, to the ball you should keep your eye on. And this will naturally lead you to what DeVore calls a positive sensory orientation.

Shepard uses the term "resonance" to describe the pay-attention process. When you keep your eyes, ears, and other senses open, the external data resonate with your internal resources.

DeVore's Own Videotape

One phase of resonance is perceptive observation, as when you watch chemistry experiments in school, "feel" good dancers make certain movements, sense your opponent's tennis form, follow good cooks around their kitchens. You don't remember it, but that's how you learned to walk and talk; even babies (perhaps especially babies) know a lot about resonance. Virtually all of our creative business leaders and students experience resonance as they closely observe others who serve as models or mentors for them.

The life of Steve DeVore, whose SyberVision Systems provides videotape models for people to use in improving their performance in various sports, is a saga of attention-paying and resonance.

DeVore contracted polio when he was two, and his parents refused to allow the operations that would confine him to a wheelchair. Instead his mother massaged his legs for months, until he could stand with a walk bar. But he had forgotten how to walk, and hospital therapists weren't helping him. At that point his mother instinctively began to encourage a kind of sensory visualization that DeVore himself many years later applied in his business. She put him through an intense program of sensing and paying attention that would help him to walk again. As DeVore tells the story:

For a year and a half she took me to a park every day. She had me watch people walk, and it went beyond watching. It went into sensing how people walked, and picking up the sound and the rhythm of the footstep, and getting caught up in the feeling and the sense of motion. As we watched, she incited my emotions by saying, "Look how easy it is. You can be doing that yourself."

It created a sense of motivation, and after that hour in the park every day, we used to go home and go through the sensing exercises. She'd get me relaxed. Then she'd have me mentally replay the events of what we saw that day: the timing, the sense of rhythm, the sense of movement, the sounds. And we got to a point where I was able to regain my walking skills in a very short time. By the time I was five years old, I was playing baseball, basketball, kickball, foursquare, and everything with all the other kids. I was probably more coordinated and stronger than the kids my own age.

To make a long story short, by the time I got out of high school, I was offered scholarships to play college baseball by two universities. This experience was very catalytic in my life. I view this experience as almost a life mission. There's something there to be learned and applied.

DeVore's first job after receiving his Master's degree in organizational behavior was with the Union Carbide Corporation in New York. He became manager of corporate golf outings. On the surface it was a challenge in developing systems, since it was his job to put together senior-management teams from major corporations with leading golf pros. But once again DeVore found resonance within himself.

The most appealing thing was my chance to learn how these senior executives function. I did have the opportunity to observe about half of the Fortune 500 CEOs and presidents, and it was a very fulfilling job.

Unfortunately (or perhaps fortunately for DeVore) there was a slump in the economy and his program was eliminated; he declined the alternative position offered to him. The following out-of-work period was difficult but gave him some real exercise in a new kind of resonance:

The unsuccessful job-hunting became very frustrating, and I became very depressed. So much so that I made myself susceptible to a virus that resulted in spinal meningitis. And I was laid down flat in bed for three months with no income coming in. Nothing coming in at all and a wife who was pregnant, mortgage payments that were overdue, and every time I started to stand up my head just throbbed, and I couldn't do anything. All I could do was read. And so I had my wife go to the library.

I said, "Get me every book you can on every great person, every person who has been successful." In these three months I devoured about twenty-five autobiographies and biographies of great people. And every time I read these biographies or autobiographies I identified with these people. These people became models. Then my wife brought home this magazine called Success Unlimited. *It has stories about the successes of entrepreneurs, about how they came out of nowhere and became successful, how they overcame obstacles and hardships. There's one story in particular about one fellow whom I really identified with because he was broke. He pulled off to the side of the road one day, desperate, broke down in tears, and started praying and everything else because his business was going bankrupt. But that turned him around, and he began to become a success. At the moment I read that, something came over me. A sensory impression or desire came over me: a conviction. I said, "Someday this magazine is going to write about me, because I am going to do something worthy that this magazine is going to take cognizance of, and they are going to write about me!" And since that time that magazine has written two feature articles on me, and it wasn't because I tried. At that point I forgot about it—until that magazine three years later called to interview me.*

Every Stick Has Two Ends

Most of our speakers agree with the philosopher G. I. Gurdjieff that a situation that at first glance seems to be either good or bad carries the opposite characteristic too. This means that no matter how painful a situation seems, it bears the seeds of progress and creative development—if only we can pay attention as diligently as does Steve DeVore.

Robert Medearis, entrepreneur and Silicon Valley Bank chairman tells this story:

I recently asked a friend who has his own thriving consulting business, "What's the most significant event that's happened to you since you left business school?" "Well," he said, "it's very clear what the most significant event was for me. You remember when that cable slipped?" He was in the Squaw Valley cable car disaster. He and his wife and daughter were separated when the cable came down. He fell a hundred and sixty-five feet and bashed in his skull, broke all the ribs on his left side and both legs. He didn't know if his wife and daughter were dead. They didn't know if he was dead. He fell down a cliff, and he scrambled up hand over hand. When he arrived on the top, he said to himself, "You know, life is so fleeting that one must really enjoy every moment." He told me that "I had a serenity about me then that I've never had before, because it was so beautiful! The snow conditions, the storm, even the disaster scenario was a very beautiful event for me. I realized that we're never going to get anything that we can't handle, and secondly there is absolute beauty in everything—because that fall, that experience in the snow, was so incredible."

His idea came out right then. He said to himself, "I must leave my present company, and I'm going to start my own business because that's really something I've always wanted to do." And he did it the minute he got out of the hospital. Now I'm not going to say that that accident occurred to impact that one person, but I am going to say that the cause-effect ratio within every event in your life is something you always have to be tuned in to. Even sickness, by and large, is just a method by which your body is telling you to do something or change something.

If you can continue to pay attention during painful or crisis situations, you can make breakthroughs to your own potential. Philip Lipetz of General Molecular Applications provides another example of this. In a mountain-climbing accident he found himself hanging by a rope that for several hours almost completely cut off his oxygen supply. He says:

As my body was undergoing the physical process of death, something very interesting happened. A small, brilliant dot of blue light appeared before my eyes. My consciousness merged with this light, whereupon it exploded and spread outward in all directions. I experienced a joy unlike any joy I had ever before experienced. Everything was suddenly one reality. I could still understand and function in the world of differences, could still experience my body dangling from the rope, could still see my friend panicking above me and a crowd of people from a nearby town gathering below me, anxious to witness my impending death. However, the different aspects of the scene appeared as the various reflections of one underlying essence. Death no longer had any meaning for me. I saw that life and death were one, and that the passage from life to death involved no fundamental transition. It would be fine if I lived, and it would also be fine if I died.

At about this time a rescue party reached the top of the mountain, and I was hauled to safety. I went into convulsions as I regained normal consciousness. I am told that the first words I said to my rescuers were, "Why did you rescue me? I was perfectly happy where I was. In fact, I have never been happier."

Syntex's Marc Steuer calls the awareness of these difficult situations "breakdowns" or "breakopens." He says that the environment provides everything you need for creativity, but you need some stimulus to make you aware of these materials. Say that you get a flat tire. The first thing that you might do is curse or groan. Your expletive—however blasphemous, scatological, or pornographic—is a signal, says Steuer, of a breakdown. It symbolizes your awareness of the problem. And suddenly you pay attention to items in your environment that you paid no attention to before: the side of the road you must head for, the tools and the jack in the trunk, the tightness of the tire's lug nuts—all the background aspects that now provide the materials for creative solution. Steuer sums up:

You can't invent anything that's not in the domain of possibilities, and the domain of possibilities is hidden in the background unless something brings it forth.

Did you ever walk through a field and get burrs, the little things with the spikes and spines, on your clothes? Pain in the neck, right? So the background that you have is: My clothes shouldn't get burrs in them, it looks stupid, it looks silly, it hurts, whatever else. That's the background of your approach to them. So you've got these burrs. You can either be upset when you have burrs on your clothes, or you can invent Velcro®.

So is that a shift in the foreground? No. The burrs are the same burrs. Is there a shift in the background? Yes. So what are we doing? We are focusing on the foreground and the background. So when life really gets tough, my assertion about creativity is: Change the background.

And this is all a matter of paying attention. It doesn't even require a very active analytical process. Rather it involves a *sensing* of your environment.

Yet from childhood on your VOJ encourages you to steer away from difficulty; to fret about or overcontrol your environment; to attempt to solve problems by ignoring them; or to submit passively to traditional intrusions in the way of persons, places, and things.

So a conflict eventually develops within, between the VOJ's habitual, comfortable, programmed attitudes and the Objective Intelligence's perceptive, attentive, and joyful alternative. This conflict initially produces some upset or discomfort, some of which you might experience in reading this book. Faced with change, the internal VOJ gives you a lot of trouble. Don't worry about it. Yell back, and smell the flowers.

Sharpening Your Ear for Business

There is no doubt that paying attention in the form of *listening* greatly affects the American economy and psyche. For the lack of listening, billions of dollars of losses accumulate: retyped letters, rescheduled appointments, rerouted shipments, breakdowns in labor management relations, misunderstood sales presentations, and job interviews that never really get off the ground.

One of us (Michael) spent much time helping a company fill an important and specifically detailed position. Finally an East Coast candidate qualified for a session of West Coast interviews. During his visit he overflowed with ideas, making many, many suggestions and comments on the operation. Unfortunately he was so effusive that in several meetings eyes glazed over as company officials gave him his due. Later the division's head summarily closed the candidate's file with just two words: "Doesn't listen."

Many companies find the quality of listening important enough to brag about it in their advertising. In one magazine we found these headlines and slogans: "We understand how important it is to listen," "I'm probably the best listener you'll ever hear," and "What's the point of talking? You don't listen anyway." A 1985 *Fortune* article carries the title "How to Sell by Listening."

But what is true listening? Check a dictionary and you'll find a real difference between "hearing" and "listening." The definition for hearing is "the capacity for auditory sensations." The definition for listening is "to pay attention, to give heed, to apply oneself to hearing something." So hearing is the capacity to receive the sounds, while listening is the act of paying attention to the sounds themselves.

Most of the sounds we hear are words. By developing these words into phrases, then into sentences, then into paragraphs, you do something called communicating. Questions and answers, statements and responses. What could be simpler?

In practice, communication is the most complex of all complex activities of human existence. These sounds called words produce emotional despair, wild elation, tenderness, tears, relaxation, hope, fury. These little things called words create divorces, barroom brawls, embattled societies, and global wars, in addition to success and failure in business.

To some extent it is true that you improve communication by improving your speech. But it is a far better thing to listen well than to speak, write, or even present ideas well.

Communication, as the theorists and practitioners tell us, is simply a moment of overlapping fields of experience. We make a connection with another person or even a whole audience when we experience the same thing together. And at least half of the effectiveness of communication must come from the listening side, from paying attention.

From our speakers' discussions, we discovered that good listening is the basis of the creativity of many of them. Both Tom Peters, with his idea of "managing by walking around," and Rene McPherson, with his emphasis on "managing from the bottom up," base their approaches on true listening. When Peters' managers walk around, they listen to what people are saying. McPherson describes his own open-ear management in this way:

Oh, that's easy. Start before everybody. Work later than everybody, and just use all the people-assets. There are hundreds of them all around you. All kinds of people surrounding you who are willing to help you, and nobody ever asks them. And you go ask them for some help, and you work with them, and they just love you to death, because you came and asked them "What do you think?" and you are genuine about it.

Claude Rosenberg of Rosenberg Capital Management says:

To be creative, if you talk less and listen more you will do very well.

Syntex's Marc Steuer says:

I submit to you, creativity's not talking; it's all about the ability to listen.

Organizational development specialist Don Prentice makes clear the link between listening and creativity:

The only thing that I can come up with is that the real source of creativity is truth. The truth is endlessly creative. The problem with that is I don't know what the truth is. Even less do I know what your truth is. What's creative? It's that truth. So how do I put this idea of creativity into practice? All I know is you listen to what's going on at that moment, and you follow the truth of what's going on in that moment—that's how you do it. The essence of creativity is to listen. You have to listen. Just forget yourself, whoever that is; leave yourself open and let it be. That's creativity.

ADVENTURES IN ATTENTION

Each of the following exercises can give you an intense jolt of clear perception, though it might take some practice.

Lose Your Head

In a yogic story, God in the form of Lord Shiva was about to manifest a new universe when His advisors complained that He was too remote in the last one. They wanted Him, this time, to be around more visibly and more often.

Shiva promised that in the new universe He would be present wherever people were present. It would be easy to find Him because He would always appear as a body without a head.

And, says the story, *this* is that new universe, and *you* are the body without the head.

This story is a bit of a yogic joke, but its imagery offers a fine technique for learning to pay attention. Actually, you're relearning the kind of headlessness you had as an infant, when you were unselfconscious and saw everything through a thought-free state.

Some thirty-five years ago an Englishman named Douglas Harding experienced the phenomenon of headlessness while he was walking in the Himalayas soaking in the mountain scenery and thinking about God. For one instant, the outside universe was inside his head—was his head. That experience governed his life work from that moment on. He developed a number of approaches for regaining such moments and for making such an experience available to others. Among his favorites were Zen *koans,* cryptic statements that challenge self-blinding concepts. See if your head can survive this one:

Find the face you had before you were born.

When you think about it, you realize that you have a head only when you consider yourself a separate, free-floating object; you are especially aware of your objective isolation when you see yourself in a mirror or photograph. This kind of aloofness is a hotbed of judgment and difficulty, because you perceive others as separate objects too; as a consequence you slip into the vanity-chafing habit of seeing yourself as you think *they* see *you.* One yoga teacher said in the magazine *Siddha Path:*

We allow ourselves to be objects "over there," in others' eyes. The headless one is full and complete; the person as object is always subject to the judgment of others.

One segment of the following exercise directs you to see as though you were looking through a hand-held movie camera. Movie directors use this as a technique to move the audience into the mind of a character, to see through his eyes. When you as part of an audience do this, you no longer judge that character as a separate, questionable being; you move *into* his experience to become one with him.

And that's headlessness: You are one with all you behold.

It isn't a conscious act of saying, "I am going to be one with this mountain or tree or lake or person." You simply unite naturally with universal truth: the beauty of all creation, and the boundless intuition, will, joy, strength, and compassion that Essence makes available to every living being.

A guide for doing this was provided in the November 1984 issue of *Siddha Path*. The point of this dharana is to throw us back on our own subjectivity. After you understand it, use it many times a day as a reminder.

Posture: Practice this with your eyes open while you are walking around, performing your daily activities.

Thought: "I am the headless one."

Two suggested ways of visualizing headlessness: "The world issues out from my shoulders;" or "The world is in my head." (Isn't the perception of the world only in your head? When you sleep the world doesn't exist for you.)

A variation: "My eyes are a hand-held movie camera and I am filming whatever I see."

See as an Artist Sees

Every great work of art—no matter the medium—comes from a clear perception on the part of its creator that resonates within a clear perception on the part of the audience. In our sense of unity with a masterpiece, we lose our heads, forget all the trivial mind chatter, meet our own Maker. As the Sufis say, "Painting and Painter are one."

Constantin Stanislavski, the originator of method acting, stresses the importance of paying attention for actor-artists. In his book, *An Actor Prepares*, Stanislavski exhorts:

An actor should be observant not only on the stage, but also in real life. He should concentrate with all his being on whatever attracts his attention. He should look at an object not as any absent-minded passerby but with penetration. Otherwise his whole creative method will prove lopsided and bear no relation to life....

Average people have no conception of how to observe the facial expression, the look of the eye, the tone of the voice, in order to comprehend the state of mind of the persons with whom they talk. They can neither actively grasp the complex truths of life nor listen in a way to understand what they hear. If they could do this, life, for them, would be better and easier, and their creative work immeasurably richer, finer, and deeper....

How can we teach unobservant people to notice what nature and life are trying to show them? First of all they must be taught to look at, to listen to, and to hear what is beautiful.... Nothing in life is more beautiful than nature, and it should be the object of constant observation.... And do not shun the darker side of nature. Look for it in marshes, in the slime of the sea, amid plagues of insects, and remember that hidden behind these phenomena there is beauty, just as in loveliness there is unloveliness.

Art teachers delineate three kinds of seeing: operational, associational, and pure. Rochelle illustrates those approaches by showing how three students react to a strange velvet ball-and-sphere object placed in their classroom.

The operational viewer would veer around it to make way to his proper seat. His only real awareness of it would be his recognition of the necessity to avoid it. He makes no error; but he does by-pass a chance to expand his horizons.

The associational viewer sees a bit more deeply. After he reaches his seat, he lets his recognition of the ball trigger some pleasant free associations: basketball season, which reminds him of a girl who watched him make a free throw, which reminds him of her father who once helped a herpetologist catch snakes, which reminds him of a San Antonio youngster who almost died of snake-bite, which reminds him of a doctor he once knew who quoted Leacock and Aristophanes ... He makes no error, either, but he by-passes an opportunity to focus on something immediately within his ken.

The pure viewer enters completely into the moment:

He observes the shapes of both the sphere and the pedestal, and the way in which the sphere rests. He sees how the curved surface turns back the light, how the color varies from the top to the underside of the sphere, and how the texture of the velvet contrasts with that of the pedestal. He moves around the sphere, looks at it from high and low points of view, and he sees how its appearance changes with his own movement. He experiences the perfection of the spherical shape, how it always turns back into itself, never leading to anything beyond itself except at the point of tangency with the top surface of the pedestal. He is inclined to touch the sphere—to test, as it were, his visual response against the tactile, or touch, response. He is not primarily interested in determining what this object is or for what it might be used. He is interested in how it is. He is not primarily concerned with the cost of this object, nor is he, in this early stage of seeing, concerned with where it came from or why it happens to be standing in his path. First and foremost, this person who exercises his vision in this pure way is taken up with the specific qualities of the particular objects before him. He may even become interested in the temperature of the velvet surfaces compared to the temperature of the harder, more closely textured surface of the pedestal. He may wonder how heavy this never-before-seen velvet sphere is, and he may lift it, or may try to.

To this person, this object is worthy of his sight, worthy of becoming known to him—for whatever reasons or nonreasons. He discovers the object, as it were, in looking at it. Instead of projecting his biases or preferences into the object, he makes himself available to the specific set of conditions that make up the particular object. In a broad sense, he is learning from the object; he is not committing the folly of trying to teach the object what he thinks he already knows. His expectations follow along with his deepening discovery of the quality of the object and they are largely determined by that quality. And so, if he is looking at a velvet sphere, he does not expect the conflict of hard right angles; nor does the absence of a glossy surface disappoint him or make him melancholy.

Teachers tell art students to pay attention to already existing work. In the following excerpt, the late Minor White—who taught photography at MIT using meditation, astrology, I Ching, and philosophy—assigns to his students the "simplest exercise possible." In later elaborations he suggests a preparation that starts with meditation, moves through detailed observation, and ends with structured remember-and-share sessions with others. You can develop such aspects on your own. Remember as you practice that the point is to apply the same kind of vivid attention to everyday situations.

Here is White's simplest exercise:

Select a photograph that you can look at for a long time with pleasure. Set aside some time, a half hour or so, that can pass without a single interruption. Set the picture in good light and yourself in a comfortable position. Look at the picture for at least ten minutes without moving even one small muscle or "giving in" to even one tiny twitch. Keep your eyes and mind on the image, instead of following long chains of associations; keep coming back to the picture. You can expect that many things will be found in it, not previously noticed. After ten or fifteen minutes, turn away from the picture and recall what you have experienced, step by step. Make this as visual as possible; review the experience visually rather than with words. After the thirty minutes have elapsed, more or less, and the experience has become a kind of flavor, go about the day's work, trying to recall the taste when you can.

No one can predict what you will experience. The trick is to accept whatever the experience is for what it is. Then one will face a moment of truth, tiny though this moment may be, relative, limited, or even negative and unexpected. It is only when one anticipates explosions, ecstasy, breakthroughs, thundering visions, that an actual, real moment of truth will be overlooked and therefore missed. If you habitually bring the notion of God into your activities, listen for the whisper. To our weak perceptions even thunder may reach us but faintly.

(Minor White, "Extended Perception Through Photography and Suggestion," permission, Minor White Archives)

Listen as a Therapist Listens

The most direct way to become a creative listener would be to become a professional listener—a clinical psychologist or therapist who uses listening as a tool for healing.

When therapy works, we say that the patient gets better because he expresses his emotions. This is only partially true. The full truth is that fine-tuned listening encourages the realization that heals. By mutual consent patient and therapist, through the instrument of listening, tune in to an operative reality.

Basically, a therapist tries to get at the patient's viewpoint. The professional listener says: "I am totally listening to everything that you say. You are not totally committed, nor do you need to be, to listening to everything that I say. You might hear many things that I say, that you say, or you might hear little of both. But we are each engaged in arranging different things. You are in a process of rearranging and integrating your new perceptions as they unfold. I'm in the process of rearranging your old perceptions and calling attention to new ones for you to arrange and integrate."

The therapist's goal is the healing of the patient. This seems a strange perception to consider applying in business, but it is certainly one that will lead you to riveted listening, and its efficacy is based on the wisdom of "Physician, heal thyself."

Dr. David K. Reynolds, a leading American practitioner of the Japanese Morita psychotherapy, points out that listening as a therapist listens does a great deal of good for the listener. In his book *Playing Ball on Running Water,* he tells of his treatment of a patient named Tamura:

> *Mr. Tamura was instructed to make efforts to act with "a therapist's heart." That is, he was to utilize the expertise he had unwittingly gained through the years of therapy for the benefit of those around him. Rather than complain to his wife about his own troubles, he was to return home and ask about* her *problems with housework and the children and ask how* he *could help. Had there been time, we would have done role-playing with my acting as Mr. Tamura's student.*
>
> *Mr. Tamura was surprised to hear that within him was a latent therapist. He was also surprised to learn that patients "treat" therapists. That is, treating patients helps therapists with their own problems, creates confidence within the therapists themselves, and holds all sorts of additional benefits. Teachers need their students at least as much as the students need teachers.*

So find your therapist's heart, and see how it enriches your business life. Here are five basic professional secrets that will sharpen your therapeutic ears. Practice them, as you would an exercise, on your next business encounter:

1. Give yourself permission to listen by giving up that part of you—your mind chatter—that wants to be more important than the speaker. Surrender to the moment that the speaker sees as *his* reality, and absorb it with all of your senses.

2. Quell your desire to talk. Like internal mind chatter, your desire to hold forth is nothing but self-puffery. Such an impulse might sell itself to you as the virtue of social responsibility; when the VOJ tells you that, remember that your own voice is your own biggest block to creative listening.

3. Suspend judgment. Now that you know about the VOJ, you also know a lot about stifling it. Don't let your own conclusions, opinions, notions, and emotions fill your receiving airwaves with static.

4. Search out what is truly important to the speaker. As you listen, learn to walk in his shoes. You will learn early that to identify with others you must quiet your own mind and call upon (dwell within) your own Essence quality of compassion.

5. Focus on the main event. Use the flashlight technique: Scanning the details of what someone says ("I lost a big account," "I've missed my deadlines," "My wife's cranky"), but stop and consider deeply the most important conclusion ("I am so depressed"). Think of your listening as a light that scans and indicates the total picture in its detail and also allows your concentration on the most important point.

Take a Fantastic Voyage

Remember the movie called *Fantastic Voyage?* In it, miniaturized scientists penetrate—as if it were a continent—a human body. The little adventure we present here is not quite as fantastic, but it does connect you with another person in a brand new way.

In this dharana, you focus upon a friend in the same way that you focused earlier upon a photograph. Minor White instructed students to do their looking without muscular twitches; in this exercise, you must try to look into the eyes of another person without blinking for about two minutes. You will find it very difficult to maintain eye contact for more than a few seconds. Remember that you're an intrepid explorer; against all odds, push on calmly to make a remarkable eyeball connection.

Try not to have expectations. Some people find familiar faces; others find a glowing light; a few find only an unbreakable chain of thought. Whatever you find, keep trying; White pointed out that tiny observations can be important in the long run. At the very least, you will develop some ability to make eye contact during conversations. That will make you a better observer and a better listener.

You might prefer to do this exercise initially with someone you feel comfortable with—a spouse or a close friend.

Sit facing the other person with your feet flat on the floor and your hands comfortably in your lap. You might want to do some relaxation exercise such as sensing your arms and legs and breathing deeply. Set a timer for one or two minutes and look into each other's eyes without blinking or moving your eyeballs. Don't worry if your eyes blink or twitch involuntarily. Relax, this is not a competition.

When the bell rings, close your eyes for a brief period and savor the experience you have just had. What did you see? Did you have an experience of unity or diversity? Did you have any special feeling toward or impression of the other person? What thoughts went through your mind at that time? Or did your thoughts stop?

When the two of you open your eyes, share the experience with each other. After some time you might want to try it again.

Variations: You can do this exercise in a group with a number of pairs or in a solitary fashion using a mirror. Some say that placing a lit candle between your face and the mirror produces a very strong effect.

Visit Ancient Egypt

Paying attention means making a connection between the outer reality and your inner resource. It's a three-link chain; object, perception, and creative transformation (into idea, solution, breakthrough, or whatever you need).

Various devices provide you with a rich source of external objects that invite such transformation. A very simple one is the assembly of Egyptian hieroglyphics on the next page. Before you study it, choose a particular problem that you'd like to solve. Then glance at the hieroglyphics, write out your problem on the top of the page, and meditate on your problem for a few moments.

When you open your eyes, write out your translation of each line of hieroglyphics as if they were written in ancient times expressly to help you deal with your present situation.

To make this exercise work for you, you must pay attention in a nonexpectant way. See each line as a brand new message from the past to you. Don't over-intellectualize; have fun with each separate line.

And pay attention further by finding within your daily environment other opportunities to speak to your self through the inner transformation of external mysteries.

Become a Brain Surgeon

As you pay clear attention to your external world you begin to be able to pull this outer stimulation inside. This is the direct approach offered by biofeedback, in which you can learn to turn down the activity of your

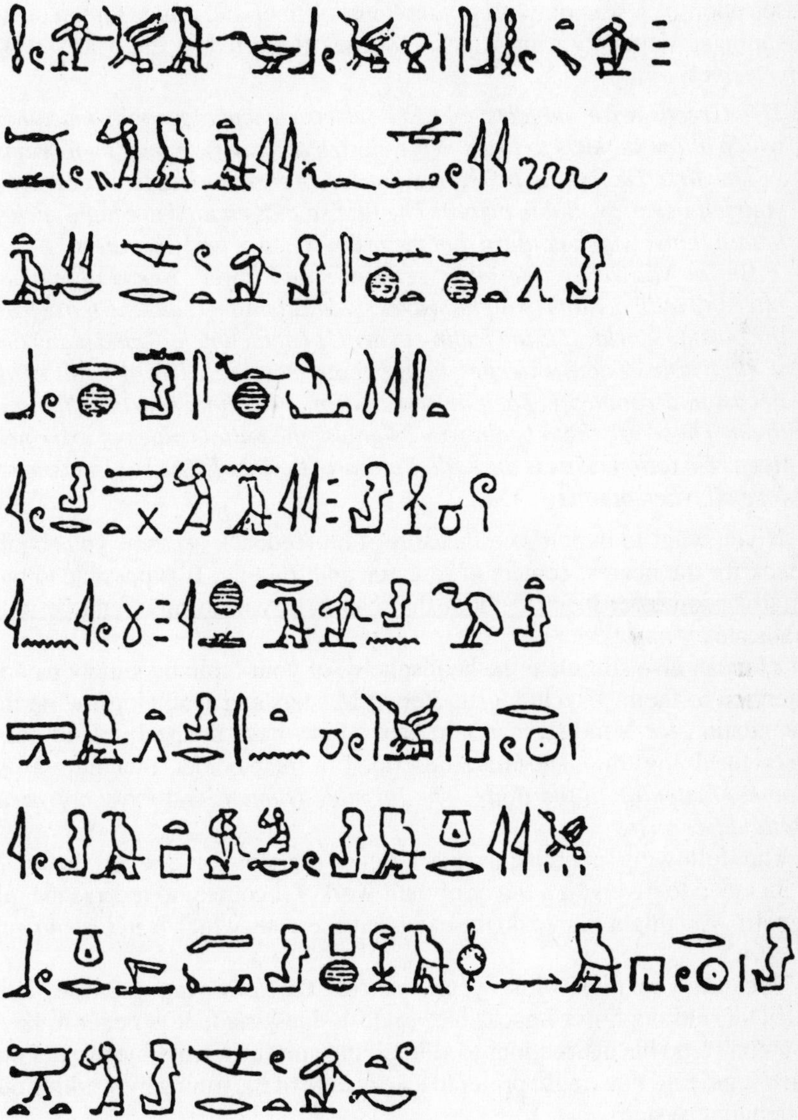

involuntary nervous system so that you can get into a mental state that is something between sleep and waking. In that state, you can get messages from your own creative resource.

Biofeedback is a little like brain surgery without the instruments, particularly when you receive feedback on your brain's activities. Witness this description of a session with psychologists Elmer and Alyce Green of the Menninger Foundation in Topeka, Kansas (reported in the March 1982 *American Way*).

> *The Greens wire subjects to EEG (electroencephalograph) machines, which allow subjects to listen to the electrical activity of their own brains.*
>
> *The first EEG is a bit eerie. You are receiving subtle clues about yourself never available before. The first sounds emitted are high-pitched beta signals, which confirm that the brain is active and fully alert.*
>
> *But as you relax, the tones get lower and lower. Beeps of medium intensity indicate lots of alpha waves; your attention is cutting loose from the outside world. It is the feeling of drift, of detachment—and many find it enjoyable. Then a deeper tone begins to sound, like the fall of an occasional raindrop. Then more raindrops. In short spurts, a flood of them. These are theta brain-wave signals, the telltale clues of extremely deep relaxation. This is the twilight zone of the mind. The subject tends to lose all track of time.*

If you want to experience this sort of biofeedback session, you should check for the nearest centers of research and training. It is possible to buy small-scale biofeedback devices that can help you to relax and get into that state.

You can also stimulate the hemispheres of your brain by simply paying attention to them. Psychologists Robert Masters and Jean Houston, at the Foundation for Mind Research in New York, have devised several exercises for doing this. These are described in their books, including *Mind Games, Listening to the Body, The Possible Human,* and *Psychophysical Method Exercises*.

The following exercise is a shortened version of one of theirs. It is included to give you a flavor of their work. Of course, to receive the full benefit, you might like to do the extended exercise, which is in *Listening to the Body*.

Because you must close your eyes for the following exercise, it is difficult, although not impossible, to do it unassisted. It is better to have someone read the instructions to you, giving you sufficient time to carry out each segment. You might prefer to take charge of the timing by working out a signaling system.

Seat yourself in a position—preferably on the floor—that you will be able to maintain with minimal discomfort and without shifting. Closing your eyes, try to become as aware as possible of your left eye. Keeping your eyes closed, look down at the floor with your left eye. Look up toward the ceiling with it. Now look to the right with your left eye, then look to the left. Keep doing that—up and down, right and left. Try to be as aware as possible of the shape and weight of your left eyeball.

Now do the same thing with the right eye, keeping your eyes closed. Look up and down several times with your right eye, then to the left and to the right a few times. And try to be aware of the shape and weight of your right eyeball.

Shift your attention to the left side of your brain, above your left eye. You should be focusing on the space inside your skull where the brain is. Do that for a few seconds.

Now shift your attention to the right side of your brain and keep it there a little while. Shift now to the left side, then bring it back to the right side again. Keep shifting your attention back and forth between the two sides of your brain.

Now look up at the left side of your brain and imagine the number 1. Look over to the right side and see the letter A. Look to the left and see the number 2 and then look right and see the letter B. Next on the left is 3 and then on the right is C. Continue to the number 26 and the letter Z if you can, taking your time and seeing the number on the left and the letter on the right.

Now let's do it the opposite way. Look to the right side of your brain and see the number 1 and then to the left the letter A. Now the number 2 is on the right and the letter B is on the left. Keep on going as far as you can to the number 26 and the letter Z.

Keeping your eyes closed, think for a moment about what you just did and whether you did it any better on one side than on the other. If there was any significant difference, you might want to work with the numbers and letters frequently until you have equalized your performance on the left and right sides.

(Adapted with permission from Robert Masters and Jean Houston, *Listening to the Body*, Delacorte Press)

Tune In to Your Dreams

One important thing to understand about dreams is that through them the unconscious mind delivers messages. Another is that dream and dreamer are one.

There are many approaches to dream interpretation. The Dream Work section of Chapter 2 gives some very good ways to tune in to dreams. The Senoi Indian technique involves literally asking and challenging each component of your dream for its meaning or message. The Gestalt approach has you consider every dream character as an aspect of yourself. Some dream interpretation approaches are based on symbols, with every part of your dream acting as a symbol for some profound value or idea. Other approaches include working in groups, brainstorming without judgment, and drawing pictures of dreams and passing them around for group interpretation.

You do best to develop your own interpretation of your own dreams, based on paying attention over a period of time. Then you can begin to understand your own symbols without reference to somebody else's psychological theory. With the Senoi technique, you can confront aspects of your dreams. Or you can begin to look for the message that keeps coming back to you in a repeating dream. To start with you might use a book such as Gayle Delaney's *Living Your Dreams,* but the main thing is to pay attention and understand that you are the total creator of your dreams and that the message comes from yourself.

Once you have written out a dream, you might try translating it through dream-work consultant Alissa Goldring's method:

Here is a method I use for retelling a dream so that I experience its message directly, by-passing my mental habits. It is the basic first step I can always count on, no matter how baffling the dream appears. And while the mechanics of doing dreamlanguage *occupy the mind, the dream experience is sinking in and doing its work.*

I'll start with an example so that you can see how I use dreamlanguage. First, here is how I originally wrote my dream of the little bird: "I am looking at a little fuzzy yellow bird held in the palms of my hands. This is an unusual bird. It can read and speak. I ask it to show me. There are some smudges with little marks on them on the wall. This is the bird's language. Slowly, the way children who are learning to read sound out words, the little bird sounds out, 'Friend.' "

To rewrite this dream in dreamlanguage, I do the following:
1) Change verbs to the present tense and begin each verb phrase with the phrase "I have" in the sense that "I have my hair cut every month." Example: "I have myself looking *at a little fuzzy yellow bird . . ."*
2) Add the phrase, "part of me" after every noun or name. Replace pronouns with the nouns they refer to and follow these with "part of me." Example: "I have the little bird part of me be an unusual bird part of me." (After I get the hang of it, I find the abbreviation "p/m" just as useful as writing out "part of me" between.)
3) Add "in me" or "of me" when doing so will intensify your feeling that all of the dream is going on in you at this moment, and perhaps continuously. Example: "I have the little bird part of me able to read in me *and speak* in me."
Throughout, "I" and "me" remain the same, representing the dreamer who watches all the action while at the same time participating.
Dreamlanguage is improved with creative intuition. For example, phrases in a dream like "it is" and "there are" distance you from your dream. Changing such phrases can bring the meaning closer to home. For example, "It is stormy" becomes "I have myself *stormy."*
In dreamlanguage, then, the little bird dream becomes:

"I have myself looking at a little fuzzy bird part of me. I have myself holding me in the palms of my hand part of myself. I have this little bird part of me be an unusual bird part of me. I have the little bird part of me able to read in me and speak in me. I have myself ask the little bird part of me to show me. I have smudges-with-little-marks parts of me be on the wall part of me. I have the smudges-with-little-marks part of me be the bird-language part of me. Slowly, the way I have the children parts of me who I have learning to read in me sound out words parts of me, I have the little bird part of me sound out the 'friend' part of me in me."

After doing this dreamlanguage, I sat quietly at the typewriter while feelings opened up in me like the pealing of bells. I had no need to understand or elucidate. Again I felt blessed, as I had on the day I received the little bird dream. A few weeks after I had this dream, I saw this poem:

"I looked for my soul, but my soul I could not see.
I looked for my God, but my God eluded me.
I looked for a friend, and then I found all three."

For me the way to heaven is on earth, with people, and this dream speaks to me of the part of me that is learning new ways to be a good friend. The little bird also reminds me of all the responsibility, opportunity, and power I carry in the palms of my hands. By tuning myself to my inner self, I am taking my life into my own hands. I feel myself tender and tiny, held in the open hands of life, learning to read what life tells.

Don't worry if, when you first use it, dreamlanguage seems silly, difficult, cumbersome, gimmicky, tedious, confusing, or technical. It works. What you want is to feel the dream as you-in-process. It's not an academic exercise. There is no single "right way." Yet it is worth staying simple or else you may fall into an intellectual game. It is easy to block the experience by being pedantic or clever with yourself. Go slowly enough to allow yourself to savor each new experience in the dream, letting it sink in and percolate in you.

Soar out of Your Body

Just as you create your own dream world, so you create your waking one. If you can penetratingly observe the process you will achieve the ultimate in paying attention: You will rise above your own body to see with detachment from on high what is actually going on.

This is not as mystical as it sounds.

You can do it by observing yourself as if you were a group of actors in a movie—the whole cast.

In the last chapter we called your attention to the way the VOJ speaks to you and through you. In this one, we ask you to notice that other voices speak too. Your childlike aspects—some positive, some negative—speak through your emotions. Your parental-teacher ones reprimand your children, keep your employees in shape, speak sharply to the cabbie. Pleasure and pain speak through your body—through tension in your shoulders, spasms in your stomach, tics in your extremities, headaches back or fore. Your loving aspects speak through your enthusiasms, your hopes, your daily devotions, your hateful ones through the things you fight, or the things you avoid, or the things you uncharitably notice in others.

For this exercise, the trick is to see yourself as a whole cast of characters: the good guy, the bad guy, and all the intermediates. By asking yourself "Who's speaking now?" you isolate the you within the cast that's elevating himself to stardom. If he doesn't deserve that stardom, you must upstage him with a better you.

Eventually, you will come to the point of wondering who it is that is soaring on high, watching the action from up there in the blue, making observations and cast decisions—the Big Who that detaches itself from the lesser cast of little, squeaking, vainly front-and-centering yous.

That Big Who is called by many names: witness-consciousness, the observing self, the Ultimate Observer, Essence. By asking yourself, "Who's speaking?" regularly during your work day, you are evoking this aspect of you that directly perceives, directly knows, and instantly creates and decides.

It is this part of you that is always awake to experience your dreams when you are dreaming. It is the part that uses the possessive form when you say "My body." And it is the part of you that takes over when you open the door to the creative-questioning approaches of the next chapter.

5

ASK DUMB QUESTIONS

To take the leaps? A provocative question is the only way that I've found.

James F. Bandrowski
President
Strategic Action Associates

Most young people going into a meeting are afraid to ask questions. They're afraid they'll appear stupid. It's a lack of confidence. So I try to get my people to write out at least two pages of questions before they go to any meeting. Actually have them written out. You rarely get through the first page. You find that those questions lead to other questions. But if you get people into those meetings with a questioning mentality, you find that they really get going.

Regis McKenna
President
Regis McKenna, Inc.

The Only Dumb Question Is the Question You Don't Ask

Sign in a high school science lab

Implicitly or explicitly, creativity always begins with a question. And in both your business and personal lives, the quality of your creativity is determined by the quality of your questions—by the way you frame your approach to circumstances, problems, needs, and opportunities. A creative approach makes life a questioning process, the same kind of adventurous quest a knight embarked upon when he went out into the field, seeking challenges and welcoming problems. The knight made no demands upon his day in terms of specific expectations. His job was just being a knight, doing what knights do.

In the same way, when you bring creative questioning into your life, you don't care what you find. You do it for the adventure itself, without defining expectations. Even if you rather expect red, you're as pleased to find blue.

If you pursue a questing question, the end is usually creative, even if it's unexpected. Columbus's question was, "Is there a sea route to India?" His answer was the astonishing discovery of a new continent and revolutionary evidence about the shape of the world.

It is certainly true that some people considered Columbus crazy, and equally true that his adventure was a tough one. Asking questions as dumb as his—the kind you fear people might dismiss with "Of course not, dummy"—often takes a great deal of initial courage and eventual endurance. You have to draw deeply upon your Essence quality of strength because you are flouting public opinion, swimming against the current, defying your own VOJ.

Preschool children ask dumb questions about everything. We wrote down some questions a four-and-a-half-year-old named Scott asked in less than an hour:

What's behind a rainbow?
What color is the inside of my brain?
What's inside of a rock? A tree? A sausage? Bones? My throat? A spider?
Does the sky have an end to it? If it doesn't, how come you can see it?
Why are my toes in front of my feet?

You once asked questions like that, too. That's how you learned about the world. But sooner or later your authorities—parents, teachers—gave you the message that such questions were not welcome. You became more careful. Your inner VOJ began to build a defense against questions. You internalized adult laughter, scorn, and irritation, and learned to avoid the questioning creative process. Pretty soon the questions stopped coming to you; perhaps cynicism set in instead.

Our students, most with prior business experience, confirm that business school, too, discourages dumb questions. One student said:

I think that I have slowly but surely been socialized out of asking dumb questions. Particularly at the business school, it appears that in order to ask a question, you should have already equipped yourself with the answer. One asks a question to illustrate knowledge, not to gather it. I have asked far fewer questions in business school than in any other period of my life, much to my dismay and consternation.

Czech novelist Milan Kundera is ruthless with those who don't ask questions.

I ask questions. The stupidity of people comes from having an answer for everything. The wisdom of the novel comes from having a question for everything.

Philosopher Abraham Heschel is equally hard on our tendency to think we already have the answer. He cautions:

An answer without a question is devoid of life. It may enter the mind; it will not penetrate the soul. It may become part of one's knowledge; it will not come forth as a creative force.

Our speakers consistently declare that questions are essential to the joy they find in business life. In listing the characteristics of creativity, Regis McKenna names "wonder" first of all. Tandem's Jim Treybig says that the way to find each day's excitement is to "Stay on the steep portion of the learning curve"—that is, continually to ask questions. Marc Steuer states flatly that "Creativity has to do with the ability to question," and elaborates in this way:

> *How many people in business school get graded highly for keeping questions open, rather than for finding the answers? We're real quick to jump at the answer. Notice how the answer closes out a domain of questioning. Take the guy who invented McDonald's: If he said, "Hey, they already have hamburgers in the world, I don't need to do that," he wouldn't have invented McDonald's. But he questioned, "Where can I get a consistent hamburger on the road?" So that's how he invented McDonald's. Not by having the answer, but by keeping the question open.*

Joe McPherson, director of Innovation Programs at SRI International, elaborates:

> *What's usually missing is going to the field and asking dumb questions, and smelling and feeling and getting in bed with the problem so that you understand the other side of it.*

Try it. Ask a dumb question at least once a day. If you wish, begin fairly timidly—just ask them of yourself, internally—but be sure, then, to pursue actively the answer. Once you start, the answers you find will tap into a strength and excitement that have been there all along. As your excitement in discovery builds, so will your courage to ask dumb questions aloud.

And courage is what it takes to ask dumb questions in public. But you'll find that it's a lot like jumping into a cold lake: After the initial shock, you discover that you are surprisingly comfortable in your native Essence element.

But What Are Dumb Questions?

That's a very good dumb question.

An even dumber one—more courageous and more basic—is "What is a question?"

Would you have the nerve to ask that question out loud? What would stop you? The fear of sounding stupid, or the conviction that you already know the answer?

If you're like most people, probably a little bit (or a lot) of both. But both fear and noncurious conviction are blocks to your natural creativity.

In this chapter we suggest that, like a medieval knight, you go a-tilting for some of the dragons that lurk as fierce convictions in your thinking. To go on a quest for truth, you must acknowledge that you don't yet know truth; to learn to ask questions creatively you must recognize that you don't yet know what a question is. So let's probe a bit into the question of questions.

One of us (Rochelle) was asked to discuss the nature of questions. Having spent her life examining that very subject, she quickly came up with these definitions:

- A question is an opening to creation.
- A question is an unsettled and unsettling issue.
- A question is an invitation to creativity.
- A question is a beginning of adventure.
- A question is seductive foreplay.
- A question is a disguised answer.
- A question pokes and prods that which has not yet been poked and prodded.
- A question is a point of departure.
- A question has no end and no beginning.
- A question wants a playmate.

Read the list again, thoughtfully, and try to add some definitions of your own.

Any luck? If not, perhaps you were striving. Rochelle meditatively planted the question "What is a question?" with her Essence, and then recorded what came.

Now that we know more than the dictionary knows about *question*, let's pick up on one of Rochelle's definitions and poke, probe, and prod *dumb* questions in a new way.

"Look. The emperor doesn't have any clothes on. How come everyone says he does?" That child was asking a dumb question that opened the eyes of others.

"Is it possible to depict the human form in some other way?" Picasso was asking a dumb question that led to cubism.

"Do mistakes have meaning?" Freud was asking a dumb question that established one of the foundations of psychotherapeutic practice.

"Gertrude, what's the answer?" Alice B. Toklas is reported to have asked that dumb question of her good friend Gertrude Stein, who was on her deathbed. Stein's final answer was a *truly* dumb question: "What's the question?"

Let's look closer. A less dumb question from the child might have been "Why is the emperor naked?" That's not a bad question either, as dumb questions go, but this kid was just dumb enough to consider his audience; he directed his question to the attitude of those within earshot, not to the psychology of the exalted emperor himself.

A less dumb question from Picasso might have been "*Should* the human form be depicted in another way?" That would have gotten him deeply enmeshed in unanswerables, and aborted cubism at the outset.

A less dumb question from Freud might have been "Why do you make such silly mistakes and keep ending up on my couch?" A question like that has the supposed advantage of putting the other guy on the spot.

A less dumb question from Toklas might have been "Do you know how much I'll miss you?" That's the kind of question the VOJ delights in— broached from the base of social niceties.

And a less dumb question from Gertrude Stein would have been, "What kind of question is that to ask at a time like this?" Note that it would have worked equally well for either Toklas question—and therein lies its pleasant, dead-end uselessness.

As you see, dumb questions can be born of observation, curiosity, rumination, aspiration, or acknowledged ignorance. Someone else might interpret the source of the above questions in less charitable terms: tactlessness, foolishness, deviltry, tasteless snoopiness, and deafness. What's worse, so might your own VOJ belittle your own dumb questions.

Going backwards, we can see what a dumb question is not: It is not dead-ended, etiquette-oriented, accusatory, argumentative, or shallow. Do any of those adjectives apply to the questions young Scott asks at the beginning of this chapter? The best adjective for his first three questions is *specific*. He's after descriptions of the things that he can't see, but that (remarkably, if you think about it) he knows must be there. The best adjective for the last two is *probing*. He's searching for the cause-and-effect logic that governs the things he can't see as well as the things he can.

So a dumb question is dumb in the same way a child is wise. Such questions have no expectations, assumptions, or illusions; they leap over hearsay and convoluted thinking to go straight to the heart of the issue. See what happened to one student:

This was the week that I had to decide between two job offers. I kept trying to weigh the pros and cons of each. Since each had both pros and cons, I really wasn't getting anywhere. One night as I was close to sleep, I thought of the ask-dumb-questions credo. I tried to think of what question a little four-year-old child would ask me if he was told I was trying to decide which of two jobs to take. The question that popped into my mind was, "Why do you have two jobs to choose from?" And the answer came to me so fast I couldn't believe it, because the first job I was offered never seemed right to me and I kept looking for another one. It became instantly obvious that, although each job could be analyzed into its pros and cons, the first job never felt right, and I shouldn't take it. If it had felt right, I wouldn't have kept looking.

I've made the decision. All the intelligent questions in the world couldn't have produced an answer (just vicious circles), but one dumb question did it.

But not all dumb questions are childlike only. They can be extremely dramatic, and can even be humorous. Lily Tomlin, echoing Gertrude Stein, said, "If love is the answer, what's the question?" We laugh, but we laugh nervously, because we know it's a serious question. Psychologist Carl Jung, echoing both Stein and Tomlin, said, "The meaning of my existence is that life has addressed a question to me.'' Sigmund Freud, in a lighter mood than usual, said, ''The great question, which I have not been able to answer despite my thirty years of research into the feminine soul, is 'What does a woman really want?' '' Socrates asked questions that continue to reverberate in mankind's eternal quest; among them, ''Which matters most, body or soul?''

At their most dramatic, dumb questions can turn a life around. This was certainly the case with R. Buckminster Fuller, the inventor of the geodesic dome. In 1927, thirty-two years old, he was on the edge of Lake Michigan, reviewing his life with despair: a daughter dead at four; five factories failed. He was facing bankruptcy, with a brand new baby. Before he did what he came to do—end it all in the water—he entered into a dialogue with himself.

He first asked if there was a greater intelligence operating in the universe. Yes, he decided, on the basis of ''the exquisite design of everything, from the microcosm of atoms to the macromagnitudes of the galaxies.'' He then asked, ''Do I know best or does God know best whether I may be of any value to the universe?'' In view of the answer he had just forged, he decided that the very fact of his existence meant that he had some purpose, some value. But what? In answer, he found within himself this next very personal question:

What does my experience tell me needs to be attended to, which if attended to completely will bring advantage to all humanity, and which if left unattended can very readily have all of humanity in great trouble?

He turned from Lake Michigan, and spent the next fifty-six years answering that question, eventually earning the description of ''a twentieth-century DaVinci.''

That qualifies his question as a magnificently dumb one. Dumb questions lead you deeper into reality, truth, and purpose. They inspire and expand you in some significant way. A Nobel laureate, explaining his success, said, ''I went for the jugular question.''

Dumb questions are efficient questions; they increase your ability to see more clearly, multiply your choices, encourage exploration. Above all, they show you how to look at old things in a new way. You, too, are endowed with the creative curiosity that will lead you to actively wonder why no one has noticed that the emperor is naked.

Ask a Dumb Question and You Get a Smart Answer

Philosopher Alan Watts said that if he were to establish a university where real learning could take place, he would ask each student on the first day of class just one question, and then use that question as the basis of that student's next six years of learning.

His question would be: ''What do you consider a good life?'' If the student answered, ''A beautiful home,'' Watts would ask him a series of questions: What is a home? What do you need to know about architecture?

Construction? How many architectural styles are there? What are they? When did they occur? What are the essentials of building? Of landscaping?

If another student answered, "Good health," Watts had another program of questions: What is disease? What do you need to know about psychology? Anatomy? Neuroanatomy? Neurophysiology? And so on.

Watts's point was student motivation, but his process exposes much about the appeal of creative questioning: Once you begin, it's hard to stop, and you find yourself asking questions that grow from questions that grow from questions.

And his opening question, "What do you consider a good life?" is a first-rate example of a meaningful, creative question. It doesn't ask for premature action. It's not judgmental, advice-giving, or aggressive. It's simple, brief, and open enough to motivate exploration. It's interesting enough to both parties to encourage an answer, yet it in no way suggests a preconceived one.

Peter Stroh of Innovation Associates uses a similar question in their Leadership and Mastery program. He asks participants, "What do you really want in life?" At first their answers usually involve secondary and enabling goals such as money; with further exploration they get to a fairly deep understanding of their life purpose.

Book titles, too, offer many fine examples of creative questioning. Note the excitement and interest these titles generate:

- *Who Is Man?* by Abraham Heschel
- *What Is Zen?* by D. T. Suzuki
- *Does It Matter?* by Alan Watts
- *Where Are You Going?* by Swami Muktananda
- *Is Paris Burning?* by Dominque LaPierre and Larry Collins
- *The Impossible Question* by J. Krishnamurti
- *Where Did You Go? Out. What Did You Do? Nothing.* by Robert Paul Smith
- *Does God Exist?* and *Eternal Life?* by Hans Küng
- *How Real Is Real?* by Paul Watzlawick
- *The Creativity Question* by Albert Rothenberg and Carl R. Hausman
- *The Three Questions* by Leo Tolstoy

These were Leo Tolstoy's three questions:

When is the best time to heed? Now.

Who are the most esteemed people? He with whom you are.

What important pursuits are to be undertaken first? That which does good to him.

Tolstoy's summary question bears similarity to Fuller's key question:

How may I be allowed to be of service this day?

Many of our Stanford speakers told of questions that were important to their business lives: Wayne Van Dyck, stuck in a snowed-in mountain home without power, asked, "Is this what the world will be like when we run out of energy?"—and was motivated to found Windfarms, Ltd. Don Prentice's organizational development firm grew from his beautifully dumb question, "What would a cooperative organization look like?" Jim Bandrowski asked, "Can creativity be part of strategic planning?" Willis Harman's 1984 publication of *Higher Creativity* came from a question he asked thirty years earlier: "What is the potential of the individual human being?" Bob Swanson, in the early days of what was to become Genentech, listened to the technical experts say that applications of genetics research were many years off. He asked openly, "If it's going to be that long, what is it that technically has to be accomplished, that will make it *not* happen for that length of time?" The emperor had no clothes. Genentech was born.

THE QUEST OF CONGRESSMAN ZSCHAU

It's not just the big dumb questions that make a creative life, however. It's the attitude of creative questioning that leads to dozens of small but significant questions every day. Before we get into the mechanics of asking penetrating questions, let's look at one person who has this attitude of quest: Congressman Ed Zschau.

Zschau often works with questions in his mind, much like the thought-picture experiments of his idol, Albert Einstein.

My ideal when I was a kid was Albert Einstein. And that really got me thinking about creativity, because the process by which Einstein came up with relativity theory and particularly the General Relativity Theory was very different from the usual scientist's. The typical scientist gathers data, then tries to explain the data with a hypothesis, and tests that. Einstein used the process that he called thought-pictures. He would conceive of an experiment in his mind and what the implications would be, and then someone else went on to test it to see whether it was right or not. Relativity theory came through this method.

When Zschau was in graduate school at Stanford, his inner questions led him to take a wide variety of courses. He says:

I was like a kid in a candy store, I took courses in electrical engineering, mechanical engineering, chemical engineering, computer science, economics, human potential (Willis Harman's course), history—just went around the university having a wonderful time.

I think creative people are curious people and are interested in everything. There was always the hand that would go up in class and the question was, "How is that relevant to what we are going to be doing in the next five or ten years?" I recall that I didn't really care whether it was relevant, I wanted to know about things. That's why I took all these courses, because I figured that if I knew a whole bunch of different things, I would be able to bring that background to bear on problems in a way that people who had only a narrow background couldn't. And I found that some of the analogies that I used in solving a mathematics problem might have come from mechanical engineering.

I find that I use analogies a lot from one field or another to help me think about things. I can recall that the key to my dissertation, which was on mathematical programming, came from reading an article on convex polyhedral cones. I was reading that article because I was so frustrated that I couldn't make a breakthrough. I went over to the book store just to relieve my mind and read some stuff, and I picked up a book written by a professor I had had at Princeton. I thumbed through, I came to an article and started to read it, and there was something in it that was like what I was worried about. I bought the book and read the article. And that article and the mathematics in it became the key to my dissertation. It was serendipity. I think creative people are curious, and they're not always asking the question, "How is that relevant to what I'm going to be doing?"

You can see how Zschau's open curiosity worked when, while still a businessman, he was appointed chairman of an American Electronics Association task force on capital formation. After many questions and answers, he ended up reducing the capital gains tax significantly and providing massive new inflows of venture funds. He explains:

Usually when there's a task force like that you write a white paper. (When you call it a white paper, that makes it sound more important than just a paper.) The white paper tells what should be done, and then you've completed your duty as a member of the task force. I never looked at it that way. I looked at it as, "We are going to change the situation for risk capital. What's required to do that?" Tax policies seemed to be a high-leverage area, so that's the way we went.

Zschau writes songs as a hobby. He wrote *The Old Risk Capital Blues* when he was working on the capital gains issue. And when he was teaching and trying to help business students get the concept of linear programming, he wrote a song called *Doing the Old LP*.

How do I write my songs? Because that is a creative process. Well, some people don't think that's so! (Laughter) *When you start, you don't know what's going to come out. Then finally in the end something comes out that didn't exist before, and so in that sense it's a creative process. For instance, I got the idea for* Doing the Old LP *from Tom Leher, who had a song on the new math. The way I worked was to try to make the last line of each stanza humorous or unexpected. So I found myself writing the last lines first, then writing the part that leads up to it.*

Zschau seems to work on songs just the way he works on his life.

There will be some times when you work down a path and rhyme scheme and then you can't get the last line. Rather than beating my head against it, I wipe all that out. I have to start fresh. Giving up what you have created is really hard to do. You've worked all the way down to a point, but if it's not going to work you have to throw it all out and have to start from scratch. When I sit down to write a song, I know I'm going to have one. I know it's going to be okay, and it's going to take me two or three hours to do it.

But when I get up from that, I'm exhausted. The creative process is hard. It's hard to be creative. It's hard work because you have to push yourself into the unknown, to take risks. It's so much easier to do something the way everyone has always done it—and that's why I think that most of the time most people aren't very creative.

THE BASICS OF CREATIVE QUESTIONING

You might actually think that you're too dumb to ask the kind of dumb questions that Ed Zschau does, or that Tolstoy, Fuller, and Nobel laureates do. Don't let your VOJ squelch you. Like any other creation, though, the artful dumb question takes motivation, understanding, and lots and lots of practice.

Dumb questions have a pattern of their own: a circular or helixical spiralling upward to new levels of understanding and creativity. Like this:

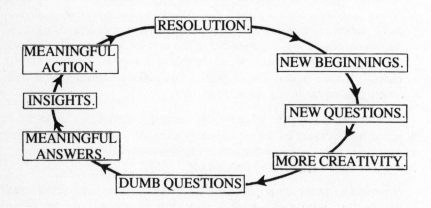

You'll find, we think, that it pays to keep this promising diagram in mind; it will help you remember that you are going to the trouble of asking dumb questions because they can lead you upward into reality and truth. Let it be a guide as you personally begin the practice of the following skill-perfecting approaches.

Get Acquainted with Existing Questions

Listen well. If you begin to notice questions every day, you will soon begin to see how active they already are in your daily life, whether you ask or answer them. Write down the good ones; analyze them all; become aware of their patterns. And don't be too quick to scorn the direct, informational ones such as "What is your zip code?" Any question that's born of ignorance is a useful one; asking them also gives you good practice in willingness to show your own ignorance in small matters.

You'll soon become adept at knowing a dumb question when you hear it. You'll recognize it by the answers it generates. A dumb question creates explosions, concatenations, cascades of insights.

This is apparent in our creativity class. When one student asked Paul Cook of Raychem if he ever used intuition in his work, we were treated to a number of insights on the crucial role of intuition in outstanding management. When student Lynee Gore asked Sandra Kurtzig what the *advantages* were of being a woman in business, Kurtzig was delighted. She said that no one had ever asked her that question before, and then she discussed at length valuable facets of her career and philosophy. When another student, Bob Strauss, asked Anne Robinson if she minded that Will Ackerman got most of the glory from Windham Hill Records, she delved deeply into an explanation of her role in Windham Hill; we suspect that she found her answers as intriguing as we did.

When Bob Medearis, real estate developer and chairman of the Silicon Valley Bank, came to class, student Jay Fudemberg asked a question that many other students probably wanted to ask: "When should we cash in on all the learning we are doing? Do we have to keep taking particular jobs for the experience?" Medearis's answer led to much subsequent discussion to the effect that learning is the main reward; the other rewards come as side benefits.

As you pay attention to questions, you'll experience a certain joy when you hear a good one. Instead of agonizing "I wish I'd said that," let it teach you to ask questions in the same spirit.

Start Small

Don't frighten yourself off with big, ultimate questions like "Who is man?" or "Does God exist?" On the contrary, start asking small, even playful questions in small, unpressured situations. Approaching issues by degrees is a fine way to begin: A better way to get to the office? A faster way to do the dishes? A more interesting thing to talk about? One of Ed Zschau's aides tells us that as a cook Zschau is constantly tinkering with his meatball sauce, trying to make it perfect. Mundane? Nonsense. It's an ongoing act of creative questioning.

Starting small includes the wisdom of starting privately. Don't feel that you must head straight out to Goliath with a slingshot. Get well acquainted with the rewards of asking yourself dumb questions before you ask them of the chairman of the board. Work your way up through your spouse, parents, best friends, teachers—the people who must put up with you.

This is no small assignment. One of the biggest deterrents to asking dumb questions is stagefright; fear of asking questions is a common affliction. Many of our students have noticed that they are especially reluctant to ask questions in class when the material is new. They think that either they should already know the answer, or that everyone else does.

But it is in the early stages of any new field that you most need the help of answers. If you learn to honor your own dumbness you might discover what this student did:

In the process of asking those questions I've had lots of responses from faculty and fellow students. Questions that I've genuinely thought stupid (i.e., asked from a position of no knowledge and great curiosity) have been praised as being inquisitive and insightful. I don't really think that they are stupid questions because I've learned a lot from asking them. If other people can learn something from my questions, so much the better.

By starting small you learn early that the dumbness of a question is not measured by the size of the audience that receives it. Some of the very best dumb questions you will ever ask are the ones you ask of yourself.

Work for Clarity

It's a matter of winnowing, winnowing, winnowing to get to the grain. But striving just gets in the way. Try asking simple questions. If your question is complicated, so will the answer be. You do best—at least to begin with—to try to find the question that will allow an answer of yes or no.

That's why questions like "What should I do now?" don't get far. They distract with too many alluring by-paths that lead to paralysis by analysis. Questions in the form of options—Which of these two is the cheaper? Which of these three is the most convenient?—are just as good as straight yes-and-no questions because they bring you to the cliff of action.

Instead of prematurely asking what you should do, try something new. Ask *no* questions rather than an action question. Try meditating, exercising, sensing your arms and legs, or any of the approaches we have suggested for putting you in touch with your inner creative ability. Then try answering any or all of the following questions.

- *What is it I don't yet understand?* This question or ones like it can penetrate the mind for clarity and understanding.
- *What is it that I'm really feeling?* When there is a problem there are usually emotions—fear, anger, hurt, or sorrow—and this question can help you become aware of them specifically.
- *What is it that I'm not seeing?* Problems usually come from not seeing clearly. By asking about what you are not seeing specifically, almost as if it consists of material objects, you heighten your perceptual ability.

• *What voice is speaking?* Is it your Voice of Judgment, your objective intelligence, your voice of childhood emotions and fears, or the voice of your Essence speaking inside of you? You can bet that if you have a problem, the objective intelligence and the Essence are relatively silent. But personifying and identifying the inner voices contributing to a problem sometimes is enough in itself to achieve the clarity needed for action.

This kind of exploratory questioning for clarity doesn't take long, especially when preceded or followed by meditation.

Evaluate Your Questions by the Fruit They Bear

With experience you will gain more than confidence. You'll learn which questions are valuable and which aren't. You'll begin to see that you get stimulating answers when your questions are direct, simple, and open-ended, coming from the heart of your curiosity. And most of all you'll learn to discover and prune out the kind of limited or even closed questions that your VOJ produces.

A judgmental question goes something like this: "Why can't you turn out a report as comprehensive as Bob's?" An implied-judgmental question is not much better: "Didn't you promise to call our Chicago distributor?"

Questions that damage other people's confidence come from your false personality, with ego and one-upmanship running the show. Not only that, they close the door on your own learning process. What kind of answers will you get if your questions build defensiveness, resistance, and hostility in their subject?

Nonjudgmental questions—"How does that make you feel?" "What was your experience like?"—encourage thoughtful answers. They also stimulate cooperation, expansion, and exploration.

Keep your questions brief: "How do you see that?" or "What could that be?" The more concise the question, the less the possibility that it will contain the verbiage necessary for judgment and aggression. And a short simple question can more easily be understood from other perspectives.

Keep your questions of others open. For instance, you can ask, "What did you notice?" and you will lead them to clarity and understanding.

A job interview might seem an especially formidable environment for a dumb question, but see what happened to this student-businessman:

It was about twenty-five minutes into the interview—right at the part where I started to run out of "intelligent" things to ask the guy. So after a few seconds of silence, I blurted out the following dumb question: "So tell me, why is it you really like this job you are doing?" At first the interviewer acted a little surprised. Kind of like he was saying to himself, "Gee, nobody ever asked me that question before!" His immediate response was just as simple as the question itself. "Because it's fun!" he said with a grin on his face. Then acting somewhat bothered by the simple nature of his response, he immediately plunged into a fairly long-winded comparison of the work he was doing now versus the work he did before he joined his present company. For some reason that rudimentary question set this guy off on a fifteen-minute stream-of-consciousness speech. As it turned out, the interviewer had been a banker previously (a profession I have been seriously considering up until recently), so it was valuable to hear about his experiences.

Keep at It

This probably isn't advice that you'll need, because once the knack of asking dumb questions starts coming back to you, your own curiosity will blaze the trail. But meanwhile here are two ploys—the ruthless and relentless game and the question-a-week program—that will give you good practice.

The ruthless and relentless game. Carry around in your back pocket these dozen ruthless and relentless questions. Flourish them whenever you feel you are not getting to the heart of a personal or professional problem.

1. *At this moment, what is my aim?* This question is about your deepest wish, not goals for the next fiscal year. Put your key life purpose on the line at that moment, not in the past or the future.

2. *If the truth be known, what's really going on?* There is a certain magic in asking for the truth. Use this question to cut through to the basics in any situation so that you can act with efficiency.

3. *What is the VOJ saying?* This question reminds you to be aware of and eliminate the negative effect of inner blame and criticism.

4. *Is this who I am, or who I'm attempting to be?* The central contradiction of your life is between the Essence and ego. This question helps silence the ego.

5. *What is it that this person provokes in me?* Instead of concentrating on questions such as: "What's wrong with her?" "Why are they doing this to me?" focus on what you can do something about: your own actions, thoughts, feelings, and sensations.

6. *What is the objective reality?* Appeal to your own objective intelligence with this one. Strip away all the rest: fears, judgments, chattering of the mind, ego, false personality. This question acts like a meditation: All that is extraneous slips away and you concentrate on what is real.

7. *What is the emotional truth?* Four emotions—fear, anger, hurt, and sorrow—cloud your thinking. If anger, or any of the emotions, is getting in the way, you must acknowledge that truth first rather than blame other people.

8. *What pain am I avoiding?* Over and over, our speakers, students, and clients point out that real learning and progress arise from pain and difficulty. This question teaches you to pay attention to the pain in order to gain insight.

9. *What stubbornness am I holding on to?* You know intellectually that the only constant thing is change, but you might find it difficult to live this truth. Change isn't the problem; holding on to stubbornness is. Acknowledge and understand that with this question.

10. *Is this choice the same as my real choice?* Your real problem might be different from the apparent one.

11. *What is it that I don't yet understand?* Again, if you feel upset, there is something that you do not understand. If other questions fail to lead you to this understanding, you can just ask yourself directly.

12. *Who said that, my mother or my father?* This question smokes out the VOJ.

The question-a-week program. You can use questions to take stock as well as to deal with ongoing problems. You will find that if you ask yourself a review question at the end of each week, you will gain much clarity about what is actually going on in your life.

Try asking one of these questions each week, and then go back in subsequent weeks to the ones that prove productive for you.

- This week who or what was my teacher?
- This week what did I learn?
- This week what did my VOJ say?
- This week what did I observe?
- This week what did I forget?
- This week how did I take care of myself?
- This week what was my relationship to time?
- This week what permission did I give myself regarding emotions?
- This week what did I notice about love?
- This week what truth did I find?

Pick a specific time period and day on which you can do this review every week. Do it whether or not you feel you have any problem that week. Do it for the fun of it, to "take care of yourself" as the question above said. Let yourself get into the question-answer process without expectation. Let the process lead you where it will. Notice that you make discoveries. And don't be afraid to add questions to your question-a-week program. For instance, while you are living with this chapter's credo, you might ask, "This week what dumb questions did I ask?"

Ask Your Essence First, Last, and Always

The answers to all your questions—especially dumb ones—are within you. Your biggest job in life is to learn to trust your Essence to provide all the answers you can ever use.

Time after time, students pose questions in the beginning of their weekly papers, and by the end of the paper they have answered the questions themselves. It appears that by asking something or somebody beyond their own intellect, they free their own inner creativity to supply the answer.

Much the same thing happens when you ask someone to help find something after you've searched for it in vain. At almost the moment the other person agrees to help, you remember where you left it—as if, the moment you relax, the Essence says, ''I thought you'd never ask.''

Children are good at asking dumb questions because they don't seem to differentiate between themselves and the outer world. Before their VOJ develops, they blurt out every question that comes to them.

As an adult with a full-fledged VOJ, you might find it difficult to blurt out any questions at all. But start asking them of yourself, inside, and you will be amazed at the answers you can get. Plant your questions with your Essence—as Rochelle planted her question on questions—in a fairly formal, structured manner, and new worlds of creativity open up.

Your question can be as mundane as ''What does the report need now if anything?'' Place the question inside your very being. Make it impersonal. Once you've planted it, don't think about it or form expectations. Let it stew a bit in your own creative juices.

Go on to something else if you wish. Finish this chapter, or meditate, or take a nap. See if you get anything back. If not, try again. Plant your question or a new question deep inside yourself before you go to sleep, and see what you get in the morning. If there isn't anything at first, keep trying. Once you begin to receive and recognize answers, you'll develop the confidence to ask questions regularly during the day.

Everyone seems to have a key question. It might change from time to time as life patterns change, but whether you know it or not your question of questions can be a guiding star. Key questions can be generally all-purpose, like ''What's the point?'' Or they can be as specifically pointed as ''What can I contribute this very minute to world peace?'' Whatever degree of detail you ask for, your key question can monitor every moment of your business or personal life.

If you don't know yet what your own key question is, ask your Essence. It might take a while for you to understand the answer, but be patient and persistent.

Do you want to try a more structured approach? In this one, you ask a question with your left brain and answer it with your right as a demonstration of your unused resources within. Since each half of the brain controls the opposite side of the body, the idea is to stimulate a part of the brain that you don't normally use by using a part of the body you don't normally use.

Ask yourself a question by writing it down with your usual writing hand. Then empty your mind. Don't try to think out an answer. Remind yourself that the answer lives within you, and that all you have to do is record it with your *other* hand. Let that other hand function as a recording tool. And have fun seeing what you have to say to yourself.

*   *   *

Did you surprise yourself? Most people find that the answers they get from this procedure are quite different from the ones their surface mind would provide. These answers are similar to the surprising creative answers that come when they allow their inner ability to operate.

We asked our students to submit this question to their other hand: "Lee Iaccoca says that MBAs know everything and understand nothing. What did he mean by that?" Here are some of their other-brain answers:

- *He meant that they never did anything for him.*
- *MBAs too concrete!*
- *MBAs have thought too much about too many things.*
- *Woof* [sic] *killer instincts. They don't function.*
- *We don't have a feel of things, especially what's important.*
- *MBAs are stupid.*
- *Lee Iaccoca's VOJ is talking.*
- *Life is confusing, unlike school.*
- *They don't do.*

Of course this is just a demonstration of opposite-brain functions. Use any method that works for you. You don't need a pencil to get home to your Essence.

Reap Your Rewards

We are constantly amazed and excited by the rewards—insights, break-throughs, significant new knowledge about their own daily world—that our students find in living with this chapter's credo.

One young man saved money. He had decided to commute to school by bicycle, and every biker he knew owned a foreign-made ten-speed. When he asked the salesman just one dumb question—"What's the purpose of ten-speeds?"—he discovered he didn't need those expensive gears.

Another student, Eric Patel, lost weight:

This evening, I asked my wife, "How come we eat dinner every evening?" "It's because you want to!" "No I don't. I eat too much anyway." Consensus: That we'll eat when we're hungry in the evening, not just because it's dinnertime.

Cliff Robbins discovered that it's no sin to show ignorance when he visited a high technology company on behalf of a venture capital group.

In preparation for the meeting, I had done some research on semiconductor and computer technology so that I could interact with people at the company. However, when I arrived I decided to employ the credo. Consequently, instead of faking it and fighting to understand what the engineers were saying, I simply said, "I don't understand this or that, please explain it to me." Much to my surprise, I found that the engineers were happy to talk about their work in layman terms, and I came away

*from the meeting with a better and clearer understanding than ever before.
I am definitely going to ask dumb questions in subsequent meetings.*

Other students reported other rewards when they came up with the
questions on the following list. Instead of defining each personal reward,
we submit the list as an exercise for you in practicing the art of creative
questioning. Imagine yourself asking each in an appropriate situation, or
even an inappropriate one. Would you have the nerve to do it? Also imagine
what the rewards of the real-life askers might have been, and then what the
rewards could be for you.

- What's a preposition?
- How come you have to fill up to get a free car-wash when a fill-up costs
  fifteen dollars for some people and only five for others?
- What is "net present value"?
- How does this company make money?
- When you swim, how do you breathe?
- What do you actually do in your job? Tell me about your day-to-day
  experiences. And what don't you like about your job?
- What makes me want to run my own business?
- Have you been negotiating your salary?
- Why shouldn't I be with someone I enjoy?
- What is the real problem with the plans? What is really bothering me?
- What's so good about company growth?
- What does it mean to be worthy?
- How do you feel working in a company with half a million employees?
- What are my skills?
- How come I feel I have to be as capable as my father?
- What is missing here?
- How are board members selected? What determines the number of
  directors on the board?

You can be every bit as dumb (wise) when it comes to asking questions.

The basic ten questions. We have found that the ten questions illustrated
on the next page are very effective in moving people along the cycle of
creative questioning. We've also found it productive to visualize the
process as a mounting wave that breaks on the breakthrough.

The introductory questions establish the nature of the problem. Questions one through three begin the buildup, with successive explorations into
your goal, personal solutions, emotions, and thoughts. Questions four and
five hit the peak of the wave, where most students receive insights.

Question four calls your attention to the fact that you stick with present
solutions because you receive some side benefits from it. By putting this
question to yourself, you require yourself to see through the comfort to the
restrictive habit-of-mind that ties you to the situation. Welcome the surprise
of whatever discovery bursts through.

Question five encourages you to explore your own objective intelligence for the reality of the situation. This helps you to get beyond the illusion that may have been set up by your emotions and mind chatter.

Once you achieve insight from questions four and five, you begin to ride the wave to question ten, which is likely to lead to another set of questions.

By its very nature, a creative life must be a questioning one. And by their very nature, questions will land you on the shore of understanding.

THE BASIC TEN QUESTIONS
LEONARD

Introduction

Q.   What would you like to get clear about today?

A.   I'd like to get clear about my relationship to *WIFE AND FATHER*

Q.   What is it about *THIS RELATIONSHIP* that isn't clear? *MY FATHER LIVES IN CLEVELAND. HE'S OLD AND NEEDS MORAL AND PHYSICAL SUPPORT. I'D LIKE TO MOVE BACK THERE, BUT MY WIFE IS NOT LIKELY TO BE ABLE TO PURSUE HER CAREER THERE.*

The Questions

1. a) What is the GOAL you would like to achieve? *A HAPPY SOLUTION TO MY WIFE'S CAREER AND MY DESIRE TO HELP MY FATHER.*

    b) What solutions have been attempted so far? *I HAVEN'T SPENT TIME WITH MY FATHER, BUT MY WIFE AND I HAVE TALKED ABOUT THIS ENDLESSLY.*

    c) What was it about these attempts that didn't work? *NOT SPENDING TIME WITH MY FATHER HAS JUST INCREASED MY ANXIETY. SO HAVE THE TALKS WITH MY WIFE.*

2. What is your feeling regarding the situation? *I FEEL FRUSTRATION, ANGER THAT WE JUST CAN'T MOVE BACK. I FEAR THAT I WON'T BE ABLE TO LIVE WITH MYSELF IF HE DIES AND I'VE LET HIM DOWN.*
    (Feeling means an *emotional* state — i.e. anger, hurt, fear, sorrow)

3. What is your attitude regarding the situation? *I THINK I'M GOING TO MAKE THE WRONG DECISION AND LOSE MY WIFE OR MY SELF-RESPECT. I BLAME MYSELF FOR PUTTING US IN THIS SITUATION.*
    (Attitude means a state of *mind* — i.e. contempt, judgment, criticism)

4. What benefits do you receive from having this situation? *I BENEFIT BECAUSE I CAN BE LAZY AND NOT THINK ABOUT MY OWN CAREER UNTIL MY WIFE HAS SEARCHED FOR JOBS AND WE'VE MADE A JOINT DECISION. ALSO, ALL OF THIS MAKES ME MORE IMPORTANT, MORE IN THE*

5. What is the reality of the situation? *SPOTLIGHT. IF I WANTED TO HELP MY FATHER, I WOULD HAVE SPENT AT LEAST SOME TIME WITH HIM. I'M HAVING TROUBLE BREAKING MY SUPERFICIAL TIES WITH HIM.*

6. What would you like to see happen? *FOR ME TO GET CLEAR ABOUT MY RELATIONSHIP WITH MY FATHER.*

7. What else would you like to see happen? *MY WIFE TO FIND A JOB SHE LIKES.*

8. What do you need to do at this time? *TALK WITH MY FATHER. SPEND SOME REAL TIME WITH HIM. CONSIDER OPTIONS OTHER THAN OUR MOVING THERE. STOP MAKING MOVING THERE AN ISSUE WITH MY WIFE.*

9. How would your life be different if this situation were changed? *I WOULD BE MORE AT PEACE WITH MY PLACE IN THE WORLD.*

10. What one thing are you willing to change to make this be what you would like it to be? *MY POINT OF VIEW. I'M WILLING TO STOP HURTING MYSELF AND MY WIFE SO SEVERELY.*

THE BASIC TEN QUESTIONS

Introduction

Q.   What would you like to get clear about today?

A.   I'd like to get clear about my relationship to _____ .

Q.   What is it about _____ that isn't clear?

The Questions

1.   a)   What is the GOAL you would like to achieve?

    b)   What solutions have been attempted so far?

    c)   What was it about these attempts that didn't work?

2.   What is your feeling regarding the situation?

    (Feeling means an *emotional* state — i.e. anger, hurt, fear, sorrow)

3.   What is your attitude regarding the situation?

    (Attitude means a state of *mind* — i.e. contempt, judgment, criticism)

4.   What benefits do you receive from having this situation?

5.   What is the reality of the situation?

6.   What would you like to see happen?

7.   What else would you like to see happen?

8.   What do you need to do at this time?

9.   How would your life be different if this situation were changed?

10. What one thing are you willing to change to make this be what you would like it to be?

INSPIRATION AND IMPLEMENTATION

6

DO ONLY WHAT IS EASY, EFFORTLESS, AND ENJOYABLE

The test of a vocation is the love of the drudgery it involves.

Logan Pearsall Smith

I never thought of achievement. I just did what came along for me to do—the thing that gave me the most pleasure.

Eleanor Roosevelt

It is your work in life that is the ultimate seduction.

Pablo Picasso

If it doesn't absorb you, if it isn't any fun, don't do it.

D. H. Lawrence

Don't just do something. Stand there!

Rochelle Myers

This chapter is—more than anything else—about love: love of work, love of life, love of self in the very best sense. It's the kind of love Paul Cook of Raychem has for his daily life:

> *I'm having the time of my life. I wouldn't change it for anything. I'm doing what I've always wanted to do, and it's every bit as exciting as I thought it was going to be when I wanted to do it. It is a thrilling experience, doing new things and leading the new technology to create new products for society. I couldn't want anything more.*

It is the kind of love that almost every one of our speakers expresses in his own way for his own work. It is characterized by energy and excitement on one hand, and contentment and peace on the other. It has all the uplift of romantic love, which brings out the best qualities in the people and things around us.

Jim Treybig speaks of enthusiasm so powerful he doesn't sleep. Regis McKenna speaks of the fun and challenge that keep him running full speed hour after hour. Nolan Bushnell, Steve Jobs, and Sandra Kurtzig exemplify the joy of complete absorption in each new task.

So how do you get what they've got? How can you love what you're doing with that kind of productive passion? One way is to start living by this chapter's heuristic: Do only what is easy, effortless, and enjoyable.

"Attractive but impossible," muttered one business student, possibly visualizing the same thing you're visualizing: sitting around with a case of beer watching television. That kind of self-indulgence—which can generate lots of self-hate—is the last thing we have in mind. To help define what we mean, reverse the thought. Do nothing without enthusiasm.

"Enthusiasm" is based on a Greek word that means, roughly, to be possessed by a god. We are suggesting that you become totally absorbed in those activities that express your own Essence.

But do not be fooled into thinking that the goal of living with EEE (easy, effortless, and enjoyable) is ease, effortlessness, and enjoyment. Surprisingly, EEE turns into a discipline for achieving a higher goal: the discovery of your true purpose in life.

Each individual has a meant-to-be, a particular blending of talents and capacities that can guide him to achievement. Everyone you recognize as creative—not only our speakers but also such luminaries as Einstein, Picasso, Beethoven—has in common the amazing ability to express his own unique purpose here on earth. They have found that true creativity is being themselves. When Leonardo DaVinci was asked to name his greatest accomplishment, he answered, "Leonardo DaVinci."

Living with EEE is a several-step process that is really a circle. First, to find out exactly who and what you are, you must look within to your Essence. That discovery delineates your purpose. As you live out your purpose, you live with ease, effortlessness, and enjoyment. To continually renew the cycle you must continually return to your Essence. There can be no drudgery in work that is a matter of growing self-expression, and no boredom in days that are permeated with the knowledge of your own boundless base, demonstrated in each personal task.

When you live with EEE you find almost a spiritual purpose for your life. You know that you are practicing your true vocation when you love all the hard work, responsibility, and tedium that goes with it. The trouble for most of us is breaking into that circle of looking within, discovering our purpose, and living out that purpose with EEE. On the one hand, there is no clear-cut first step because the circle is a continuous, self-feeding one. On the other, it seems apparent that solving the problem of purpose is the cornerstone of personal and business creativity.

So let's get down to business.

FINDING YOUR PURPOSE

It is no easy thing, living out a credo of EEE in a business world that often imposes the credo of DDD—difficult, distasteful, and depressing. This situation attracts the attention of many experts. In *Transforming Organizations* (edited by John D. Adams), organizational consultant Richard McKnight says:

I work with executives to help them to focus on the purpose or lack of purpose in their lives. Ultimately, they learn how to reflect humanistic values and to become quite spiritual in nature. These executives are reminded that life centered around a clear purpose is totally integrated. Our principles, values, and behaviors stem from and are consistent with our purpose. There can be only one purpose at a time or conflict results.

To educator Warren Bennis, doing the right thing is more important than doing things right. He found this to be true of the nearly one hundred chief executive officers and innovators he interviewed. He says:

When we love our work, then we don't have to be managed by force or fear. We can build systems that facilitate creativity, rather than be preoccupied with checks and controls on people who are motivated to beat or exploit the system. I believe that everyone wants to find both quality and love in work.

In working with his organization, Perspectives, Don Prentice asks people in groups to state their real goals. Initially, he found, most people became evasive or lied out of fear that their true goals would be attacked by others. One company president who was in constant conflict with his people finally admitted that all he really wanted was to make a couple of million dollars and quit the whole thing. To his surprise he found that his co-workers were willing to support him in that. Further probing revealed that his real goal was not so much the two million dollars as it was the end of the harassment; what he really wanted was to connect with the people in his organization. In Prentice's opinion, that EEE activity would have gained him five million dollars instead of just two.

Managerial psychologist and educator Harold J. Leavitt offers these sage comments:

One thing I would like to say about problem-finding is that it's not just ideas that are important; it is ideas you love. One of the issues here is finding something with purpose, something you can really put your soul behind, not just another good idea. And I think it's also important to have some independent criteria of love.

It worries me that one of the ways we learn to love something is by being socialized into it. For instance, many of us love our own virtuosity in problem-solving. We really don't care very much what the problem is. We get our kicks out of saying, "Look, that is a complicated problem, I can take it apart and put it together, and I just love the fact that I'm so skillful." That is, we learn to love the things we do well. So when we learn to do them, we not only learn them, we learn to love them. We don't know whether we learn physics or learn to love what physicists imply is lovable.

So I think it's important to develop an independent criterion of love in which we can say, "Look, what are the things I really want to do regardless of what the external world is saying? Regardless of whether or not I learn to be skillful as hell at it? Skillfulness is nice, but let me not be seduced by that: by feeling that the right things to do are the things that I know how to do. Or by feeling that the people who don't know how to do those things are somehow wrong."

There's got to be some kind of independence. You should be able to say, "Regardless of what I've learned or what I'm skillful at, I'm not going to be a true believer. I have some emotions of my own."

Start Living by Quitting

You can begin to get a handle on the problem of finding your purpose through psychotherapist Arthur Deikman's book, *Personal Freedom*. In a chapter called "Quitting," Deikman tells of a time when he was deeply troubled. He went to the woods to contemplate his situation, and a fantasy came to his mind. He saw himself as a troubled young man asking a teacher for help. When he promised the teacher to follow whatever advice he gave, the teacher replied:

"Very well, but I'm afraid it may be too difficult for you. It is this: Whatever you do you must enjoy, or you may not do it. No matter what it is, if you find that you are not enjoying it, you must stop right at that moment. It doesn't matter if you are driving your car, or eating, or doing your work, or doing anything else. If you are not enjoying it, you may not do it. It is up to you to find a way to enjoy anything that you do. Do you understand?"

For a moment the young man's eyes were wide, incredulous, then they narrowed and his brow wrinkled in annoyance and disbelief. "That's impossible!" he exclaimed. "No one can enjoy everything, besides, there are damn few things that are enjoyable. You are just trying to trick me or having a joke!"

The teacher smiled. "I was afraid it would be too difficult for you, and now you see what I mean. Nevertheless, I know of nothing else that would be of help to you. You must go away now. See if you can do it for a year and then come back."

A year later the young man returned. His face was open and glowing. "Good," said the teacher. "Now that you love the world, perhaps you can be of some use to it."

When the real Deikman returned home he told his daughter about the fantasy. She encouraged him to try that kind of quitting for a year, and he did. Each time he was unhappy he noticed that he was centered in his own thoughts, worries, and concerns. Then, just as we suggest, he would destroy those judgments and focus completely on the task at hand. In so doing he began to appreciate the world again, and his daily life became easy, effortless, and enjoyable.

The trick seems to be to experience and love everything from your own inner Essence rather than from the demands and directions of the VOJ. Here Deikman explains his approach in greater detail:

Consider: How long do you work? Eight hours? Not likely. Chances are you work every minute you are awake. And part of the time while you are asleep. Consider all the orders you receive and all the ways you labor to meet the stream of commands. From your boss: "Finish today." From yourself: "Make it neat." From your leg: "I hurt—move!" From the waiter: "Choose." From a sign: "Buy me." From a centerfold: "Screw me." From the radio: "Remember this!" From your spouse: "Listen to me." From your mind: "How?" From your desires: "Fantasize." From your fears: "Worry." From your skin: "Scratch me." From your car: "Fix me." From your room: "Clean me." From your mind: "Talk with me." From the golf club: "Swing me." From a bottle: "Drink me." From a problem: "Solve me." Even from your vacation: "Enjoy me."

Deikman recommends this rewarding meditative exercise as an immediate quitting tool:

Would you like to try quitting? You may have never done it before, never really taken time—any amount—just for you. You may never have said, "The next ten minutes are just for me" and stopped doing. Consider: ten full minutes in which to be aware, just for yourself, not doing anything, just being aware of your existence . . . Try it now. Realize that no matter what problems are facing you and no matter what work you have to do or what people need you or what your body wants, for ten minutes there is nothing you must do. That's true. Realistically, no matter what your situation is right now, it can wait for ten minutes. The Big Bump may be coming, but the next ten minutes can be yours.

So set the alarm clock or ask someone else to let you know when the time is up so that you don't even have to worry about that. Then quit. Sit comfortably. You needn't be solemn. You don't even have to close your eyes. Just quit. Feel how tired you are of saluting all those commands, or placating all those anxious messengers, so threatening, so seductive with all their flattery and their bribes. Rebel. Does your foot hurt? Say to it, "To hell with you, I won't move!" Does your nose itch? "Sorry—go scratch yourself." In the middle of thought you may suddenly realize that you've been thinking—well, just sag inside, let go of the thought and drop it to the floor. It's too much work to finish the thought, too much effort even to be annoyed, just too much. But don't go to sleep; that would be a swindle, that's what they are always doing. Every time you start to stop and see what it's like they send you to sleep so you never get to know. This time quit and stay awake. Be curious: What is my experience when I stop doing? What is it like when I'm just being? Try it now. Just ten minutes. Stop reading. Stop. Quit now.

*

What was it like? You probably didn't stop just now, but kept on reading. You may have felt that you didn't have time, that you wanted to finish. That's the whole point: You are driven. So stop now and do it. Even if you have done meditation and think you know all about quitting, it is important that you stop now and do it anyway. Don't go on reading. Quit now, for ten minutes right where you are.

*

You may have found a world emerges that seems different. When the outward pressure of your mind relaxes, it leaves space that can be filled. Don't be afraid. Let the world move in and fill that space. See what it's like. Savor the color and the fragrance. Experience the rich, massive presence of the emerging world. Later, realize that Time was gone and so was your personality. Some part of self may have stayed to register anxiety or ask questions in your mind, but only from the back row. Satisfaction is the main event. How complete is the moment world! When you let it in, comparison collapses, for memory is gone, displaced by the fullness of the chair, the tree, the air, the sounds. You have been peering out the door at the world and now, in the twinkling of an eye, the world jumps into the room. Let it stay. Get acquainted with your guest. He won't stay too long; he is very sensitive to the host's concerns and will be gone before you voice the thought. Enjoy him. Be entertained. Even rest your head a while on his strong shoulder. Then you can come back to thinking, to doing.

As a distancer, Deikman's quitting technique is similar to what many business people do to stir up their creative juices. That is, they quit their everyday activities by getting away into something else. Many, like Jim Treybig, find the night a good time for such distancing. Paul Hwoschinsky calls the dark, quiet, early morning hours his prime time; during it he takes stock, contemplates, and writes books. Howard Palefsky regularly awakens at about three o'clock and reads—primarily history books—until six.

But make no mistake about it. Quitting is not procrastination. If you have a passion for a particular purpose in life, you do not procrastinate. You see what has to be done and you do it. What others see as difficult, distasteful, and depressing, the truly creative person views in terms of the bigger picture of his or her purpose.

No, quitting is not procrastination. Quitting is letting go of the VOJ and the external blocks that stand between you and your meant-to-be. You quit not to avoid work but to refresh your approach to it.

Be Yourself

Those two words contain a universe of meaning and are usually followed with the question, ''Who is that?'' Only you can answer that question, but there are ways to approach it that will make the task easier.

Marc Steuer, director of Field Support Systems at Syntex Corporation, takes a Taoist approach to both his work and personal life. The Taoist cycle of the universe is *be, do, have*. To illustrate that cycle Steuer asked a group what they would do to help a sister who wanted to be a ballet dancer. Some said she would need to *have* a tutu. Others said she would need to *do* lessons. But Steuer echoes the suggestion of this chapter by saying that the source of creativity comes from the domain of *being*. He elaborates:

What happens if we started with be? *I want to* be *a ballet dancer, I mean really want to be a ballet dancer. So you actually come from* being. *And I do ballet dancer stuff. I mean I do it, as if I wanted to* be *it. What are you likely to have at the end? You're likely to* have *the satisfaction from* being *a ballet dancer.*

Do you know why a lot of fat people don't lose weight? You've got to be *fat before you can lose weight. And a lot of people don't like to admit that they are fat, so they start with* have. *And they* have *weight programs, and they* do *weight programs, and they're still heavy. If they said, ''I am going to* be *a skinny person, and I'm going to* do *what skinny persons do, and I'm going to* have *the satisfaction of being a skinny person,'' they would actually have that experience.*

Paul Hwoschinsky talks about being yourself in terms of quality:

What we need to do in our lives is lead from quality and not get stuck on form. So that if you're in finance, you're in finance. What's the quality you're reaching for as a financial person or a marketing person or a production person or any other kind of person?

Hwoschinsky continues with constant exhortations to be yourself. Discover what that is, he says, and everything else falls into place.

But how can you know yourself? Brian R. Zwilling of Spalding Sports answered that question from students in this way:

I'm talking about directing your attentions inward. Ask yourself, ''What about me is different? How do I feel about that when everybody else is feeling another way?'' Know that you feel different. That's all. My god, for years I heard people say, ''You're so intense!'' (Pounds the table with fist.) ''You're so serious, Mr. Intensive.'' Now I say, ''That's cool. I'll buy it.'' That's where I get my new product ideas. I will turn my own intensity on myself, and I will not quit until I can come up with a better invention, something that does the job better than anything out there.

Make an EEE List

By making a list of the activities that you already find easy, effortless, and enjoyable, you will begin to look at yourself in a new way: through the things that you like to do. Get a piece of paper—right now is as good a time as any—and write out as quickly as they come to mind all activities that you find EEE. Don't worry about putting the activities into three separate categories; there is no contradiction between the three Es.

* * *

One way to learn about yourself is to examine your list as if it were written by someone else. What is the person like who made this list? What are his qualities? What kind of activity or career should he pursue? What is his purpose or meant-to-be in life? What kind of career should this person pursue?

If you're like most people, you enjoyed making this list, but this is not just an idle EEE game. You can develop real insight from it. You might flex your own analytic muscles on this list from a business consultant:

Running, stretching, karate kata, climbing, free-style karate—when I'm not consciously striving to improve...Working in the early morning with a hot cup of coffee...Interviewing for jobs...Talking/communicating...Doing dishes...Spending time with my wife and close friends... Organizational behavior-type problems: recognizing and solving them...Starting projects and getting them off the ground...Meeting new, interesting people...Selling myself...Writing computer programs... Developing, presenting, and writing up marketing and strategy solutions...Giving slide shows, talks, and presentations...Making people laugh and telling stories...Going to bed early, getting up early...Creating new climbing problems, karate katas, and running loops...Shaving and showering...Driving long distances, especially early in the morning...Attending Creativity in Business class.

The list of a businesswoman, who found within herself an "excitement when a lot of disjointed thoughts or images suddenly jell," is no less revealing and no less valuable. Consider her feelings as she wrote this list—and then apply a stringent analysis to your own list.

Chatting...Reading...Driving my car on highways...Going to dinner with friends or with new acquaintances...Swinging a golf club...Washing dishes...Making cookies, breads, or desserts...Christmas festivities...Roaming through library stacks...Aerobic exercise...Coloring...Doing handwork such as crocheting, needlepoint, hand sewing, or quilting...Drawing graphs...Talking to family...Playing with dogs... Talking to young children...Play-acting...Exercising or running to music with a strong beat...Anything at the beach...Climbing on jetties...Eating crabs...Algebra...Learning about new things (assimilating trivia)...Playing with color chips, fabrics, swatches...Washing walls...

Refinishing furniture...Numbers work...Attending concerts...Developing organization of data, etc. ...Wandering in supermarkets...Building things...Shelving books.

Above all, make such a list in joy. Honestly approached, an EEE tally brings you face to face with your true Essence. One lady we know said, "What a wonderful way to count your blessings!"

Take a Long View of Your Life

A key to discovering your purpose, your meant-to-be, is to look at yourself as though you had reached the far end of your life. Ask yourself leading questions based on the assumption that you have had broad experience and acquired great wisdom. Step back and examine yourself as though you were a stranger. This is the yogic "witness-consciousness." Bob Murray, a businessman who lived with this chapter's credo for a week, shares his method of taking the long view.

One method I employed to make things easy, effortless, and enjoyable was to play a little imagination game with myself. This involved imagining that I was in actuality seventy to eighty years old, sitting in a room staring out the window. I'm aware of myself, my inner self, and it is no different than when I was twenty-seven. The difference is that my body no longer functions as it once did. Somewhat disturbed by this, I think back to the days of my youth, to the days at Stanford, secretly wishing I could return for a just a few moments. Then suddenly those two instants in time are tied together and for some unknown reason I am allowed to return. Not just for a few moments. But rather, I am here again, able to live out my life a second time. Everything between the ages of twenty-seven and eighty has been blanked out, though. I'm aware of that instant in my life fifty-three years from now, but of nothing that has happened (or will happen) from 1984 to 2037. Now there is something inside that compels me to live out my life with as much enjoyment and fulfillment as possible.

The perspective of being old, and probably wise, can help you appreciate your current efforts in EEE, even if they seem fruitless at present. Father Jim Henry, pastor of Holy Cross Church in Santa Cruz, California, talks about Jesus' parable of the farmer who sowed seeds. In this parable only some seeds fell on fertile ground, the others fell on stone. Father Henry compares this to the experience of some of his older parishioners:

Elderly people often tell me this. They say that they would labor for a long time throughout their youth on something without much point and then later in their lives find that those efforts found fruition.

Paul Hwoschinsky, after recommending that you do "whatever you're going to do from the point of view of learning," suggests these exercises.

Take your prime time, a time when you can be alone and free of distractions, usually in the early morning hours, and write your own obituary. "Paul Hwoschinsky died in 1986 in his sleep." Now, what sort of person was he? And when I did my own obituary, it took me about two hours and I cried in the middle of it. It was an incredible experience.

Talk to someone who is very, very old, who has your best interests at heart, who has no axe to grind—they just like you. And ask them what, looking back, they see in their lives, what they've learned. And then you can be like Scrooge. You can wake up and Christmas hasn't happened yet. You can still do something about it. I did that once. It was fascinating. I talked to someone in his mid-eighties. He was a friend of the family's. It was very, very interesting. He had a lot of regrets. It was interesting to hear about those and integrate those.

Marc Steuer of Syntex says that the following revealing exercise opens up the *be* segment of the Taoist cycle, and takes ten minutes or less.

Section off a couple of pieces of paper with decade headings: "Birth to 9"; "10 to 19"; and so forth. (We suggest that you take it to its outer limits—"90 to 99.") Then do a Who's Who description of each decade. Each entry can be as brief as "Born in New York, bored at school, got decent grades, enjoyed sports."

If you do it right now, you will better appreciate some of the class results.

* * *

Most of the students who tried this exercise were about twenty-six years old. Their comments reflect that perspective. Here's what some said:

I didn't know what I wanted to be as I got older. I wanted to kill myself at about age sixty-five.

I'm having a really difficult time once I reach the age of sixty-five or seventy. I just can't picture being that old or what I would be doing.

I learned that there are some goals I have now that I suspect I'll have all through my entire life; just simple things like working out, staying healthy, having a good marriage—high priorities that I can't see changing.

I'm very present-oriented. I mean I want everything by the next ten years, and beyond that it was travels around all the countries. Right now it looks like I expect to achieve everything I can think of by age forty, and then after that it's "What do I do now?"

I seem to feel that I will have all my successes early and then go into government because I will be able to afford to do that kind of thing. That would be an experience of having a lot of power without having to concern myself with making money.

After age forty-nine I didn't really know what I wanted to do.

I found myself compartmentalizing aspects of my life. One part was very career-oriented. I'd write that down. I'd go through many of these decades doing that. Then all of a sudden I realized, "Hey, how about the personal side of it?"—that was a separate compartment. Now I know that it's important to me to integrate those two parts of my life.

One thing I realize from doing this exercise is that instead of career planning being a primary focus, it should be life planning. My career is going to be no good at all if it doesn't fit with my natural inclination and urges in terms of life.

Again—as with your EEE list—try this exercise several times; you will learn more about yourself from each attempt. Don't chintz on the over-sixty decades; and don't sublimate aspirations that are beyond your present job. Putting the big, overall view into thoughtful details will allow you to begin to crystallize your own meant-to-be, and vitalize your potential for EEE.

Draw a Mandala

Many students find this the most rewarding of the find-your-purpose strategies; and most are surprised at what they learn about themselves by playing, within a small circle, with crayon, chalk, or colored pens. Try not to be put off by your VOJ's scorn of your artistic ability. In making a mandala, your goal is to bring out images and symbols of your personal viewpoint.

The Sanskrit word *mandala* means both circle and center. The traditional elements are the soft line and the hard line, or the arc and the angle, the circumference and the core. As both a shape and a discipline, mandalas occur throughout Christian, Judaic, and yogic traditions, in American Indian sand painting, Tibetan art, Aztec calendars. Once you become aware of the mandala, you sense it everywhere: in the patterns of music, literature, poetry; in the shape of the solar system, the earth, the ear lobe, the sea shell, the cell and the molecule; and in the circuits of your thought.

Throughout history, the mandala has acquired a multitude of interpretations. Within the circle there's the soft and the hard, the indefinite and the definite, the immortal and mortal, the masculine and feminine, the Yin and the Yang, the eternal and the transient, the long and the short.

In their outstanding book, *Mandala*, Jose and Miriam Arguelles say that a mandala has three basic properties: a center, symmetry, and cardinal points. Only the center is constant; symmetry and cardinal points can vary. Thus, you can see yourself as the center of a mandala, with your visible surroundings as the symmetry, and north, south, east, and west as the cardinal points.

You have probably already drawn hundreds of mandalas. Child psychologists and art teachers notice children drawing mandalas at a very early age. Though you are likely to find in your doodles evidence of the basic mandala form, you should realize the difference between a doodle and a mandala. In doodling, you draw aimlessly while engaged in some other activity. In drawing a mandala, you are fully absorbed, surrendering to

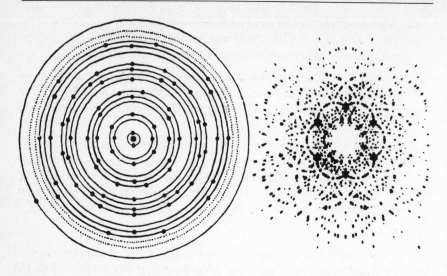

Mandalas in nature. Left, a flat representation of Gold. Right, X-ray diffraction pattern of Beryl.

whatever comes from within you, destroying judgment of what you are developing, and totally curious about what your Essence reveals.

Probably the most vigorous Western proponent of the mandala as a meditative form of self-discovery was psychologist Carl G. Jung, who is said to have drawn a mandala every morning when he awoke. Our students (some of whom made as many as seventy-five during a ten-week academic term) reported that each time they felt as if they were in a meditative state, completely relaxed and centered during the process; and each time they gained a new insight into themselves.

Most of our students used the mandala to help deal with a difficult situation—as a tool for discovering their true feelings at specific times. When Heidi Roizen, who is now head of T/Maker Corporation, was attempting to live with this chapter's credo, she was also in the middle of some difficult work. She says:

I asked myself what I wanted to do right at that moment, and the answer was "Draw a mandala." Since I allowed myself to do what was at that moment EEE, I spent two delicious hours concentrating on a mandala, and I am very happy with the result because whenever I look at it I recapture the joy I felt creating it.

(Interestingly, one of the hottest products of Roizen's new corporation is ClickArt, a program that provides graphic images to be used with Apple's MacIntosh Computer. ClickArt is her own development, and we like to think that it was stimulated by her experience of doing mandalas.)

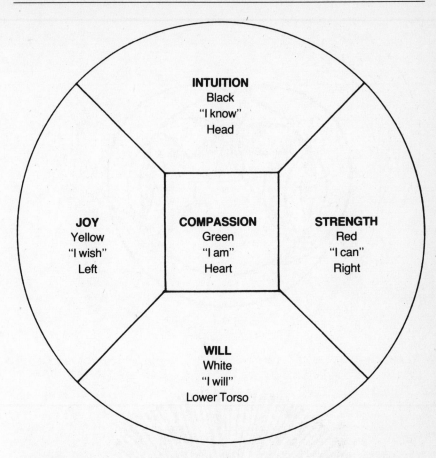

A guide Mandala corresponding to the qualities and colors of Essence as expressed in a Sufi tradition.

Are you ready to try a mandala? If you wish to start in a structured way, you can use the above illustration as a guide. We've constructed it to correspond with the Sufism personification of Essence; in some Sufi traditions each quality of Essence has its own color and message, and resides in a specific body area.

While this Sufi system adds some dimensionality to the qualities of Essence, you should work instinctively with colors and forms. Afterwards, use the ratio of your colors and the emphasis of the qualities as a guide in interpreting your mandala. The more you explode the rigidity of the form, the more you will discover about your own true nature.

In our class we suggest that students draw their mandalas on graph paper since it offers timid artists a bit of structure and comes in tablets that

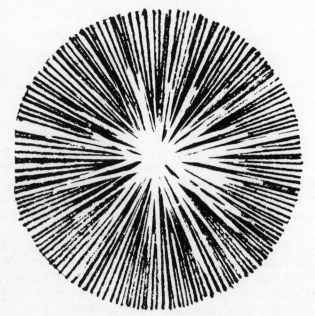

Student Mandalas, above, are photographed from original color drawings.

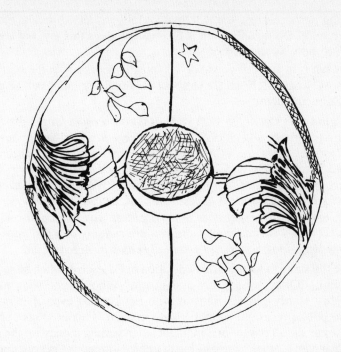

encourage multiple efforts. We also suggest that they use a compass and ruler if they wish. But the only materials you really need are paper and colored pens, pencils, or crayons.

Nor do you need music, but many find it helpful. We find baroque music especially evocative. There is a wonderful tape by Daniel Kobialka called *Path of Joy*. It is a mandalic fugue built out of Bach's *Jesu, Joy of Man's Desiring*. We also highly recommend George Winston's album, *Autumn*.

Approach mandala drawing as you would a meditation. Start by sitting comfortably with your eyes closed, perhaps noticing your breathing. Pay attention to your breath, and go deeper and deeper into the space between the breaths. When you are comfortably relaxed, centering on the mandala of your existence, open your eyes and let your Essence flow out onto your paper.

The interpretation must be left up to you. You'll find that it helps to know that the Essence that guides your hand will also speak to your thoughts as you try to deepen your understanding of your own true nature and purpose in life. (Of course, if after a good try you find that doing mandalas is DDD for you, by all means quit.)

Do What Is in Front of You

The personal and professional parts of your life become balanced when you are aware of your purpose and consider the aspects of your personal life worthy of total attention. If you see each task in the light of your own overarching purpose, then you will do it joyfully, as an expression of your own true nature. Doing only what is EEE can produce this joy, but how do you start? Simply by *starting*.

Doing what is in front of you to do is typically necessary at the start of a new business. Regis McKenna talks about the small beginnings of the giant National Semiconductor:

> *I locked the doors at night, and we built the storeroom for the products out of two-by-fours and chicken wire on weekends. It's kind of hard to remember (you drive down Central now and you see all those buildings), but it really started out very, very humble. We had a pretty unimpressive building, but we had a big sign made. It said "World Headquarters," and we had that put over the doors. National, as I said, grew very, very rapidly, and my own experience in my business was similar. It really is fun, and it really is challenging and you are running at a fast pace and you work long, long hours. But you really enjoy it. At least I did.*

You see the same kind of joyful dedication in Ed Zschau when he says to a constituent, "Okay, what's my assignment? Who do you want me to call?" Vicky Hardy pitches right in with dedication, even if it means mopping a public restroom hours before a concert is about to take place. Robert Marcus didn't pause for a moment when getting money for the start of Alumax meant a grueling trip to Japan to face immediate negotiations.

It's a matter of surrendering, in many little ways, to the work at hand. Take the case of Will Ackerman and Anne Robinson, the founders of Windham Hill Records. Today it is a mini-conglomerate with international revenues of approximately twenty million dollars, known for developing a new category of popular music: soft jazz. But the beginnings of the company were simple EEE, to say the least. Ackerman says:

> *We never meant to start a record company. The entire thing was a fluke. And the first record was my own. The second was that of my cousin and long-time friend and associate in the building business. We weren't out to do anything commercial…We were simply doing music that mattered to us. There was no eye for commerciality whatsoever. When I decided to do the Winston album* [George Winston's album *Autumn,* which has sold over five-hundred-thousand copies], *every independent distributor moaned and groaned and talked about how that was the kiss of death: a solo piano album was destined to be an absolute failure financially. And that didn't matter.*

Robinson describes the beginnings of Windham Hill in more detail:

> *Will is a guitar player and had written some music for a production of Romeo and Juliet. (Incidentally, I designed the costumes.) And a lot of people were really taken by the music and really wanted it, and they kept saying "Come on Will, come over, play in my house and I'll make a tape." Will got real fed up with it, so he went around to everyone he*

knew, and he said, "Give me five dollars, I'll bring you a record in three months." He managed to get five bucks out of sixty people. Three hundred dollars. When the day came to pick up the records, he was twenty bucks short, but I had it—I gave it to him.

We had to make five hundred records because the pressing company would not make less than that. We felt, "Oh, this is ridiculous. We are going to have these records for a long time." The first thing we did was take them down to the bookstore where I was working, and we sold a few.

Then Will ran into somebody he had grown up with here in Palo Alto who was doing radio work, and the guy said, "Give me ten records, and I'll take them to radio stations." And I remember it was a big battle, "Should we or should we not give this man ten records that he didn't pay for?" (Laughter) And we gave them to him after some soul searching, and found out that six radio stations had added it and the response from people was phenomenal.

Things began to fall together for them, even though they didn't seem to know what was happening. They didn't incorporate the business until 1981, five years after they cut the first record, *The Search for the Turtle's Navel.* And Ackerman didn't stop his construction work and concentrate on the record business until 1978. Robinson didn't stop working at the bookstore until 1979 or 1980. So in the early days they were just doing what came naturally to them. Anne Robinson continues:

At any rate these radio stations added our record and started playing it, and people would call in and ask about it. Will had the foresight to have his name and address on the back of it, and people started to write us letters. And we would sell them records at five bucks a pop and within three months we had sold all of the records with no advertising, no distributor. We had gotten rid of all five hundred. We got kind of cocky, "Oh, we'll make some more." And we did.

Will was really great about working the telephone, getting on the telephone to radio stations saying, "I'm delighted you are playing the record. It's clear there are people who will buy it. What are the record stores?" Then he'd get on the phone with them. That's basically how it developed. We had, I think, within one year, two distributors, one here and one in Boston.

Eventually Ackerman and Robinson signed a distribution contract with A&M Records, expanded beyond records to wine and publishing, and developed videos of their music with both Japanese and American partners. But it all started with EEE and continues with EEE. Ackerman is very direct about it.

It's hard to come into a biz school and talk about love being the motivation of what was going on, but in very simple fact that's what it was. I was doing my own music. It was an opportunity to have my own music presented and that of my cousin initially. And the graphics and the quality we put in—the half-speed mastering with Stan Ricker and the record pressings that were and still are vastly superior to anything else within its price range—all that was simply a reflection of: "This is mine. I care about it." And Windham Hill still remains mine, and I care about it. Is that too corny?

Anne Robinson shares the same deep feeling. She says:

In a lot of ways, Windham Hill is the child that Will and I had, if you'll forgive me if it sounds sort of saccharine. But it's really true. That's what we made together, and we really gave it our hearts.

This kind of dedication to what there is to do is at the heart of every business success story we know. And it can be that way for you too—your own distinctive life purpose.

LIVING OUT YOUR OWN LIFE PURPOSE

As you see, one secret to bringing creativity into business is truly to love what you are doing at every moment. Everything becomes EEE if you are very clear about your purpose in life—if you can relate each necessary daily activity to that purpose.

This Zen story captures the way to an EEE life.

A student approached the master in his zendo, bowed, and reverently asked, "Master, what is Zen?"

The master replied, "Zen is eating when you eat, working when you work, and resting when you rest."

The student was astonished. "But master, that is so simple!"

"Yes," said the master. "But so few people seem to be able to do it."

How about you? Do you ever watch television at the same time you are supposedly enjoying your family at the same time you are eating and—even—at the same time you are reading the paper? As the Zen story suggests, trying to do four things at once might well mean doing nothing at all. And it certainly means that you are loving none of those activities.

Finding your purpose has a domino effect: it reduces stress and promotes efficiency; it brings your personal life into better balance with your business life; it strengthens your sense of self-worth. The lesson of the Zen master, like the credo of EEE, is simply this: to find, in the light of your life purpose, that each task, act, and situation is worthy of your total attention.

Our speakers and our students have worked out many approaches in applying EEE to each task. Here are some of them.

Rank tasks in order. For many business people, the problem isn't the task itself but that so many tasks clamor at once for immediate attention. Questions of which task to do first, which to do next, which to temporarily shelve, and which to delegate become a kind of mind chatter preventing the accomplishment of any task. Ranking tasks with EEE as the criterion, imposes immediate order and throttles the clamor. Some people rank their tasks from most pleasant to least pleasant, not minding if the day ends before the tasks do. Others rank them in the opposite order, considering each ensuing task a reward for the last. Either way works admirably, and so does alternating the EEE's with the DDD's. The point is to make the decision only once, then enjoy the result of a chatterless mind.

Break tasks into small pieces. This is in recognition of the discovery that many tasks are DDD only in anticipation. Once started they often become EEE almost by their own volition.

Steve Westley, now Northern California chairman of the Democratic Party, once dismally faced the prospect of making fifty telephone calls asking for support; he saw it as a sort of begging. But by breaking the task down to a single phone call to a friend, he got himself started and even began to enjoy it.

Another student, facing a mountain of fix-it jobs at home, applied EEE by deciding to do only three each Saturday. He completed the first three in fifteen minutes with great efficiency and a sense of accomplishment. It wasn't always that quick, but it was always EEE.

Do one thing at a time. Remind yourself as you work that what you are doing is the only thing you are doing. Drive the point home by knowing that it is also the only thing you need, should, or could be doing. That shuts up the mind chatter that keeps you from living in the moment. One man, working on the balance of his personal and professional life, says:

I am me, a husband, a father, a student, a member of the Sloan compadres, an employee of X Company. Conflicts arise among the roles, and resolutions can be un-EEE. But the ultimate resolution is EEE. Once the decision is made, I enjoy where I am and forget about where I could be.

A business woman had to type eighty slightly different letters to eighty people. The only time available was late at night. So she made typing a reward:

At 10 p.m. you can turn your brain to low frequency and go into a nice haze, typing for three hours. It really did work. I've now been doing it for six nights. A benefit that I hadn't anticipated was that each morning, having a dozen or so letters to drop off at the post office, I felt so productive and proud that I was ready to launch into the new day happily, knowing that at the end I would get to do something (typing) that would earn me more psychic benefits the next day.

Change your attitude. This, of course, is what every chapter's heuristic is all about, but it is still worth spelling out as a specific method of learning to love your work. If you step back mentally to take a longer look at what you are doing, within the larger picture, you are also likely to see the activity as a necessary step toward your overall goal.

One student changed the way he was relating to his wife by considering the overall purpose of their marriage. He found himself hugging her instead of arguing with her, and their discussions flowed much more smoothly. Another student was having difficulty getting to a paper for our course. Instead of approaching it as a formal theme, she turned it into a friendly letter—with EEE results as well as excellent ones. Another student was handed a midterm assignment on Friday to do a paper on money and capital markets by Monday. He says:

> In order to make it enjoyable, I had to find a way to avoid letting it ruin the weekend. I decided to go down to my grandparents' house in Carmel for the weekend. My grandfather is very interested in what I'm doing here at school, is also in the middle of restructuring his investment portfolio, and has been asking if anything I had been learning at school would help him in that endeavor. Thinking about real life money is much more interesting than thinking about money in the abstract, and it put me in the proper frame of mind to do my midterm. I think this approach relates to the advice you gave us in class—put a problem in the perspective of how it relates to what you're trying to achieve in the future. The midterm itself was not enjoyable, but being able to help my grandfather out with his problem was, as was seeing that the things I'm learning are useful in the context of the real world.

Know when to quit. To know this, you must pay close attention to the experience you are having. You might find, as did this student, that a self-indulgent activity is not an EEE one after all.

> Whenever I wanted to do something (when something was EEE), I did it. In the case of watching a TV football game, I did it. But I found that after a while it was no longer EEE, so I went to do my work. After I had the relaxing time of watching the football game for a few minutes, my work was much easier, primarily effortless, and enjoyable. This way of looking at things and doing things was really valuable and contributed to my enjoyment of life tremendously. Maybe I did not do the volume of work, or spend the hours I did before, but my retention and understanding has increased quite a bit. As with so many other things of this sort, one has to pay close attention to one's true thoughts and feelings and avoid internal lying. My present rule—and this is new to me this week and came out of the EEE idea—is to stop doing something when it becomes uncomfortable. This is so easy if you tune in to your true feelings. At least it has been so far for me.

Be good to yourself. When one business woman was trying to apply the heuristic to some work she found difficult, she remembered the Mary Poppins line, "Just a spoonful of sugar helps the medicine go down." So she rustled up a doughnut and a cup of coffee, and got down to work. It turned out that she forgot the treat, because she became so absorbed.

Another student, liking the idea that an alcoholic drink might loosen up his writing muse, soon discovered that this created problems. He began to question the nature of his writing difficulties, and discovered that his dislike of rewriting was discouraging him from doing any writing at all. So he rewarded himself with a word processor and unblocked the flow.

Business people have come up with many other self-rewards: pleasant surroundings, background music, a mid-task stretch or coffee break. The last two symbolize a sort of temporary quitting, and often prove unnecessary as the task proves to be EEE.

Make a game of it. About seven years before he took our course, Christian Peterson was a Mormon missionary in the rugged highlands of Central Honduras. He says it was one of the most creative and satisfying times of his life. Clearly he had ranked the passions of his life and had ''successfully integrated those passions (from the world of thought) with my life (in the world of action).'' And he already understood a lot about living with EEE. As he tells it:

The room I shared with another missionary measured ten feet by seven feet and featured a cement floor, cinderblock walls and a tin roof that drummed uproariously during rainstorms. I had enough to eat, but nothing to spare. My bed, barely wide enough for my shoulders, consisted of a grass mat spread over wooden planks. I could sleep well, provided I didn't try to roll over in bed. I found that rolling around gave me bruises on my hips and shoulders, so I learned to sleep motionlessly. I made a game of gingerly getting into bed each night, carefully arranging the blanket against the cold, and folding my hands over my stomach. After checking to see that my weight was evenly distributed and resting on the padded parts of my body to avoid bruises, I would close my eyes and go to sleep. The challenge was to wake up simply by opening my eyes, having not shifted my weight or moved my hands during the night. My first expression after a motionless night was always a broad smile—a sort of celebration of the complete relaxation I just enjoyed. The only parts of my body made cold or numb by the wood planks were the center of the back of my head, my shoulder blades, my bottom, the back of each calf, and my heels. I always catalogued the condition of my entire body and especially these five locations before beginning any motion.

My first motion of the day usually was a check of my watch to see how my timing was. Within one or two minutes, I always awakened at 6:30, the time at which I had set my internal alarm clock the night before.

The next game was exercise. Each morning I took fifteen or twenty minutes to work on the muscles that were not challenged by the extensive walking I did as a missionary. Leg lifts, arm circles, trunk-twisters and push-ups were the mandatory touch-points in my game, and I bettered the previous day's output each morning.

The exercise was followed by a shower. Here the game was to stand directly under the nozzle and turn on the cold water without flinching. This was not needlessly cruel and unusual punishment. There was no hot water to be had in this village. I got tired of dreading the shower, so I decided to play games with it. I sometimes convinced myself that it was warm. Other times I concentrated on the abrupt temperature change as the cold water hit my warm body. The steam rising off my sweating body in the crisp morning air was extinguished instantly by the flood of good, cold water. I usually could avoid flinching, which made me feel good, because it meant that I reveled in the hot and cold temperatures joyously instead of freezing to death resentfully. No flinching meant that I had chosen to be in that situation, not that I had fallen into an inescapable unpleasant experience.

Use a mantra. A mantra is a sound, a group of syllables or words, that can turn your thoughts inward to your creative Essence. As a focusing tool, it is effective not only in helping discover your true purpose but also in helping you live out that purpose in an EEE way.

Your mind is already full of repetitive modern-day mantras: the negations of the Voice of Judgment, the jargon of your profession, the snatches (both tune and words) of popular songs and commercials. Everyday human interaction has programmed us all with dozens of words, phrases, and clauses that we repeat dozens of times daily, and this can affect the very nature of a culture—sometimes harmlessly, but sometimes not. The trick is to reprogram yourself with an intentional mantra that works for your good.

According to the science of mantra there is a *spanda*, sound vibration, at the base of the universe and at the root of your mind. Physics agrees, saying that the universe began with the Big Bang, and that the sound continues as a ceaseless vibration. The yogis say this basic sound is *Om*, pronounced "ohm." To get in touch with this universal vibration is to get in touch with your Essence. In their book *Rhythms of Life*, scientists Edward S. Ayensu of the Smithsonian Institution and Philip Winfield of the University of London say that "Rhythms are the key to self-knowledge and to knowledge of our surroundings. They put all life into a timely perspective."

By simply repeating a mantra in your mind while doing your everyday activities, you can block out the useless chattering of the mind, allow your true creativity to manifest itself, and become blissfully absorbed in your task. Try it on your next telephone call when you find your mind wandering, and in any tense situation when you want to concentrate on the moment. You might also be surprised by the results of using a mantra to combat such problems as writer's block, fear of flying, and tension in traffic, classroom, home, or office.

Group chanting can also be very effective. One student describes this experience:

The experience with chanting in last Thursday's class was different from my usual meditation experience. The chanting was very soothing, and I felt the resonance throughout my body. The best part of the experience was a feeling of deep heaviness in my body—it felt as if my arms and legs were filled with warm lead. It was as if the relaxation had permeated the deepest recesses of my muscles. The feeling of group cohesiveness was also nice. I visualized a huge group of people chanting in unison in the warm sun.

Munich artist Mahirwan Mamtani plays a tape of a chant while a group of his students do mandalas. He says:

One could feel that the mantra sound vibrations were creating ever-new patterns, and the children in particular were captivated by this creative process. I noticed that our wild school children had remained on the spot for over an hour and had obviously found peace and joy working together. One of the eldest and most sensitive participants shared that while working she felt that she was being conducted by someone invisible, someone within herself, to choose the right colors at the right time. People said that they still felt very intoxicated and high even after the workshop was over.

Our students have found that chanting a mantra promotes grace and ease in athletics as well as creative interaction. One says,

I have used it on many occasions and discovered the comfort and peace of mind that comes with the repetition of the words. The mantra has helped me live with an EEE outlook. I think there's hope for me yet in this wild and crazy world.

Reap your rewards. One reward of learning to love the task at hand is that you do usually manage to get the task done—but that is the least of the rewards of living with EEE. The bigger rewards are in what you learn about yourself, your work, and your place in the world around you.

Business and law student Lynee Gore, in applying the EEE credo while driving to the mountains for a break, reaped this exalting reward:

I finally experienced EEE—I saw a beautiful rainbow and a condor in flight. I stopped the car immediately. I was particularly intrigued by the bird's flight pattern as it struggled against the high winds. It would fly into the wind and get pushed back. To counteract the negative force of the wind, the bird changed its altitude up and down until it found the path of least resistance. Things fit more into place for me; I had given myself time for myself and was rewarded far beyond my expectations. I was able to relax for the remainder of the weekend with the knowledge that always following the path of least resistance will produce tremendous results.

A businessman's reward was less highflown but equally satisfying:

I had always thought that it was impossible to refuse to scratch where the body is itching. It was impossible until I considered that this part of the

body was not me, I did not have to obey its orders, only my own being was important. I was. I was not ''in relation to.'' My being was not related to any stimulus. I was amazed how easy it was for me to ignore itching. It was pleasurable too. I thought: I am here.

One student found much food for thought:

There seemed to be a number of common themes throughout the talks given by creative business leaders: If you do what you love to do it is more likely you will be both successful and happy, because success does not come to those who look for success but rather to those who are passionate about their ideas; the right way to do something is the way that feels best to you; and, finally, the more you just do what is there to do and avoid becoming involved in extraneous issues and concerns, the happier and more successful you will be. There was a very childlike quality to many of the people, as if they were kind of surprised that everybody was making such a big deal about what they did. They felt they were just doing what they wanted to and didn't understand what was so amazing about that.

Another very critical thing seemed to be that they allowed themselves to make mistakes; they were not self critical but rather felt the process, and all its facets, was a lot of fun. It was very clear that the main criterion of these successful, creative businesspeople was to do what they like to do; it seemed equally apparent that when something was no longer fun they would stop doing it.

IN SUMMARY: EEE MADE EEE

Once the great meditation master Swami Muktananda was asked for some guidelines for living. Reportedly his eyes twinkled as he seemed to consider the question and what answer would be correct for that person at that particular time. His words: ''Do what's convenient. Do what you want to do. Do what's true to your nature.''

The person to whom these remarks were directed took them as a sort of Zen koan, which he understood more and more as he began to apply them. As you apply this chapter's heuristic you will come to the point where you are naturally practicing the one of the next chapter: Don't think about it.

7

DON'T THINK ABOUT IT

If your mind is empty, it is always ready for anything; it is open to everything. In the beginner's mind there are many possibilities; in the expert's mind there are few.

> Shunryu Suzuki
> *Zen Mind, Beginner's Mind*

When you are completely caught up in something, you become oblivious to things around you, or to the passage of time. It is this absorption in what you are doing that frees your unconscious and releases your creative imagination.

> Rollo May
> *The Courage to Create*

The minute I ever start thinking that I'm successful, or begin thinking about what I do... I'm in big trouble.

> John Madden
> TV football commentator

The Small Business's Three Worst Enemies...Thinking Too Big... Thinking Too Small...Thinking Too Much...

> Advertisement, Control Data Business Advisors, Inc.

Why is it I get my best ideas in the morning while I'm shaving?

> Albert Einstein

True creativity seems full of paradox. It simultaneously involves analysis and intuition, order and disorder, judgment and nonjudgment, and—as you will see in the pages ahead—fullness and emptiness, thinking and nonthinking.

But the last paradox slips away when you realize that not thinking means being free from worry, doubts, and expectation. As soon as you wipe away the VOJ and the chattering of your mind, even for a moment, your Essence appears. And when you live from an uncluttered mind and Essence, you experience creativity not as an isolated event but as a continuous pulse: alive, real, direct, now.

Consider, for example, Willie Mays. On the night he hit his six-hundredth home run, a radio announcer asked him about his goals. His answer:

Goals? Man, goals are baaad! If I had any goals when I started in this game, I wouldn't have hit thirty in my whole career.

Like John Madden and Albert Einstein, Mays has apparently discovered that nonthinking frees him in some important way. Sri Aurobindo, a twentieth-century yogi and scholar, said:

If the power to think is a remarkable gift, the power not to think is even more so. Let the seeker try it for just a few minutes, and he will see what stuff he is made of.

In the *Siddha Yoga Correspondence Course*, meditation teacher Ram Butler says:

Of course, if the mind stopped thinking, we might experience something else. This is why we meditate—to get a glimpse of that space between thoughts, which is the space of the Self. A person is so afraid that if he stops thinking he'll miss something, or that he'll be bored. On the contrary, it's when we are thinking that we miss something, and it's our own thoughts that bore us. A person couldn't possibly be bored if his mind were tranquil and still, but most people have no idea whether this is actually true or not. Very few people will dare to discover the truth for themselves.

PEANUTS®   **BY CHARLES SCHULZ**

© United Feature Syndicate, Inc.; by permission

In the last chapter we focused on recognizing your creative Essence. In this one we develop new techniques for controlling mind chatter—the thoughts that the heuristic "Don't think about it" aims at eliminating. The Peanuts cartoon tells you a lot about this kind of mind chatter; Buddhist Tarthang Tulku in his *Openness Mind* gives further compelling insight:

When a thought arises in the mind, we attach ourselves to it as if it were our child. We feel ourselves as a mother to our thoughts—but this is actually a trick that our minds play on us. In fact, if we watch carefully and try to remain unattached, we can see that each thought arises and passes away without substantial connection to the succeeding one. Thoughts tend to be erratic, to leap from one thing to another, like kangaroos. Each thought has its own character. Some are slow and others fast; one thought might be very positive and the next very negative. Thoughts are just passing through like cars passing by on the highway.

Tulku suggests, in effect, that we all tend to identify as "my" thought what we should recognize as a homeless wanderer from the collective consciousness. The VOJ tries to keep past successes and failures alive by masquerading them as present thoughts, but both good and bad memories bring with them all kinds of emotional baggage: resentment, hostility, self-pity, regret, longing, nostalgia, self-puffery.

More insidiously, the ego-mind tries to keep you from present achievement by masquerading as your thinking—as your hopes, plans, dreams, expectations. If, as you read this chapter, you are partially occupied with what you will do when you finish this chapter, you are mothering a child that does not belong in this moment; it's only a distraction, pretending it's a true thought.

False thinking, as Erich Fromm points out in his *Beyond the Chains of Illusion*, delivers you into bondage.

Often one believes he has thought through something, that his idea is the result of his own thinking activity; the fact is that he has transferred his brain to the idols of public opinion…. He believes that they express his thoughts while in reality he accepts their thoughts as his own…. He is their slave because he has deposited his brain with them.

Freeing yourself mentally demands, paradoxically, a good bit of don't-think-about-it mental effort, but it's simpler than you might expect. We see the struggle as a two-part but concurrent process. The first, emptying your cup, has its roots in Eastern approaches. The second, living in the eternal now, in Western.

EMPTY YOUR CUP

A university professor once visited a Japanese master, asking many questions about Zen. While the professor went on and on in his intellectual, scattered, convoluted, and pedantic way, the Zen master made and served tea. He filled the professor's cup, and tranquilly continued to pour.

The professor finally noticed the overflow. "Stop!" he cried, alarmed. "The cup's full! There's no room for more!"

"Exactly," said the Zen master, putting down the pot. "Just like this cup, you are so full of your own views and opinions that there is no room for new understanding."

Lee Iaccoca says much the same thing with "MBA's know everything and understand nothing." So do India's Kashmir Shavists when they point out that it is your precious knowledge that gets in the way of inherent creativity. Shavists call it "limited knowledge" and say that you must get rid of it.

That's what Suzuki is talking about in his opening quote. A beginner's mind that's as empty as a cup—of preconceptions, judgments, opinions, memories, expectations, striving, fear, chatter—is a mind that's clear of emotional clutter. That was Charles Schwab's attitude when he founded the first discount brokerage firm in 1975. His company, which he sold to the Bank of America in 1982, is now the largest of its type in the world. He says:

> *Sometimes I look back on it and say I was really stupid at the time.... A really smart person probably wouldn't have done what I did. I can attribute it to not having too high an IQ. I don't know what it is. You've got to have a sense, a feel, and also probably a zeal.*

Suzuki and Schwab bring the word "naivety" to mind. In its present usage, naivety doesn't quite say it, but its Latin root, *nativus*, meaning native, regains its original clout as an expression of Essence. This naivety, this lack of rigid expectation, shows up too often as a quality of our speakers for us to ignore its importance in business creativity.

Steve Jobs and Steve Wozniak had this kind of naive openness when, as school drop-outs, they sought help from lawyers, venture capitalists, and advertising agents in the early stages of Apple Computer. Paul Cook says this about his now giant Raychem Corporation:

> *When we started, we didn't know what we were going to do. We didn't know what products we were going to make. All we knew was that the first commercial radiation machine was about to come to market from General Electric Company.*

Each step of Congressman Ed Zschau's career seems to be grounded in a bit of don't-think-about-it naivety. He thrust himself into business-school teaching before he precisely knew what he was getting into. Then he started a business before he knew what his products or markets were. He launched his chairmanship of a committee of the American Electronics Association by working to actually lower the capital gains tax instead of first preparing a white paper on the problem.

Like Zschau, James Bandrowski of Strategic Action Associates often barges ahead without thinking about it, and finds out later what he has accomplished. At twenty-three, with only a bachelor's degree in chemical engineering, he blithely and successfully gave presentations to the national convention of clinical chemists—virtually all Ph.D.s or M.D.s. Later he developed a procedure for bringing creativity into the strategic-planning process; it is so successful and unique that it has been featured in a variety of business publications, including an American Management Association monograph and *Fortune* magazine. Of this procedure he says:

It wasn't formalized for a year or two—until I had to stand back and look at myself and say, "What are you doing?" And then it dawned on me.

Dean F. LeBaron, president of Batterymarch Financial Management, knowingly takes a Zenlike approach to his everyday business management, so it is not surprising that a version of "Don't think about it" underpins the firm's investment strategy. Rather than building portfolios stock by stock, based on intensive analysis, Batterymarch uses broad investment strategies (such as buying stock of companies that bought their own stocks on the theory that corporate boards know their stocks well) and plugs them into a computer, allowing it to direct their buying and selling. LeBaron says that his study of Zen teaches him "to be relaxed about things."

What might be surprising is that this system works so well. Batterymarch has beaten or tied the performance of Standard and Poor's 500 in all but two of their first fourteen years of existence. Its annual return over that period was fifteen percent—six points higher than the market.

Although many of our speakers, in looking back over their careers, seem surprised by the almost impossible things they accomplished with their empty cups, they recognize the value of their own don't-think-about-it naivety; and many have developed a certain awareness of its processes. From their experiences we have drawn two effective mental disciplines that will help you empty your cup and keep it that way: Pull out the plug; and stop worrying.

Pull the Plug

It's a nice coincidence that we can visualize Archimedes doing just that when his Eureka! struck. But his sitting *peacefully* in his bath is the significant point. Most of our speakers often mention the importance of both mental and physical ease for inducing creative thoughts.

We've touched on this point before in terms of quitting, distancing, and withdrawing. James Treybig, Charles Schwab, Howard Palefsky, and Paul Hwoschinsky all recognize that their regular, peaceful, pull-out hours are sources of new ideas and solutions.

Nolan Bushnell, who developed the video game "Breakout" while idling on a Hawaiian beach, often takes groups of employees to a California beachfront for idea-generating sessions. Paul Cook solves many problems while half-dozing on airplane trips. Vicky Hardy tells us this:

I have to allow myself free time. And by free time I don't mean an evening at home watching television. I'm talking about totally unstructured, unorganized, undisciplined free time. And that free time is frequently spent at a cabin I share with some people out on the coast, where I can wander on the beach for several hours, chop wood, or do physical labor—very, very much unstructured and not what you would normally think of as intellectual activity.

For some of our speakers, pulling the plug is a bit more structured. James Benham finds that improvising on his trumpet is a form of meditation. Molecular biologist and venture capitalist Phil Lipetz also practices meditation. He was meditating when he made some of his initial discoveries about how the shape of the DNA molecule relates to cancer and aging. In some instances his meditation put him within the DNA molecule where he made observations that were later verified in the laboratory. Lipetz says that meditation helps him in business, too. If he gets a meditation sensation while discussing a venture-capital project, he knows that he should look into it further.

Scientific research sheds new light on the mental phenomenon of pulling out. In his book, *The Bond of Power*, Joseph Chilton Pearce tells of the research of psychologist Burton White of Harvard's Child Development Center. After finding that about one child in thirty is brilliant and happy, White did a great deal of research to determine what demographic or psychological characteristics distinguished those children. But the children came from a wide variety of backgrounds—rich and poor, small families and large, broken and stable homes, poorly and well-educated parents— and from all parts of the U.S. Finally, through extensive questioning, he determined that the bright and happy children had only one thing in common: All of them spent noticeable amounts of time staring peacefully and wordlessly into space.

The ability to shut off irrelevant mind chatter, to empty their cups as these children seemed to be doing, is critical to experiencing creativity in everyday life. You might be comforted to know that you do just that every night when you go to sleep. Unfortunately, that is probably the only time your mind ceases its chatter.

Meditation masters say there are four states of mind: the waking state, the dream state, the deep-sleep state, and the meditative state. In the waking state you have the greatest influx of mind chatter and fear. In the dream state you partially experience an inner mind that produces fleeting dramas and (sometimes) solutions to problems. In deep sleep the mind is at total rest, bringing peace and renewal.

In the true meditative state, the mind is also completely quiet. The advantage of meditation is that you are still aware. As meditation master Swami Muktananda says, "We do not meditate just to relax a little and experience some peace. We meditate to unfold our inner being."

When we asked Robert Marcus of Alumax whether he meditated, he said that he did smoke an occasional cigar. After laughing, we asked him if that helped. He said:

You know it may. It may. You know that smoke, it's nice. In fact, when I negotiate, I like to smoke a cigar. In addition to making a cloud in the face of the people you're with, it relaxes you. You know, who's to say? It may help. It puts you in kind of a dreamy state.

You might have your own way of efficiently pulling the plug—by showering, running, gardening, playing an instrument, listening to music, or smoking a cigar. But meditation can help you to concentrate your creative energy.

Be warned, however, that we all have deep sources of personal fear that can drive us constantly toward a life that always seems too busy. In his book *The Denial of Death*, Ernest Becker says:

> The "normal" man bites off what he can chew and digest of life, and no more...as soon as he lifts his nose from the ground and starts sniffing at eternal problems like life and death, the meaning of a rose or a star cluster—then he is in trouble. Most men spare themselves this trouble by keeping their minds on the small problems of their lives...These are what Kierkegaard calls the "immediate" men...They tranquilize themselves with the trivial so they can lead normal lives.

The VOJ likes you best when you're tranquilized by its full cup of trivialities.

Stop Worrying

One of the ways that creative people in business exemplify the don't-think-about-it credo is by refusing to dwell on past mistakes or future worries.

Mistakes, they find, are something to learn from. Real estate developer John Waldroup was so struck by the positive influence of his own mistakes that he quoted from Francis Bacon: "Prosperity doth best discover vice but adversity doth best discover virtue." He also repeated, as good advice, "When you have lemons make lemonade." As one example of adversity he profited from, he told of borrowing money to buy a bookshop. When the lender reneged on the contract, Waldroup found another spot for the shop by developing a concept for an innovative shopping center. The result was his phenomenally successful Barnyard complex in Carmel, California.

Paul Hwoschinsky, too, has found that there's more to learn from pain than from pleasure. Not that he totally approves of such ground rules; he said that if he ever meets the heavenly committee who set life up that way, he would be happy to give it a piece of his mind. But he does believe in failure as a refining tool. When a representative of a foreign government asked for advice on setting up a replica of Silicon Valley in his own country, Hwoschinsky asked, "Will you be allowed to fail repeatedly?" The foreign visitor exclaimed, "No. Absolutely not!" Understanding the need to learn from failure, Hwoschinsky said, "Well then, that's it. End of conversation."

Nolan Bushnell sees fantasy as a productive alternative to dwelling on mistakes or worrying about their impact on the future—the kind of "Did I choose wrong?" trepidation that can fill your mind with the fear of tomorrow. He suggests that before making a major business decision you go through exercises he calls "fantasy win" and "fantasy loss" by imagining the ultimate of both results. Once you make the decision to go ahead it is no longer necessary to think about success or failure. You are free to concentrate on doing your best in each moment.

Decision science techniques, market research, and quantitative analysis are all useful tools, but they are also in a very real sense "worriers" that can lead to paralysis by analysis.

Professor David Kreps, a decision science expert at Stanford University, says his field should actually be called "decision arts and crafts," and that techniques such as decision analysis should be used to guide intuition, rather than be followed blindly to a conclusion. He believes students who take his course would be better off rejecting the techniques than accepting them totally. Even better off, he says, are those who use decision analysis as one tool among many, including intuition.

Successful businessmen are legion who say that market research is similarly overused. And, as a group, our speakers seem to have little respect for career plans. Howard Palefsky says that instead of making step-by-step outlines for himself, he stayed on the lookout for jobs with mentors from whom he could learn. Sandra Kurtzig puts her approach to career planning succinctly: "I never give it a thought." Michael Bilich says about his aversion to career plans, "I don't want to limit myself."

Of all our speakers, Robert Marcus of Alumax might best represent the spirit of this chapter's credo in the way he runs both his business and his private life. In a 1984 *American Management Magazine* an investment banker credits Marcus for "the Company's financial success since it was formed in 1974: not an unprofitable quarter in nine years, and record earnings for five years, including...the all time high of 1981, when the recession was eroding the financial base of the industry."

Marcus speaks quietly and with wit. Like a Zen master he exhibits a lack of apprehension, anxiety, and mind chattering. This don't-think-about-it demeanor is also seen in the rather lean way he runs Alumax. He said:

We're an efficient company in terms of people per dollar. Although we're a two-billion-dollar company, we have only eighty-four people in headquarters, which isn't too many. We're doing the same thing, but we're not as big as Alcoa or Alcan. We're about a third of their size, but we have about a tenth of the number of people in headquarters. It seems to work pretty well, so we're going to stick with it.

We grew from a billion dollars in 1982, and will be about two billion in 1984. So that's quite a growth. I think we added twelve people in headquarters. You have to add some.

I'll tell you some of the things we do. We don't have a lot of meetings. We don't write a lot of reports. We make quick decisions. You know, if it takes you a long time to make a decision, if you have to have a lot of meetings and write a lot of reports, you need a lot of people. We communicate very rapidly. We do it all by word of mouth. I don't write letters. I don't write reports. In fact, I don't know what I do. (Laughter) *We don't use outside consultants. At least we didn't for the first ten years. This year for the first time, because we don't know anything about computers, we had to bring in an outside consultant to explain how to set up computers. Otherwise, we don't use consultants. Public relations? We have one man who does all public relations: government relations, all the publications—you know, one man. He's got a lot of free time. We play squash often.* (Laughter) *I think a lot of these things are overdone.*

Marcus's tranquility has produced an easy relationship to time.

I don't let the time I allocate to some big parts of my life interfere with each other. I confine my business time, which is pretty much nine-to-five or eight-to-four-thirty, to business. And I don't bring my work home with me. I don't think it takes a hundred-hour week or an eighty-hour week. You should be able to do what you have to do in forty hours if you delegate properly, and you trust the people around you, and so forth. I allow time for a squash game at lunch. I go out to play three times a week. And I don't feel really pressed by business. You must have a good priority system. Always make sure you do the important things and do them well. And allow enough time for them.

But how can you achieve that kind of peace in relation to time? It's very simple and also difficult: Just shut down the mind chatter and live in the eternal now.

LIVE IN THE ETERNAL NOW

That's an exalted thought and a magnificent goal, but how can you apply it to your daily business life? Time-management experts present time as a limited commodity that you must learn to expend more and more efficiently. This viewpoint often leads to chaos and stress as you attempt to give projects less time than they need, worry about deadlines, and cram more than one activity into each time period. In 1983 *Business Week* ran an article called "Putting Your Time to Work Before You Reach the Office." It told of executives who take portable radios into the shower to listen to the news and financial reports, and who watch television while doing their morning exercise, and who read business reports while eating breakfast.

If your goal is freedom to live with your fullest creative potential, you should remember that you are not free when you are doing contradictory things. In line with this chapter's don't-think-about-it credo, doing contradictory things includes having contradictory thoughts. And a contradictory thought is any thought that does not apply directly to the present moment.

Remember too that many of your thoughts, especially the ones that recall past events or make up future ones, consist of a series of images that run like motion pictures through your mind, complete with motion, sound, color, and tugging emotions. To fully live in the eternal now, you must cut down on such endless visualization.

One way to stop the motion pictures in your mind is to analyze the source of their power over you. Isn't it in their continuity? They keep your attention over long periods of time because they seem to present an unbreakable story line, built on cause and effect, action and reaction, onset and outcome, build-up, climax, resolution. But just as the continuity of a real motion picture is illusory (it's composed only of separate stills) so is the motion picture in your mind.

More important, so is the continuity of your real life. Just as a line on paper is composed of a series of minute dots, so is the sweep of your life composed of one moment after another. The trick is to take your hypnotized focus off the line and put your complete awareness on the dot. Living your life in the eternal now means living fully in each moment—because there is in reality no other moment in which your creativity can operate.

It also helps to realize that all moments are created equal; that is, a moment has no duration, no limitation, but is simply your point of contact with eternal time. No moment can reach backward or forward. It just is. You have almost unlimited freedom in what you do with each moment, but you don't change the nature of the moment itself; you change only its content. Ultimately and transcendentally, you *are* that moment.

From the Sublime to the Practical

Right after you read this paragraph, take no more than a minute to define for yourself your basic problem with time. Put down this book, close your eyes, use any relaxing meditation technique you wish, and ask yourself, "What is my own distinctive problem of time management?" We ask our students to frame their answers in the form of a penetrating question, and to write that question down.

*   *   *

Do you have your time question? Consider these questions other business people have come up with. Do any apply to your situation?

Is time really a constraining factor? Can it be a benefit rather than a constraint?

What does it mean to be very busy?

How do you break cultural ties to time?

What relationship to time do I have now? Which should I choose?

Does time really limit us, close doors?

How do I stay in present time when I am given deadlines?

It always gets done. But is there some point at which I can't take on any more?

Am I attracted to giving myself pressure?

How can I get in sync with the pattern or underlying rhythm of my life?

How can I experience "flowing" or "oneness" or "timelessness" all the time?

Any one of these questions could be a good start for an investigation of your own relationship to time and job stress. Most are budding realizations that time in itself really isn't the problem; self-push or self-image is.

A typical complaint about time goes something like this:

I never seem to have enough time. It goes by so quickly. I start projects that I don't finish, during the week I get home from work late, the weekends go by so fast, the months go by so quickly. Before I turn around it's summer, and before I know it it's Christmas again. Each season brings its own special pressures. Time does seem to have me by the tail.

But each problem contains the seeds of solution. You can see in the next typical statement that expectations often cause the problem.

Well, I guess if I think about it, in one way or another things have been in a state of flux ever since I can remember. Even when I was very young, I remember wanting to go to school the way the older kids did. And when I went to school I could hardly wait to get out of school. When I graduated from high school I could hardly wait to go to college, but when I was in college I didn't enjoy it that much. I was always so busy trying to make it in the world that I really didn't have time to enjoy it. I got married, but I was so busy earning a living I didn't have much time to enjoy being with my wife. When the children came, I felt tremendous pressure to be successful, and I spent more and more time at work and less and less with my family. I didn't really enjoy those years because the children were growing and changing so fast, and I wasn't really a part of the whole process. It was as if I was an outsider. So I started looking forward to the day when I would be financially stable and the kids would be grown up and then I could enjoy the things I worked hard for. I'm forty-six years old now, the children are grown up enough, my wife is developing her own career, but I'm still looking forward to the day when things will be stable and I can enjoy my life. Now I find myself thinking: "Maybe when I retire that will happen."

Why wait? Right now, in the present, you can stop the overthinking that is the cause of the time problem. In our Stanford class we recommend several techniques for bringing current business problems of time and stress into line with the eternal now. Here are some of them, along with student experiences.

Meditate. One student developed his own form of meditation in order to better function in a don't-think-about-it way.

First I break any job up into tiny sub-tasks. The next problem is how to concentrate. This technique sometimes works for me: I hold a thought in my mind of what I want to do, and listen to the clock or to nothing. It is almost like meditating but I don't really try to get deeply into it. I just relax for fifteen or thirty seconds or so, just holding the task in my head. When this works, which isn't all the time, I find that I can really concentrate on the job at hand, because that is all that I am thinking of. This has three positive effects. One, the little jobs are more interesting because they have a beginning and an end, both in plain sight. Two, I can get that little fill-up of self-congratulations from the finishing off of any one little task. Three—and the best aspect of this when it works—is that I do a better job in less time than it takes me when my mind insists on mulling over the last science-fiction book that I have read, or what I am going to have for dinner.

Here's a more formal meditation, designed to deal with time and to quiet chatter. Have someone read the following to you or make a tape of it. You might also want to play some soothing music.

Sit comfortably, close your eyes, and listen to these words from Rochelle:

We are living in a culture that is entirely hypnotized by the illusion of time in which the so-called present moment is felt as nothing but an infinitesimal hairline between an all-powerful past and an absorbingly important future.

We have no present because we are almost completely preoccupied with memory and expectation. We do not realize that there never was, is, or will be any other experience than present experience.

We are therefore out of touch with reality. We confuse the world as talked about, described, and measured with the world that actually is. We are sick with the fascination of the useful tools of names and numbers, of symbols, signs, conceptions, and ideas. Meditation is therefore the art of suspending verbal and symbolic thinking for a time, somewhat as a courteous audience will stop talking when a concert is about to begin.

Now simply listen to all the sounds around you, without trying to name or identify them. If you find that verbal thinking will not drop away, don't attempt to stop it by force of will power. Just keep your tongue relaxed, floating easily in the lower jaw, and listen to your thoughts as if they were birds chattering outside—mere noise in the skull—and they will eventually subside of themselves, as a turbulent and muddy pool will become calm and clear if left alone.

Also, become aware of breathing and allow your lungs to work in whatever rhythm seems congenial to them. And for a while just sit listening and feeling breath. But, if possible, don't call it that. Simply experience the nonverbal happening. The reality of which you are now aware is not an idea. Furthermore, there is no ''you'' aware of it. That was just an illusion. Can you hear yourself listening?

And then begin to let your breath ''fall'' out, slowly and easily. Don't force or strain your lungs, but let your breath come out in the same way that you let yourself slump into a comfortable bed. Simply let it go, go and go. As soon as there is the least strain, just let it come back as if a reflex. Don't pull it in. Forget the clock.

Above all, don't look for a result, or some marvelous change of consciousness, or *satori* (Zen Buddhist enlightenment or illumination). The whole essence of meditation is centering upon what is—not upon what should or might be. The point is not to make the mind blank, or to concentrate fiercely, but simply to be here right now.

In the course of meditation you might possibly have astonishing visions, ideas, and fantasies. You might also feel that you are becoming clairvoyant or that you are able to leave your body and travel at will. But that is all distraction. Don't think about it. Leave it alone and simply watch what happens now.

Categorize your thoughts. One way to see the effect of the chattering of your mind is to catch it at work. To help keep a constant watch you might carry a notebook and record your thoughts whenever feasible over the course of a week. You can set an alarm or timer, and when it rings record whatever thought you have at that moment. Or you can record your thoughts during any regular occurrence. Where do your thoughts usually go when a commercial comes on? While you wait at a traffic light?

Once you capture the thoughts, categorize them. Patanjali, author of the *Yoga Sutras*, found these five classifications hundreds of years ago: right thinking, wrong thinking, dream or semi-sleep state, memory, and fantasy.

Psychologist Helen Palmer offers another classification system. On the positive side, she says, your mind evaluates, plans, creates, and considers; on the negative side, it judges, schemes, imagines, and doubts.

You can make up a classification scheme of your own, but, whatever you use, you'll probably be surprised by the results.

Lock your irrelevant thoughts away. Categorizing your thoughts builds up your awareness that, as Tarthang Tulku implies, not all of your thoughts deserve mothering, and that many deserve to be cast into outer darkness. Monroe Institute provides a set of meditation tapes designed to help you do just that. Robert Monroe opens each tape by urging the listener to put problems, concerns, anxieties, fantasies, schemes, plans, memories, and chatter into an imaginary steel security box, close it tight, and leave them there for the duration of the tape. After a session with the Monroe tapes, one business woman reported:

I didn't realize what a difference it made until, after we had taken off the headphones, someone pointed out that we hadn't been directed to return to the security boxes to retrieve our worries. All of a sudden my relaxed euphoria diminished.

Gurumayi Chidvilasananda, the current head of the lineage of Siddha meditation masters, offers this dynamic technique for accomplishing the same thing:

We have our duty that we need to perform. We have our work. You cannot let your emotions get in the middle of it, so what you do is have compartments, and you put everything there. You do not suppress them. You put them in their compartment and tell them, "Wait until I get to you. Until then, don't bother me!" It works. Do not think your thoughts do not have life. They are full of life. They have consciousness. But do not let them bother your duty, bother your work... You do your work.

You do your duty. Then you go back to your thoughts and ask them, "Okay, what's with you now?"

Then they come up, "This... this... this..." You respond, "Okay. One by one. Don't give me all of them together. I can't take everything at once. Little by little."

You go back to them whenever you have time. When you don't have time, tell them, "Go to sleep." And they do. They have conscious energy. Everything is consciousness. That is the best way to deal with them because if you do not deal with your problems they will become thorns, they will always hurt you. But you deal with them at the right time.

Draw a mandala. Since the mandala represents the universe of the person creating it, you can focus it on your past, present, or future states to develop a perspective on sources of stress. Often, the gaining of perspective means alleviating or eliminating the problem.

As always, approach the mandala peacefully. Give yourself some time and space. Assemble your materials and then meditate for a short period. You might want to play music that is appropriate to the time—past, present, or future—that you're dealing with. You might also want to record and play back the following imagery or have it read to you. Remember: In each time frame, you are in the audience, watching a movie named *This Is Your Life*. Breathe deeply and let your hand carry your sensations and emotions to the paper.

TIME PAST: The scene opens with a picture of you at age four with your family; it shows shots of your house. In the next frames you are between four and fourteen; observe several incidents of your growing-up years. The scene shifts to your high school: the building, your teachers, your friends, parties, sports events. Notice the details. The scene shifts to your college years. Appreciate the variety of activities and people in your life. Continue this reverie for a while, feeling your emotions and sensations as you bring it up to date.

TIME PRESENT: See your present home, your present place of work, the people with whom you relate. Watch yourself at work, at social events, relaxing. Dwell on specific details. Experience everything that comes for a short while longer, and then open your eyes and begin your mandala.

TIME FUTURE: Let the projector roll to, say, thirty years hence. See how you look. Your face, hair, body. Notice the house you live in. Do you have a partner? What does the partner look like? Any children there? See if you can see yourself going to work. What is your job like? What does it feel like walking into your office? What details do you notice of your personal and professional life? What is the one central question you carry?

Each mandala—time past, present, and future—is expressive of a very precious thing: the life of this human being. By expressing yourself through a mandala, you draw in the eternal now.

Reap your rewards. If through clearing your mind of clutter you begin to find moments of the eternal now, you are at the same time entering into a state of timelessness, of creative flowing. Take, for example, the experiences that Susan Shea, now vice-president for operations at F.A.O. Schwarz in New York, had with deadlines and planning in her work life:

I'm not worried, I'm not miserable. I have only a general idea of how and when I will do each task, but I simply know I will do them. I always knew that worry wouldn't help get anything done, but I still worried. What I didn't know was that planning wouldn't help get anything done either. Living in future time seemed efficient to me; planning ahead was smart. Now I know that present time is how and when I will carry out every responsibility. I have not reached a state of perfection in this, needless to say. I am still full of chatter at many times, and I still fall into old habits. But that's okay. I'm on the way to less and less struggle with time. And that, as you would say, is a glorious experience. I have my whole life to get there.

Most of our students have discovered that when they feel rushed it is because they are not living in present time. Many have also reaped a surprising bonus: When they succeed in living completely in the present, they not only become one with the moment, but become one with the task.

EXERCISES

Sensing, Looking, and Listening

This exercise helps you shut down the chattering of your mind by focusing your attention on the body. It produces the side benefits of physical relaxation, sharper sensory perceptions, and problem solving insights.

Like all meditations its ultimate goal is the unfoldment of Essence. If you have a specific problem you might want to put it into the form of a question before you start. You will probably find that an answer will appear as long as you focus on the exercise and don't strive for the answer.

We recommend that you do this exercise every morning before breakfast for a week, and observe the results. At first it will take about twelve minutes, but the more you do it the less time it takes. Eventually you will find that you can do it right in the middle of a business interaction—to clear your mind and sharpen your perceptions.

Whether you put the following on tape or have someone read it to you, it should be delivered in a calm, relaxed manner, with enough pauses to allow you to experience the movement of the energy.

Sit comfortably with your feet flat on the floor and your hands on your thighs. Slowly close your eyes and begin to relax. Breathe deeply several times into your stomach, letting the breath out with a sigh each time.

If thoughts come, just let them go. Think of them as clouds passing by. You and your mind can relax, because you really have nothing to do right now other than this exercise.

Now you can feel the energy begin to move up your right foot. You can feel all the bones in the foot and the muscles and the shape of the foot as the energy begins to move into the heel of the foot and into the ankle. And it begins to move up the right leg.

If thoughts come, let them go. All you have to do right now is to concentrate on the energy as it moves up your right leg. Your eyes are closed as you feel the energy move up the shin area, and you can feel the roundness of the leg in that area. And you can feel the energy move into the right knee, and feel the back of the knee and all the bones and the knee cap there.

And the energy moves into the upper part of your right leg. Sense the energy and that part of your right leg as the energy moves into your right thigh and your right hip. You can feel the pressure of your right hip against the chair as the energy begins to move into your right hand.

You can feel the energy moving—slowly, slowly—through the fingers of your right hand, through the knuckles, across the palm and inside the hand to your right wrist and into the forearm. The energy is moving into your elbow, and it is beginning to move into your upper right arm. You can feel the flesh and shape of your upper right arm as the energy moves through it and into your right shoulder. There is nothing to do but concentrate on the energy moving into your right shoulder, across the very top of your back and into your left shoulder.

The energy is moving now, down your left arm from your left shoulder. You can feel the upper part of your left arm, its shape and even the inner parts of it, as the energy moves into your left elbow and begins to move further down through the bones of your left arm to your left wrist and into the fingers of your left hand.

Now the energy is moving out the fingers of your left hand and into your left hip. You can feel the left hip as the energy moves into the left thigh and slowly makes its way down into the left knee. You can feel the left knee with the energy there as it slowly begins to spill into the lower part of the left leg, the shin area, and the back of the leg there.

Now you can feel the energy in your left ankle and all the bones there, as the energy gradually moves into your left foot and out the toes of the left foot. You can feel the energy moving through your left foot and slowly, gently cascading out the toes of your left foot.

Allow the energy time to continue to move down the left side of your body and into your left foot and out your toes. If you can't feel the energy moving out your toes right away, that's okay. Just relax and feel the energy moving. Sense your left foot as the energy moves out those toes.

Your eyes are still closed and now you should pay attention to your limbs on the right side of your body—right arm, leg, hand, and foot. Sense your right arm, leg, hand, and foot.

Now pay attention to the limbs on the left side of your body—the left arm, leg, hand, and foot. All at once, sense your left arm, leg, hand, and foot.

Now sense both arms and hands. And next forget about your arms and hands and concentrate on sensing both legs and feet.

Next, sense all your limbs—arms and hands, legs and feet. Pay attention just to your arms and legs, hands and feet. Sense only your limbs—arms and hands, legs and feet.

Now, keep your eyes closed until I tell you to open them. When I tell you to open them, you will continue to sense your arms and legs but you will also just...look. And also when I tell you to open your eyes and just look, you will open your ears and, while still sensing your arms and legs, just...listen.

Okay, slowly and comfortably open your eyes now. Open your ears. Continue to sense your arms and legs, hands and feet. Just look. Just listen.

Continue sensing, looking and listening for as long as you like. Then come back into the room in a normal way without sensing, looking or listening.

(We are indebted to Ron Kane, a Reichian Therapist in Berkeley, California, who first introduced this exercise to us.)

Tarot Cards

Tarot cards, available in many book and game shops, are an ancient fortune-telling device. We believe their effectiveness as a projective device lies in the richness of their imagery rather than in any mystical significance. Like dreams, they teem in imagery, and like dreams, they have the capacity to go beyond the normal chattering of our minds to the clear insight within.

You can think of this exercise as equivalent to the approach of Battery-march Financial Management. Recall that they pick a general strategy, such as buying stock of companies that buy their own stock, and then allow a computer to make the specific buying decisions. In this exercise, you put an important question in your mind (or perhaps on paper) and then allow the computer of your inner creative ability, aided by a tarot card, to give you your answer.

After you've planted your question, shuffle the deck and pick a tarot card but don't look at it; put it face down in front of you. Then have somebody read the following meditation instructions to you (or record them for yourself.)

Sit straight with your feet flat on the floor and your hands in your lap. Gently close your eyes and relax. Breathe easily and deeply from center. Go into silence. Notice the rise and fall of the abdominal breathing. Look inside. Notice the sound of the inside. Experience the quiet inside. All that is of value is there. All of your useful thoughts, emotions, and insights are inside. Your body is a container for them. Feel inside as quiet as you can feel. Now go even deeper and feel ever more quiet. Imagine yourself as an empty space with a light inside you. It could be gold or white or pink. Feel suffused with this light. Now become that light. You are light itself. You have a question. It is an important question, and you have the answer also. Know this. When you are ready, slowly open your eyes and turn over the card you have picked and look at it. Look at the picture and begin writing your answer. Whatever comes, write it. Don't worry. Don't think. Just keep writing even if it seems to be gibberish. Try to write for ten minutes.

It seems to be useful to share this experience with someone else— spouse, friend, or co-worker. You will find that you have some important insights in some almost magical way.

The Spectrum of Stress

Normally when you have a feeling of stress, you probably don't deal with it specifically; instead, you let it reign in your daily life as a nagging sense of worry, hurry, or crankiness. With this chapter's credo you learn to deal with each matter in the moment that is most appropriate for it. This exercise gives you practice in doing just that.

First list the issues that are causing you stress at this time, as on the sample form. You might list more or fewer; six is no magic number.

Once you have listed your main areas of stress, classify them as indicated. If a problem requires action, act immediately, or at least set a specific time for action and make a note of it. Know that this kind of stress is avoidable. You simply need to set priorities and handle each issue.

The second category includes all those sources of stress that need greater clarity. When stress comes from human relationships, there is usually something you don't understand. In one sense such stress is avoidable because you might be able to take some action. In another it is unavoidable because other people are not under your control. You can get clarity by observing, by questioning, and by using the nonthinking approaches suggested in this chapter.

The third category is stress that is purely unavoidable. There is nothing you can do individually about your friend's presence in the hospital or the present level of violence in your city. But you can develop a new philosophical attitude toward the situation—with the help of the nonthinking, observing, or questioning approaches throughout this book.

THE SPECTRUM OF STRESS

CURRENT AREAS OF STRESS

1.   _MY CAR NEEDS REPAIR_

2.   _MY BEST FRIEND IS IN THE HOSPITAL_

3.   _MY BOSS IS ANGRY WITH ME_

4.   _MY MAIL NEEDS ATTENTION_

5.   _MY WIFE DOESN'T WANT SEX_

6.   _VIOLENCE IN MY CITY_

A.   **STRESS THAT REQUIRES ACTION** (Avoidable)

1.   _MY CAR NEEDS REPAIR_

2.   _MY MAIL NEEDS ATTENTION_

3.   _____

B.   **STRESS THAT NEEDS GREATER CLARITY** (Avoidable-Unavoidable)

1.   _MY BOSS IS ANGRY WITH ME_

2.   _MY WIFE DOESN'T WANT SEX_

3.   _____

C.   **STRESS THAT CALLS FOR DEVELOPMENT OF A NEW PHILOSOPHICAL ATTITUDE** (Unavoidable)

1.   _MY BEST FRIEND IS IN THE HOSPITAL_

2.   _VIOLENCE IN MY CITY_

3.   _____

THE SPECTRUM OF STRESS

CURRENT AREAS OF STRESS

1. _____

2. _____

3. _____

4. _____

5. _____

6. _____

A.   **STRESS THAT REQUIRES ACTION** (Avoidable)

1. _____

2. _____

3. _____

B.   **STRESS THAT NEEDS GREATER CLARITY** (Avoidable-Unavoidable)

1. _____

2. _____

3. _____

C.   **STRESS THAT CALLS FOR DEVELOPMENT OF A NEW PHILOSOPHICAL ATTITUDE** (Unavoidable)

1. _____

2. _____

3. _____

8

ASK YOURSELF IF IT'S A YES OR A NO

When the evidence seems to be in, I like to say yes or no at once and take my chances.

> David Starr Jordan
> Founding President (1891-1913)
> Stanford University

To dare is to lose one's footing momentarily. To not dare is to lose oneself.

> Soren Kierkegaard

How do you recognize the right business opportunity for you? In my mind this question falls in the same category as "How do you know who you're going to marry?" "How do you know you're in love?" Well...you KNOW! (Laughter)

> Robert A. Swanson
> Genentech, Inc.

The interesting thing is that there are so few important decisions. You don't have to go in the "right" direction. You don't have to enter the "right" business. What you have to do is to have made a decision as to what you're going to do and then you just have to figure out how to succeed at it.

> M. Kenneth Oshman
> IBM Vice-President,
> Co-founder and President
> ROLM Corporation

Life is a lot about making decisions. Each day and hour confronts you with a flock of choices, major and minor: Buy a house or invest the money? Coffee, tea, milk? Avoid or confront? The blue tie or the brown? Branch out or merge? Do it yourself or delegate? Argue or compromise? Smile or frown? Yes or no?

Let's say for now that basically there are two kinds of decisions: good ones and bad ones. A good decision is clear-sighted and results in appropriate action. A bad decision comes from distorted perception and results in inappropriate action. If an initial decision is a good one, it either breeds further good decisions or clears the way for other matters. If an initial decision is a bad one, you are likely to try to rectify it—or, worse, defend it—by heaping further bad decisions on top of it, amassing a tower of confusion, anxiety, and tension.

Many people, for fear of making bad decisions, try to find virtue in making no decision at all. A United Technologies advertisement has wise things to say about this tactic:

Sometimes the decision to do nothing is wise. But you can't make a career of doing nothing. Freddie Fulcrum weighed everything too carefully. He would say, "On the one hand...but then on the other..." and his arguments weighed out so evenly he never did anything. When Freddie died, they carved a big zero on his tombstone. If you decide to fish—fine. Or if you decide to cut bait—fine. But if you decide to do nothing, you're not going to have fish for dinner.

One of our students, George Watkins of Conoco (UK) Limited, put it more succinctly:

Analysis allows you to say maybe, but life does not.

The secret of creative decision-making is in deciding from your Essence, particularly from your intuition. Remember that the Sufis characterize intuition by "I know." Dictionary definitions go something like "the direct knowing or learning of something without the conscious use of reasoning; immediate apprehension or understanding." Both approaches imply that the correct decision is always within, waiting to express itself.

The Essence knows, even when the ego strives and frets and procrastinates and endlessly weighs the pros and cons. Let's take a closer look.

Suppose you say to a friend, "There were five good things about the restaurant I went to last night: The food was good; the atmosphere was pleasant; the service was fast and friendly; the music was lively; and the view was breathtaking." Your friend might say, "Well, I suppose you'll want to go back." And you might say, "No, not particularly."

Has that ever happened to you? Something told you no, without explaining why? That was your intuition speaking.

Do you have a friend who bugs you in many ways, but whom you seek out anyway? Again, your intuition directs you.

Even if you make columns of advantages and disadvantages, ultimately it's your intuition that makes your choices if you let it. It's your surface mind that makes the columns; it's your intuition that makes the decision. When one of our students went shopping with her sister, they wandered into a boutique where the sister tried on a dress that caught her fancy. "Should I buy this dress?" she asked. "It's in my color, I like the fabric, and it's on special sale." Our student asked, "Is it a yes or a no?" The sister promptly answered, "It's a no," and they both laughed as they saw the beauty of the yes/no credo in action.

If you accept the premise that everything in life is either a yes or a no, you will see again and again that your intuition is your friend. It cuts straight through the confusion of what other people think, what you fear you should do, and whatever the VOJ says. Even if you temporize with a maybe, you will know deep down that your intuition is always operating on some level for your benefit.

THE CHALLENGE OF CHOICE

Few areas of decision-making are more challenging than that of achieving balance between your personal and professional lives. All too often, one flourishes at the expense of the other. But no matter how successful you are in one part of your life, you are not living creatively until you are moving toward a balance.

Life seems to set you up for the balance challenge. When you are very young, your life seems all-of-a-piece, but when you start school you begin to lead at least two separate lives. It is not uncommon to pay more attention to one life than to the other, and to begin making good decisions in one and poor ones in the other.

A recent magazine shows a photograph of a businessman sitting in his own company jet. His brow is furrowed, his collar open, his tie astray. With his left hand he holds a telephone to his ear, and with his right he poises a fork over his plate. His mouth is open as he talks—either into the phone or to someone across from him at the small airplane table. The caption describes the airplane as a good deal, costing ''only a million dollars or so. When [he] runs out of business calls, he rings his wife or one of his five children.''

Of course he might not be as scattered (out of balance) as he looks. The research of Henry Mintzberg, William Pounds, Harold Leavitt, and others indicates that managers often operate in chaotic circumstances, jumping from topic to topic—but they fully attend to each issue, one at a time. Even so, that photograph certainly seems to provide a caricature of an unbalanced life, stemming from a series of bad decisions or indecisions that sacrificed the personal side of life on the altar of business.

It's a challenge everyone in business faces—how much time and what kind of time to devote to families, friends, social activities. Does it make you uncomfortable to consider this intellectually? It's a decision you already make many times a day, either implicitly or explicitly. If you haven't noticed, it's because you are living out your choices through default, habit, or the fear of making a mistake with a conscious decision.

One of our speakers made what could be considered a mistake in this area. He and his wife separated. But this turned out to be a two-month learning experience; they were able to use the experience to develop a beautiful balance. As he puts it:

My family understands that some of the demands on me are a result of the nature of the job.... It requires a lot of travel and long days at the office.

The biggest part of the answer to that problem for me is that what counts is not the number of minutes but the quality of time that I give my family.

Others, such as Bob Medearis, disagree by saying that it's the quantity of time that counts—that quantity begets quality. But both men have achieved obvious balance in their lives through making, we think, clear, conscious, and confident decisions.

Creatively successful people make a point of noticing when their lives go out of balance. Ken Oshman, who many of our speakers named as a man who has attained balance, admitted that at the time he spoke to us his personal life needed attention. Sandra Kurtzig, in absent-mindedly giving incorrect ages for her two boys, said that this was just one symptom of her three-year imbalance as she concentrated on bringing ASK Computer Systems public. Both aired their intentions to restore balance.

At least half of the great ideas Ted Nierenberg told us about related to his personal and family life. Under the pressure of an ultimatum from his wife, Paul Hwoschinsky quickly made a momentous move away from almost total emphasis on business and toward family concerns; today he works with his wife on bringing people concerns into business. Just a week after winning reelection for a second term in Congress, Ed Zschau announced that he was not going to seek a U.S. Senate seat, even though he was thought to have an excellent chance to win. His stated reason for this decision included the desire to spend more time on family matters, and it sounded very much as if his intuition had come up with a no. "A week ago I had myself talked into it, but I never felt comfortable."

Many successful people operate on the intuition that comes from a yes/no credo. David Starr Jordan, whose statement about yes/no begins this chapter, was the forty-year-old president of Indiana University and a world-class ichthyologist when in March 1891 he was offered a rather dubious proposition: to become the first president of a proposed university in the wilds of the west. He accepted with a fast yes on the same day. When he died in 1931 at eighty, he had spent half of his life at Stanford—creating a solid foundation for the university, continuing his study of fish, and crusading for world peace.

Bob Swanson says this about the founding of Genentech:

I was offered a choice and I said, "I don't want to do that. That's not me." It was a realization. And then I went out and started talking to people. Later the opportunity to do Genentech came, among probably three or four things that I could have done. I asked myself, "What would you wish you had done if you were an old man looking back?" And the answer said, "Go!"

Intuition is often like a bolt of lightning. You *know*, without even thinking, that one course is wrong and another is right. Ken Oshman had this kind of experience when he met with the other three founders of ROLM to discuss for the first time the structure of the company they were forming. As Oshman tells it:

Someone said, "Well, who's going to be president?" Another fellow said, "Well, I will." And I said, "No, I will." We stared each other down. And that was that.

And Oshman became president.

Just before his father died, Will Ackerman asked him for advice on whether to move from the construction business into what became Windham Hill Records:

I sat down, and we sort of rocked in these chairs a little bit and I said, "God, Dad, I'm scared to death. I'm looking at this record thing and building thing and I don't know which way to go." He said, "Look, I never made a decision in my life." And at first I thought, "Well, that's inadequate!" (Laughter) But then I chose to interpret it as a very Zen statement. In other words, "Read the damn writing on the wall and follow your heart and go where you want to go." And honest to god, the next day it was just fine. No trouble. I guess I have to take some credit for having made some decisions. But it's been so inevitable. Every step has been so obvious, that, in my estimation, only an idiot could have made another decision.

Even if you haven't had a life-changing experience like Ackerman's, you can start acknowledging your Essence's decisions immediately by applying the credo of this chapter. Right now, in the presence of this moment and this book, ask yourself: "Should I continue reading now?" Use any means you find useful to stop the mind chatter and....Yes or no?

* * *

Now, be pleased with your decision. You didn't waste time making it. It wasn't right or wrong by some outside standard. It was just what you, the real you, decided to do. All the information was in and you decided. And know that even if you went against your intuition—if your intuition said "Stop reading" but you went ahead anyway—that's all right too; you still have the satisfaction of having made a yes/no decision.

You might want to examine how you made the decision. Did you go through pro and con reasons? Did you sit in vain, waiting for inspiration to hit you? Did you begin to worry, even a little bit, when you realized that you were faced with a decision? Did the reality of the decision start you thinking about irrelevancies? Did you take more than a few seconds to decide?

If you did any of these things, you will gain a great deal from applying the yes/no credo. On this kind of decision there is no reason to ponderously weigh pros and cons, to wait, to worry, to daydream, to waste even a second. In fact you make such decisions from Essence continually as you partake in any activity. You are unconsciously making yes/no, go/no-go decisions throughout your day. The trick now is to pay attention to this process, and see how it works.

You might discover what one student discovered:

I have made almost all of my most important and best decisions on a simple yes or no basis. My choice to apply to business school was a yes, as was my decision to marry my wife. My wife and I moved in together two days after our first date, and a day after that we decided that we should get married. We have never had reservations about this decision. Another example is my choice not to join X Company this year, which came down to a no, in spite of many rational reasons to join.

On the other hand I rarely make day-to-day decisions on this basis. I often unnecessarily deliberate for minutes or hours on simple issues: Should I eat now or later? What should I eat for dinner? What type of workout should I do tomorrow? Should I prepare my case assignment or watch the football game?

This week, I have started to make day-to-day decisions on a yes/no basis. It really doesn't matter what I have for dinner. It makes my life easier just to make a decision and go with it rather than worry about it extensively—especially if it doesn't matter what I do anyway.

Or you might find agreement with this student:

When I heard this assignment, computers immediately came to mind. Man, in designing the most complicated machine, made the basic element a yes/no. This fact led me to believe that life must also be this way. I have never thought of everything as yes or no. Realistically, this is probably how nature is at the smallest elements.

And I learned something interesting. The point is not whether you make the right decision. First of all, what is the right decision, anyway? The point is that your decision in the grand scheme of things doesn't really matter. Therefore, everything can be a yes or no. Just trust your intuition.

PRACTICAL INTUITION

To some people the phrase ''practical intuition'' seems to be an oxymoron: two contradictory words in a single phrase. They consider intuition highly impractical, something to be left to psychics, unliberated women, and those without the training or intellect to reason things out. But many successful people operate with their intuition, although in the past some didn't talk much about it.

It took editor James Bolen two years—from 1972 to 1974—to get together a special magazine issue on ''ESP in Business.'' What took so long? Bolen said that it was hard to get people to talk about how they used intuition. They seemed embarrassed.

For example, Alexander M. Poniatoff, founder and chairman of the board, emeritus, of Ampex Corporation, revealed to me that previously he wouldn't admit to anyone, specifically business people, why his decisions sometimes were contrary to any logical judgment. But when he learned of others who follow intuition, he didn't mind talking about it.

By the eighties, many business people acknowledged that intuition is an obvious cornerstone of business. In reviewing a book about business by two nonbusiness authors, Robert Lubar of *Fortune* says:

In this connection the authors have also discovered and made much of a phenomenon that most executives become aware of early in their careers. They learn that rationality has its limits....When it comes to the crunch, the numbers and the analysis go out the window and gut feelings take over. Solman and Friedman quote the ruminations of a former IBM executive about an important investment decision he once had to make: "Ultimately it's a gut call."

At first, in spite of the emphasis on intuition in our course, we (Rochelle and Michael) felt a bit sheepish when our students asked our speakers leading questions about meditation or other intuition-awakening techniques, and about their use of intuition itself. We soon outgrew embarrassment as the questions hit the spot. Almost every speaker had his own idiosyncratic approach to tapping his creative resources, including intuition. Even somewhat conservative speakers like Raychem's Paul Cook and Alumax's Robert Marcus answered directly in the affirmative when they were asked about intuition. Cook said:

Strangely enough, the company has made two or three big mistakes that it never would have made if I'd followed my intuition faithfully. I would not let that happen anymore. I've learned to trust my intuition. I really have. It's made a big difference.

When Marcus was asked whether they relied a lot on intuition at Alumax, he got a big laugh when he said, "I think so, yeah, we probably do. That's one of my big jobs. It doesn't require a lot of work." Perhaps we laughed because executives aren't supposed to admit that they do something that doesn't require a lot of work. Or perhaps we laughed in the delight of hearing that creative ability comes forth in such an effortless way in the form of intuition.

The Truth About Intuition

Intuition can be practical and effortless for you too. Once you understand more about the nature of intuition, you'll know what you have to do to bring it into your life. Here are some golden truths.

Intuition is a gift that must be developed. Because experiences with intuition so often seem to come out of the blue, you might assume that it is strictly a sometime thing, a matter of come-and-go lightning. It is equally easy to assume that intuition is the province of the gifted few or, less charitably, of oddballs—that it is an innate talent that you either have or don't have. Not so; this kind of debunking from the VOJ can divert you from using your own intuition.

Instead, as a quality of Essence, intuition is a skill that everyone can develop. In fact, as with any gift from your source, you have a responsibility to accept, develop, and perfect intuition.

Intuition complements reason. Blaise Pascal, the great French philosopher, mathematician, and physicist, says:

We know the truth, not only by reason but also by the heart.

Psychologist Carl Jung said:

The term [intuition] *does not denote something contrary to reason, but something outside the province of reason.*

Jonas Salk, the discoverer of polio vaccine, has recently been investigating the roots of creativity. Salk told *Time* correspondent Peter Stoler in an interview in *Psychology Today:*

I'm saying that we should trust our intuition. I believe that the principles of universal evolution are revealed to us through our intuition. And I think that if we combine our intuition and our reason, we can respond in an evolutionary sound way to our problems...

In business the stories go way back. Andrew Carnegie carried a deck of cards and played solitaire to calm his mind before making a decision. And when Conrad Hilton was bidding for the Stevens Hotel in Chicago, a number popped into his head. He used the number and purchased the world's largest hotel with a bid that won by just two hundred dollars.

But you don't have to go back decades to see the practicality of intuition in business. Every day you have to make decisions without complete data or with what seems to be contradictory information. What do you do? You use what you might call guesswork, insight, hunch, speculation, imagination, judgment (not the blame and criticism kind), gut feel, sixth sense, a feeling in the bones, good guesses—intuition.

Fairly solid evidence indicates that those who rely on intuition in their decision-making make more profitable decisions than do others. Engineers John Mihalasky and E. Douglas Dean at the New Jersey Institute of Technology found that eighty percent of those company leaders who had doubled their companies' profits in a five-year period had above-average precognitive powers (intuition). And when Weston Agor of the University of Texas at El Paso applied his test for intuitive ability to over two thousand managers he found that top managers scored higher than others.

Of course this research alone doesn't prove that all successful executives actually make decisions in a yes/no fashion, but the link is there.

No one is suggesting that decisions should be made solely on the basis of intuition. It is the combination of experience, information, reason, *and* intuition that is so powerful. Psychologist Arthur Reber of Brooklyn College, who has shown the superiority of intuitive over analytical approaches, maintains that "A blending of the two modes...is still preferable to the use of only one or the other."

Intuition is unemotional. You might mistrust intuition on the grounds that it springs from emotion as opposed to reason. But intuition does not come from emotion. In fact fear, anxiety, pride of authorship, wishful thinking—the entire VOJ gamut—get in the way of the clear operation of your intuition, which flows from an empty cup.

Arthur Hastings, dean of faculty at the Institute of Transpersonal Psychology, brings this home. In a talk on "ESP and Intuition in Business and Management," he described a hypnotist who led people to yes/no decisions from their subconscious.

He tried this with women who were pregnant, because he figured the subconscious mind ought to know whether the baby is going to be male or female. He asked them under hypnosis, "Are you going to have a boy or a girl?" And they would answer, "It's a boy" or "It's a girl." Well, they were right exactly fifty percent of the time. (Laughter) *Pretty accurate but no more accurate than if they had flipped a coin! So he changed his procedure and asked, "Would you like to have a boy or a girl?" and he got an answer to that question. Then he asked, "Is the baby going to be a boy or a girl?" and he got an answer to that question. And once he'd allowed them to express their emotional feeling, its power was discharged, and he got eighty-five percent accuracy on that time, the second time. So, let go of your emotional needs first, as much as you can, and be willing to accept whatever the answer is.*

Listening to intuition is not the act of concentrating on what you think you want. It is not hedonism, a move toward the most pleasurable short-term alternative. It is not giving vent to the inner emotional child left over from your infancy. It is simply paying clear attention, without mind chatter and emotions, to the most appropriate alternative that comes from the creative Essence.

Our speakers seem to tell us that intuition kicks in precisely when they move through the stress and the frustration to a calm, clear state beyond. At that moment, the appropriate action appears almost as a solid conviction: Take the case of Robert Medearis. Instead of emotion, he prefers to talk about energy:

I think everybody has a certain amount of energy about them. And I think that one of the critically important things is to allow that energy to take place. Don't be afraid of it, don't try to channel it. Let it emerge. Because that energy is the source, it's the food for the idea....Allow it to ferment, allow it to come out, allow it to bubble up if you will even though you might think that it's somewhat negative in origin. Allow it to manifest.

Notice in the following example how Medearis moved very quickly from rage into popping ideas for a totally new venture.

Silicon Valley Bank was started because I was pissed off at my bank. I was flying on a plane down from Calgary, and I'd been turned down on an income-tax loan and I was furious. They had changed their organizational structure so that I couldn't talk to the local manager. I don't know what happened, but I was just plain pissed. The more I thought about it the madder I got. And I don't think that was negative energy. I think it was my body sort of starting to ferment some ideas and let them come out. So I started playing around with some names. Silicon Valley has a terrific identification, so I got off the airplane—true story—I got off the airplane and I immediately went to a phone, called my attorney, and said, "Would you check the name Silicon Valley Bank and see if there is any registration of that kind of name? I'm heading down to my office right now; call me after you get a run on it." So he called me and said that nobody had registered it. I said "Register it, because I think it's a good name."

Lesson: Listen to your body, listen to your gut, allow the intuition to come forth. Because your subconscious is probably a better guide than your conscious when it comes to gut feeling. You know what they mean when they talk about gut feel decisions? They're talking about your subconscious. They're talking about listening to your body, about letting the energy come out. So listen to your intuition and believe it. You have it, but you've got to learn to believe it.

Dansk founder Ted Nierenberg dislikes the emotional term "gut feel" but speaks about an extra recognition—the kind of recognition that led him to sell his late father's business ("The fastest decision I've ever made") and get married less than a week after meeting his wife ("The best decision I ever made in my life").

Recognition, which literally means "to know again," is probably as good a synonym as any for intuition. When you have worked diligently and built upon experience in any area of business, the right decision comes instantly as a sort of emotionless recognition. Venture capitalist Wayne Van Dyck has this to say about his intuitive breakthroughs:

In business, most of the ideas that you get come out of the blue. They come only from looking at the problem and saying, "Hey, I think there is something that needs to be done." Getting down and starting to work with it. Not necessarily knowing where the answer's going to come from or even, in most cases, what the answer will be. For example, when I started Windfarms, I had this idea of what I wanted to do in terms of demonstrating that the large-scale technology could work, but I couldn't figure out what to do about it. Here was one little guy, and out there were these massive organizations. What could I do? But I kept very clear in my mind that there had to be a way to achieve the result that I wanted.

Then one day I was sitting with a friend down in Los Angeles and it happened. I can remember because it was like a photographic slide flashing on. I got this picture of what Windfarms should be. And once anything becomes really clear, you can make it happen. Then it's only a matter of doing it.

Intuition demands action.   R. Buckminster Fuller said:

I call intuition cosmic fishing. You feel a nibble, then you've got to hook the fish.

Too often you get the nibble of an idea or a yes/no leap, and you don't follow through to solidly hook the opportunity. To do this you have to unite intuition with all the other aspects of Essence—will, joy, strength, and compassion.

People who have followed through make it sound easy. They use words like ''just'' and ''only.'' Perhaps their follow-through seems easy only in hindsight. Or perhaps their decisions were so powerful that they were propelled forward into implementation. But the fact remains that if you don't follow through, your decision or idea dies.

Certainly those people who identify intuition as luck always caution that hard work is also necessary. Dana's Rene McPherson says that you can be lucky, but ''You don't get to be a slobby dog.'' Tandem's Jim Treybig argues that creative success in business comes from luck *and* hard work.

Follow-through in business is more than just hard work. It is *timely* hard work. Remember that Bob Medearis called his lawyer about Silicon Valley Bank right after getting off the airplane—and that wasn't the end of it. Within days he conferred with a banker to learn all that he could about the business, drove around the area and commissioned a market study to determine the best location, worked with knowledgeable people to discover the bank's market niche, and put together a blue-ribbon founders group of one hundred individuals who could provide capital, credibility, and publicity for the bank.

If there is one characteristic that signals creativity in business, it might be follow-through. For instance, Nolan Bushnell is only one of the people who could be credited for fathering the video game, but he often gets the credit because he was the first to bring any to market in a big way. He says:

After the creative moment I thought, ''Gee, anybody should be able to make a business out of it.'' As it turned out, anybody could. I had twenty-seven competitors so fast! (Laughter)

But timely action isn't necessarily the same thing as immediate action. Charles Schwab told us that many of the ideas for his discount brokerage appeared over a twenty-year period. But when it was time to implement them, he did so with dispatch.

Heidi Roizen, president of T/Maker Corporation, had come to such an appropriate moment when the first MacIntosh computers came out. Everybody in her office played constantly with the MacPaint art option on the new computer, but most were disappointed in the results of drawing with the computer. Was it possible, she wondered, that a computer-program version of the clip-art services available to commercial artists could fill an important need in the market? Was the idea a yes or a no?

There were at least four negative arguments. First, such a program would require a completely different distribution system than did the company's main product, a business software system. Second, the project would mean turning vital resources away from industrial to consumer markets where costs were greater and competition was fierce. Third, the twenty-five thousand dollars needed to develop and launch the program represented about eighty percent of the small company's quarterly budget, and was already needed desperately for T/Maker's established product. Fourth, the product idea was so obvious and good that other marketers were probably already producing it.

So how did ClickArt become a yes? Heidi Roizen tells us what happened.

I was sitting in a restaurant with a co-worker before going to see the movie Gorky Park. *We were talking about this new art program idea for the MacIntosh. I said, "Wouldn't it be neat if you had a set of images of household furniture and appliances that you could call up?" Furniture was actually the first thing we thought of. Instead of actually having to go move your furniture, you could have these little things on the screen. Then we said, "Wouldn't it be neat to have cars and animals and people." We wrote this list down on a napkin. And I sat through the whole movie, and I couldn't keep my mind on it because I was so fired up by this product idea. When we came out of the movie, I said, "You know something is going on when I can't pay attention to a whole movie."*

For me, though, it was enough satisfaction just to have thought of the idea. But not for my co-worker. He sat me down a week later and said, "You haven't done a goddam thing. I think it's a good idea, and I'm going to do it. Are you going to help me or not?" He was really right. If he hadn't been this real-world person saying, "Do it, you're going to get something out of it," it would probably have been one of those ideas that I would have seen someone else advertising a month later.

Follow through. Heidi Roizen did, and ClickArt became a bestseller that sold over twenty times the break-even level in the first year. Her small group got the product on the market in only eight weeks, faced off six competitors to become the number one seller, brought out a special version of the product for publication work in another twelve weeks, and a third version of the product in twelve more weeks. The line of ClickArt products brought in fifty percent of the company's revenues in the first year.

Intuition is mistake-free. Will you always make the right decision if you use yes/no and intuition? Isn't there a danger in making a yes or no decision when the situation is still only at the maybe stage? If you make a decision intuitively, how do you explain it to your family, your boss, the people who are going to implement it, your directors or stockholders? How do you defend yourself if it goes wrong?

It's not unusual to have doubts like these about bringing intuition into your decision-making. Reason, analysis, and logic seem solid and familiar; you have imbibed them well over the years. They are something that can be computerized, put on paper, discussed. And there is something mysterious about intuition.

If using intuition to make decisions is worrying you, ask yourself what part of you this worry is coming from. Remember what Ken Oshman said in the quote at the beginning of the chapter, to the effect that searching for "right" is wrong. And, remind yourself that, since good reasons usually support both sides of any argument, you'll probably have no trouble explaining your intuitive decision on a logical basis.

Claude Rosenberg of Rosenberg Capital Management banishes the fear of making mistakes by what he calls "dealing with the Y in the road."

A very learned man said to me once, "The most serious thing is to get stuck at the Y in the road. You don't know which way to go, and you stay at the Y." I think that's really true. It has to do with creativity and change. You come to the Y in the road and you think for a minute. If your instinct doesn't tell you which way to go, don't stay there and muddle muddle muddle. Think it through, but then you've got to go down one of the forks. And once you go down that fork, you will find that you've gone the "wrong" way or the "right" way and you might come back, but that's the learning experience.

Rosenberg reached a major fork in the road in 1970. He had been with the investment banking firm of J. Barth and Company for fifteen years. During that time he had become a research partner, published two books on investing, developed the largest investment research department in the western U.S., and pioneered formalized regional investment research. But now, during a downturn in the market, he seemed to be ready to go out on his own. Was it a yes or a no?

It wasn't that there was anything wrong with J. Barth and Company. I had wanted to leave and do my own thing for a number of years, but I had stayed there out of an exaggerated sense of loyalty, despite feeling that I wanted to do my own thing and that I was tired and frustrated by not controlling my destiny myself.

I remember when I told my senior partner (who remained a good friend until he died) that I was going to leave and start my own firm. The market was terrible and the investment business looked bad. He said, "Do you want my reaction?" and I said, "Yes." He said, "I think you're nuts." I went out of his office thinking, "Now there's a guy with good judgment." Normally he did have it, but he didn't in this case. It could have been foolhardy, but I was lucky. I was in the right place at the right time when we opened our business.

Today Rosenberg's independent investment counseling firm manages over four billion dollars of fixed-income and equity assets. In addition, in 1975 he formed RREEF Corporation, which purchases high quality, income-producing real estate for tax-exempt clients. RREEF is the third largest corporation of its kind with well over a billion dollars under management. An amateur musical comedy lyricist, Rosenberg gives a lot of the credit for his success in both his business and personal life to making decisions with intuition.

If you never do anything about these ideas, then you will be part of something that I don't think will do you very much good. I read an interesting article once that said that the most dangerous word or phrase was "should" or "should have." I think that's really true, so I've written a song about it called "Shoulda Coulda Woulda." I'll read some of it to you, because I think it means something. It goes:

> *Life's filled with options, those forks in the road,*
> *Requiring adoptions that change living modes.*
> *My problems, my choices, once set in concrete,*
> *Incite bleeding voices that seem to repeat:*
> *I shoulda done this, I coulda stood pat*
> *I just can't dismiss how I coulda changed that.*

And then it goes on, but the singer is really saying: "I don't want to take it that one step further. I don't want to take my creativity the next step and do something about something." What I'm saying is that you've got to find the creative things that fit with what you can do, and then do them. One conduit to happiness is this ability to keep the enthusiasm going, and to create, and to have a positive attitude toward change, which I think is really the secret to what differentiates successful people within their business experience and in their own personal lives.

Living with yes/no develops a positive attitude about change. At its base, procrastinating about decisions because of fear of making mistakes is really an attempt to avoid change. In contrast, love of change characterizes successful business people, even the change that comes from what others might think of as a mistake.

When we asked Nolan Bushnell to tell us about a time when he lost a game in life, he mentioned his having to sell Atari to Warner for twenty-eight million dollars. It was a loss to him, because he couldn't move his company into retail consumer sales fast enough. But he made the decision with reason and intuition and went on to build other companies. At the time he visited our class, video games and his old company Atari were riding high with billions in sales. But conditions have changed since then, and so has Bushnell. His name now comes up often as a backer of successful new technology.

When conditions change, creative people make new decisions. We've already reported how Ed Zschau decided not to run for the U.S. Senate. But seven months later he became convinced that the candidates planning to run against the incumbent were not going to win. So he changed his decision. He began to explore possible support for a Senate race.

Many of our speakers echo Rosenberg's positive attitude towards change. When Jim Benham quit Merrill Lynch to start one of the first money market funds, he left so quickly that he lost benefits money and had no income for three years. Mistake? Not to Benham, mainly because Capital Preservation Fund has opened up to him whole new worlds of challenge, opportunity, and reward.

Remarkably, Benham and the others don't really see the possibility of a mistake, even in a clear failure. Most people rationalize a failure when it is clearly apparent, but these creative business people use failures as learning experiences, and come back even stronger.

Not all people put the same kind of confidence, energy, and commitment into their personal decisions that they put into their business ones. But in personal life, too, you must be willing to make decisions, not worrying about making mistakes, and realizing that it is better to go down a fork in the road than to stay stuck at the Y.

Tricks of the Trade

Decisions are conscious ("I want vanilla ice cream"), and unconscious ("I want to fail in my new job"). It's the unconscious decisions that too often rule daily behavior. Bringing unconscious material to conscious knowledge is the primary movement in effective decision-making. The best way to do this is to flex the intuition muscle by consciously making many decisions into yes/no ones every day—starting with today. Here are some tricks of this essential trade.

Develop your own style. When nineteenth-century composer Anton Bruckner was asked how, when, and where he thought of the motif for his Ninth Symphony, he replied:

Well, it was like this, I walked up the Kahlenberg, and when it got hot and I got hungry, I sat down by a little brook and unpacked my Swiss cheese. And just as I open the greasy paper, that darn tune pops into my head.

Stories like that belie the work and preparation that led to that moment. No one else could have walked up the Kahlenberg on that particular day and have that "darn tune" (which some have called divine) pop into his head. Nor can anyone else have your unique ideas. Because of your experiences and work, you have the idea or decision already within you, but you must make the choice of whether to heed it or not.

How do you know whether you have enough information, enough experience? Advice on this varies widely. R. Buckminster Fuller said, "When in doubt, don't." Songwriter and pop recording star Harry Chapin said, "When in doubt, do something." And former Belgian prime minister Achille Van Ackere used to say, "I act first, then I think about it."

The answer is to develop your own style; only you know what is right for you in each situation. Each time you experience your own creative resource makes it easier to experience it again. The more you make decisions from Essence, the quieter your VOJ. And the quieter your VOJ, the sharper your observation; you begin to pay attention without worry or mind chatter, and you begin to build up the wisdom to make good decisions. And the more sharply you observe, the more profound your questions. Either you find the problem or it finds you.

You can develop your decision-making style and your ability to make creative decisions by starting with small decisions and by paying attention to what happens. Notice the conditions in which ideas occur to you. Is it in the shower, in doing something physical or athletic, in silence, in discussions with co-workers in the heat of battle, in getting away from it all, in meditation, in using some fifties creativity technique, in dreams, or in toughing it out until the idea or decision occurs? Use whatever works for you.

Replace frustration with simulation. As you pay attention to what happens with yes/no, you'll increasingly see ways to get to your intuition quickly, without the long frustrating periods of beating your head against a wall. Meanwhile, you might want to try the following four-step simulation based on some remarks by Dean Arthur Hastings. We recommend that you approach it as a meditation: sit comfortably, with your eyes closed.

First, diffuse emotional desires. Allow yourself to accept whatever outcome your intuition gives you. Our students find that reminding themselves that there is really no right or wrong way to go—that "This isn't for keeps," that the decision isn't really important in a cosmic sense or even in terms of their whole life—helps them to divest themselves of any emotional wishes or desires.

Second, clear and calm your mind. This usually means relaxing physically or using a meditation technique.

Third, put the question into your mind. Don't try to work on it or strive for an answer. Have no expectations. See the question in your mind's eye. Hear it inside. Wait for your answer.

Fourth, observe. What is the answer? What are your reactions to the answer? Imagine the outcome of the decision that comes.

When you finish with the simulation, after you have opened your eyes, act on the answer, even if it is just to write it down or to mentally affirm it. This is not a frivolous game. It is a process by which you can develop your most valuable decision-making tool. What you want to develop is the ability (which you inherently have) to make good decisions quickly and efficiently as soon as you need them, without going through any four-step technique, even in the heat of controversy and pressure.

Flip a coin and pay attention to your feelings. Since most decision situations add up, pro and con, to about fifty-fifty on an analytic basis, you might as well flip a coin. But unlike the superstitious ancients who practiced sortilege (the drawing of lots), you can still override the coin's answer with the one your Essence gives you. Sense your body. How does it feel if the coin comes up with a yes? Are you uncomfortable with it? Do you want to try two out of three? Then it is probably a no for you.

Follow the gnawing feeling. A variation of the coin-flip occurs when you sound out ideas or decisions before you fully act upon them. James Cook, president of L. G. Balfour, was reported in the *Wall Street Journal* to differentiate between "gut and guess" by observing his own reactions when his colleagues shoot down his ideas. If his feeling persists—"and gnaws and gnaws"—he is more likely to stay with his idea.

Nolan Bushnell told about presenting the idea for the video game "Breakout" to a group at Atari, where people were encouraged to be frank about others' ideas. He got an overwhelmingly negative response. But the gnawing went on and:

> *The common wisdom in the game companies at that time was that games with paddles were passé. But I just knew in my mind that the game was going to be fun. I hired a consultant who developed a prototype of the game. Once everyone played it, they said, "Oh yeah! Why didn't you say this in the first place?"*

There is a caution implicit in Bushnell's story, however. People very often confuse habit ("It worked before") with a message from their Essence. That could have been the case here since Bushnell started the video game revolution with a paddle game. Fortunately he had the check of reactions of others in his company. You can benefit from the same kind of check.

Stimulate your whole brain with a breathing exercise. Recent research indicates that our breathing is intimately related to patterns of brain hemisphere action. When you breathe predominantly through the left nostril, your right brain is more active, and vice versa.

Given what we know about right brain versus left brain, it wasn't long before researchers asked the obvious question: Is it possible to activate one side of the brain or the other by selective nostril breathing? The answer is yes, which probably explains why a centuries-old hatha yoga breathing exercise works so well in relaxing people and in opening up their inner creative resources.

You can do this exercise right where you are now, since it involves nothing more than alternating breaths across nostrils. It can clear and direct your mind while you are making a decision.

The alternate nostril breathing rhythm goes as follows: Pinch your nose as if you smell something, putting the first finger of your right hand on your left nostril and the thumb on your right nostril. Then lift your thumb and inhale easily and deeply into the right nostril. After inhaling all the way, close the right nostril with your thumb, lift the first finger, and first exhale out of and then inhale into the left nostril. Then close the left nostril and open and breathe out and into the right. Continue alternate breathing for as long as it feels comfortable, remembering to shift nostrils after each deep inhalation.

Concentrate intensely on one activity. You probably often get insights and make good decisions when you are involved in something that is unrelated to the problem. You can achieve the same effect by concentrating intensely and silently on any activity, such as eating. Simply eat alone and pay total attention to the tastes, temperature, colors, odors, sounds, and textures of the food, and to your bodily and emotional reactions to it. Don't read, watch TV, or think about anything but the food.

The sensing, looking, and listening exercise of the last chapter can do the same thing wherever you are. Whatever you concentrate on, don't *expect* anything. Just see what happens, especially when you get back to your decision problem. You might be surprised.

Cherish your revelations. As you live with the yes/no heuristic, many small revelations will occur. These came from our students:

Food seems to taste better when it is chosen by yes/no.

Yes/no saves time.

No decision is forever.

You never seem to be able to compile enough facts to be able to make a decision based solely on them.

There doesn't have to be a rational reason for your decision.

Big decisions are usually made by yes/no already.

You can do a yes to a no as long as you know it is a no (and also vice versa).

Revelations like these (you will have your own) are validation that the intuition is operating. You can keep the process going by writing down your findings and acknowledging your successes.

Ask yourself if it's a yes or a no. Surprise. We have come full circle to the trick of the trade that is the very basis of this chapter. It is truly a powerful little idea for revolutionizing your decision-making. If you're diligent in applying it, observing and even writing down your experiences, you are well on your way to making creative decisions consistently in all parts of your life.

9

BE ORDINARY

Be what you is, not what you ain't, 'cause if you ain't what you is, you is what you ain't.

> Luther D. Price

I go through periods of having serious self-doubts. All of us do, and we are lying if we don't say so. I'm president of my corporation, and we are making money. I also see what's happening and I tell myself it's happening because I made it happen. And then I figure I'm just full of it.

> Anne Robinson
> Windham Hill Records

The kingdom of God is within you.

> Luke 17:21

Almost all men...have strange imaginings. The strongest of these is a belief that they can progress only by improvement. Those who understand will realize that we are much more in need of stripping off than adding on.

> Doris Lessing

We shall not cease from exploration
And the end of all our exploring
Will be to arrive where we started
And know the place for the first time.

> T. S. Eliot
> *Four Quartets*

Sages and seers, poets and philosophers have been delivering the same know-thyself message for centuries. But how can you do that when daily business life gives you so many selves to contend with?

The self who glows in a minor triumph ("By god, I was right!") then cringes under a minor criticism ("I should learn to keep my big mouth shut").

The self who beholds the glory of an idea breakthrough ("I see! I see! After all my fussing, I really understand!") and then wallows in the hell of self-doubt ("If *I* thought of it, it can't be any good").

The self who, at one end of the room at a cocktail party, feels out of place among the elite (''Oh, lord, why didn't I go home to change?'') and at the other end feels too good for the peasants (''These people aren't even dressed correctly'').

Which is the real self that wise men say it pays to know?

None, of course. All speak of alienation, in one degree or another. Self-inflation represents the peak of the alienation scale; self-flagellation, the depths. You have probably already learned to recognize and to challenge the self-indulgent phoniness of both extremes, but you might not yet have learned that they are phases of alienation rather than characteristics of your true selfhood.

It is the job of this chapter to help you discover within your thought processes the self it pays to know—the inner, true one who is not a helpless passenger on a careening roller coaster. ''Acquaint thyself now with Me, and be at peace; thereby great good will come to thee.'' That's your Essence talking, your creative source, and it offers a strait-is-the-gate escape from the heights and depths of alienation: Be ordinary.

Be ordinary. Our words, not the Bible's. By those words we do not mean anything as namby-pamby as ''Strike a happy medium.'' Instead we mean: Connect with everything that your creative Essence bestows.

One of Muktananda's favorite stories was about the Lords' Club. As he told it, this group of lords realized almost immediately that they needed someone to administer the organization, someone to wait on them, someone to guard the door, someone to take minutes, someone to clean and maintain the facility, someone to entertain them. But they were all lords, and only lords were allowed to attend.

So every month they took turns by drawing assignments. Each did whatever job he drew to the best of his ability, but no one got attached to his monthly task, or identified with it. They never forgot that they were lords.

This, implied Muktananda, is the way you can live your life. You never know what life is going to present to you, but you can maintain a constant awareness that you are really a lord, the Essence, the Self, heir to a high estate. And that's what it is to be ordinary: to live your life in awareness of your full powers as you face everyday situations as well as critical ones. If you feel yourself slipping into the self-centeredness of alienation, remind yourself that such role-playing enticements come from your false ego. Remind yourself that your true self comes from Essence, infinitely creative, with boundless intuition, will, joy, and compassion. Affirm, with Emerson, that:

What lies beyond us and what lies before us are tiny matters when compared to what lies within us.

THE MANY PATHS TO ORDINARINESS

Truly ordinary business people don't hire a press agent. They are oblivious to fame even though they accept it if it comes. They are supremely confident without being inflated, humble without being brow-beaters. They are totally fulfilled in what they do and keep doing it with great skill through thick and thin. While there might not be many *extraordinary* people at any one time in history, there certainly are many in all walks of life, including business, who are ordinary throughout their lives. Some of them come to our class as students or as speakers or as tales told by others. Two of our favorites are the scientists Subrahmanyan Chandrasekhar and Barbara McClintock.

Chandrasekhar was twenty-four years old in 1935 when he presented, at the Royal Astronomical Society under the auspices of his friend and mentor Arthur Eddington—at that time the acknowledged dean of the field—a theory of black holes, decades before they were acknowledged by others in astronomy. Shockingly, however, Eddington stood up after his young friend's talk and demolished it, an attack that ruined any chance of Chandrasekhar's getting a tenured position. Instead he worked in six other fields, and did not return to the subject of black holes until his sixty-third year, when he launched an eight-year study. He simply came into his office at the University of Chicago and worked for at least twelve hours a day, usually seven days a week. And then, in 1983, he won a Nobel prize for the entire body of his work.

McClintock began working with Indian corn, or maize, soon after she received her doctorate in plant genetics in 1927. By 1944 she was elected to the National Academy of Sciences, but soon she was not taken seriously because of her theory that genes could "jump" around on a chromosome. She recalls, "They thought I was crazy, absolutely mad." She even stopped bothering to publish her results, saying later to *Time,* "Nobody was reading me, so what was the use?"

For nearly half a century she worked with her patch of Indian corn at the Cold Spring Harbor Laboratory—alone. One day she apologized to a late-day drop-in, "Excuse me for being so hoarse, but I have not yet used my vocal chords today."

By the 1960s, molecular biologists, using "sophisticated" methods, supported her theories and results. Through it all, she never lost direction or heart, she never gave up. She says, "When you know you're right, you don't care what others think. You know sooner or later it will come out in the wash." She said that her work "has been such a deep pleasure that I never thought of stopping, and I just hated sleeping. I can't imagine having a better life."

At eighty-one she won the Nobel prize for medicine. The committee said her work was "one of the two great discoveries of our times in genetics."

The Experience of Being Ordinary

Being ordinary is not winning prizes, although they might come. Being ordinary is acknowledging, without thinking about it, that you possess the capacity to meet, gracefully and productively, whatever situation or challenge you find on your plate.

Buddhist Lama Sogyal Rinpoche told our class about having an ordinary experience while having breakfast in Holland. As he was about to butter a piece of bread he realized what an act of reverence and perfection that act was. Another Buddhist, Chogyam Trungpa, once said:

> When we first experience true ordinariness, it is something very extra-ordinarily ordinary, so much so that we would say that mountains are not mountains anymore, nor streams streams, because we see them as so ordinary, so precise, so "as they are."

To be ordinary means, at heart, to know your purpose in life and find contentment in your daily doings, unimpressed by the accumulation of monetary wealth or public recognition.

Martin Luther King, shortly before he was assassinated, made the following statement at the Ebenezer Baptist Church in Atlanta:

> Every now and then I think about my own death, and I think about my own funeral.... I don't want a long funeral. And if you get somebody to deliver the eulogy, tell them not to talk too long.... Tell them not to mention that I have a Nobel peace prize. Tell them not to mention that I have three or four hundred other awards. I'd like somebody to mention that day that Martin Luther King Jr. tried to give his life to serving others. I'd like for somebody to say that day that Martin Luther King Jr. tried to love somebody.
>
> Say that I was a drum major for justice. Say that I was a drum major for peace. That I was a drum major for righteousness. And all of the other shallow things will not matter. I won't have any money to leave behind. I won't have the fine and luxurious things of life to leave behind. But I just want to leave a committed life behind.

Paul Michael, a former MBA student now with Charles Schwab Discount Brokers, says:

> I've come to the conclusion that I am creative when I do not think about it. I am creative when I do not feel the need to conform to someone else's expectations. I am creative when I simply let go of my preconceived notion of who I am and let myself be.

Another student, a middle manager with a multibillion-dollar corporation, admits that he often experiences feelings of alienation at social gatherings because of his generally low self-esteem—despite his surprising successes and innovative solutions for his company. In living with this chapter's heuristic he decided that:

I could no longer continue feeling the way I felt and acting the way I did, which was basically being uncommunicative and distant at these social gatherings. I resolved to just be me and stop worrying about everyone else's reactions.

One encouraging incident this past week involved a meeting I had at my company with one of our vice-presidents. The meeting held was to discuss a possible position for me. The individual was someone I hardly knew. Before I entered the meeting I told myself to just be me. In other words I was going to try not to get nervous, not assume a role, and not feel as if I had something to prove.... I was relaxed, candid, and unassuming. I felt detached from the normal feelings I would have had in the past. I was offered the job I wanted and felt very satisfied with the meeting.

Jim Collins, now an independent consultant and founder of a computer software company, was an internationally known mountain climber before attending the MBA program and our class. He equates the experience of being ordinary with one he had when he free soloed (climbed without a partner or a rope or equipment of any sort) a mountain face called the Naked Edge. A *Mountain* magazine article about the climb said:

Before 1978, everyone who attempted the Edge considered the challenge quite sufficient to warrant a rope. Then, early on a summer morning, Jim Collins decided to try it solo.

It was only later that Collins realized how being ordinary was key to that climb.

Being ordinary has helped me to understand a number of very significant events of my life. The difference between making something happen and letting something happen is the centerpiece of these incredibly meaningful (to me) experiences.

The consequence of a mistake while free soloing is instant death. Being ordinary was the key to reaching the summit of the Naked Edge without killing myself. Free soloing the Naked Edge would normally be deemed sheer lunacy, even in the climbing community. It was something that few people had ever even thought about.

Early in the morning of the day he did the climb Collins had a fight with his ex-girl friend and didn't really care about anything but getting out to climb.

The relevant issue about the Naked Edge is that I never planned to do it. I never told myself, ''I'm going to get up tomorrow morning and make a free solo of the Naked Edge.'' Instead, I just let it happen. This was taken to such an extreme that I didn't even think about doing the whole climb while I was actually on the climb. There were always easier routes to the side that I could have traversed to, until the last pitch. I took each move one by one, never thinking: "Hey I'm soloing the Naked Edge." I was simply executing each little movement one after another with no thought of the whole climb. The interesting thing is that each move by itself is nothing exceptional. If any one move was done two feet off the ground, it would be no big deal.

The other relevant issue is that my motivations for soloing the Edge were not ego-driven, but instead were very personal and internal. In fact, I never told anyone that I had done it. I simply reached the top, enjoyed the cool morning air, and hiked down the descent route. I think I went home and took a nap and read the afternoon paper. I don't think anyone would have known about it had it not been for a few climbers in the canyon who saw me top out.

Living with the Ups and Downs

The people who come to our class have certainly attained major goals. But they still face everyday irritants and challenges and seem to handle them by being ordinary. Steve Jobs came to us at twenty-five years of age, the head of what was already a two-hundred-million-dollar enterprise, and he had just had an argument with his girl friend. Anne Robinson was suffering from jet lag, having just returned from Japan, and was also facing some nagging collection problems back at the home office of Windham Hill Records. Paul Cook's company was listed on the Fortune 500 for the first time on the day he came to our class. Vicky Hardy's top assistant had just been hired away. Charles Schwab had, a week before, attended his first meeting of the Bank of America board of directors. Nolan Bushnell was being attacked in a newspaper article that one of our students brought to class and read out loud. These people and others like them are toasted one moment and roasted the next. Yet they seem to be able to handle both types of situation with creativity and grace.

Michael Bilich, the general manager of F. A. Hoyt Ltd., has faced the kinds of ups and downs that are typical in any business career or life. In particular he became one of the youngest vice-presidents in the history of Crocker Bank, but he began to see that in order to make further contributions there he would have to make sacrifices in other parts of his life. He recounts:

I left there and didn't have anywhere else to go, so I immediately started looking for a job with the basic panic that, "I should be working." Luckily (I only say this with hindsight) I couldn't find anything. At first I started getting down on myself a little bit and worrying about what I was going to do, how I was going to make the mortgage payments and all that sort of thing.

But he and his wife realized that they could get along on her income for awhile.

All of a sudden I decided not to worry about it. We have in our house a little courtyard, a very private place. In this year that I was off (I call it my "monastic period") I'd go out there and be by myself all day. I'm basically a loner anyway, and I just thoroughly enjoyed it. So I started getting up in the morning and meditating for an hour; then I would go out and run five or ten miles, then I'd come back and start reading. In this period of unemployment, I read more than fifty books—history, philosophy, religion, physics, mathematics, biology, things like that.

Through all this, I was trying to figure out, "Who am I?" "What am I doing?" "Am I in the right career?" "Am I not in the right career?" "What should I be doing?" In my meditation I came to realize that I had to decide what I really wanted to do, and had to do something about it. I finally started visualizing, in my meditation, what type of job I would want to do if I had my choice of anything in the world. I started thinking that it would be fun to run a small company. I'd like it to be owned by a wealthy person, and I would also manage his money.

Through a series of seeming coincidences, Bilich was presented with exactly that type of job with F. A. Hoyt. And once he got to Hoyt, a leaser of garbage collection equipment, he was able to triple pretax earning in four years—by applying what he had learned during his monastic period about being himself, about having compassion for himself and others.

I had come to love myself, not in a selfish way, but just to recognize who I am, that I am a person of value, and I have that value to give to my fellow-man. And in giving to that fellow-man I will get something in return for it, but the real joy is giving, not receiving. Once I discovered that, and learned that I could love myself, then I realized that I could truly love others because I knew how it felt.

This discovery helped when he was faced with the situation at Hoyt.

As I took this thing over I told myself, "What an opportunity! I've always talked about managing a corporation but have never been given the opportunity. Now I've been thrown into it, and I'd better come through with my ideas."

As I walked into the place, I could sense that there was a lot of negativism. Rather than jump on people, I started loving them to death, and I gave them freedom. I also told people that they don't work for me. They work with me. It took me about six months to get them to feel comfortable with the fact that the organization was in a state of change, that it was going to continue to change until we could really start showing some success. Every morning we'd have a little discussion. We'd talk about love and about how we can service this account or that account and deal with pertinent situations.

Ever since Steve Jobs visited our class, fresh from an argument with his girl friend, he has been on a roller-coaster ride. In one year, for instance, he he presided over the successful launching of the MacIntosh line of computers, and in the next year he was forced to resign from the company he had built on his own vision.

Through it all he always appeared to remain himself. Early on, he said to our class:

What Apple has really been to me is an opportunity to express some deep feeling about wanting to contribute something. In other words, we use somebody else's mathematics, we didn't invent the shoes we wear. The watch we have on our wrist somebody else did and it's somebody else's language, and we weren't around when the Constitution was signed...all this stuff we take. We are constantly taking. I really believe that people have a desire to put something back, to give something in a greater way than simply a one-on-one interaction. In a sense I think that that's part of the joy of Apple Computer and a lot of other companies around this valley. It's sort of a framework or glue that holds this whole environment together where, if it's done right, people really can put something back, you know. And we're very fortunate in the sense that what we are doing is being used by a few hundred thousand people and so that's very fine.

Being ordinary can carry you through the most difficult of situations. When Jobs was almost forcibly stripped of any operating role at Apple, he was asked if his company had been taken from him. His answer to *Newsweek* echoed what he had said in our class years earlier:

To me, Apple exists in the spirit of the people that work there.

So if Apple just becomes a place where computers are a commodity item and where the romance is gone and where people forget that computers are the most incredible invention that man ever invented, then I'll feel I have lost Apple.

But if I'm a million miles away and all those people still feel those things and they're still working to make the next great personal computer, then I will feel that my genes are still there.

Being ordinary doesn't mean that you just sit back and let events take their course. You are an active participant. You operate with great efficiency because you are being yourself.

The early history of Dansk Designs illustrates this. After negotiating with German producers for an early delivery of stainless steel flatware, Ted Nierenberg covered forty-six cities in two months, selling the flatware to department and specialty stores and chains. He was financed by a bank for fifty percent of every order he received, so every day he sent in his orders by priority mail to the bank. In the midst of this pre-Christmas rush an October letter from Germany postponed delivery indefinitely. Ted says:

We could have thrown in the towel...or we could have waited until February or March. But I said to Martha, "You pack me some shirts and get me a ticket and somehow we've got to solve this problem over in Germany." So she met me at Kennedy and I flew to Germany, stayed there a week and made some compromises, and they agreed to fill my order only because they knew darn well that I'd be there up until Christmas Eve if they didn't produce the stuff. So in order to get rid of me, they put the stuff back into production, and I took the shipment of four wooden cases up to Hamburg.

Ted shipped the cases on a passenger ship, because it would take half the time that a freighter would. Unfortunately when the ship got to New York there was a stevedore's strike, and the ship was going to set off again for Europe in three days with the Nierenbergs' precious cargo.

Ted thought he had the solution, however. The father of an old school friend was head of the waterfront police, so:

I went up to New York to see my friend's father, George Hahn. He always chewed a cigar. He said, "Teddy, don't worry, we're going down there." We went to the piers in a squad car with motorcycle escort. We walked up to some guys who seemed to be about 6'5" and 300 pounds each. George said, "I want you to take some cases off." The stevedores refused and gestured at us in a way I don't want to imitate here. George said, "Don't worry, Ted. Comes the night shift—a different ball game." Well the night shift wasn't a different ball game, and the day shift the next day wasn't different.

Thursday afternoon I went back home and said, "It's all over." There was no one at home. Martha had taken the two kids off in her station wagon. She said she'd be home for dinner and by the time she walked in I think I must have had five scotches and was three sheets to the wind.

She said, "I've got it." I said, "Got what?" She said, "The shipment, I've got the cases you loaded on the S.S. America in Hamburg." I said, "That's impossible." She said, "They're in the station wagon."

I went out and looked at the cases, and I said, "How in God's name did you do that?" She said, "I had Lisa by the hand and Karen in my arms and went up to the stevedores and said, 'These two kids can't eat unless you get me those four cases off the boat.' " (Laughter)

Well, she's really the founder of Dansk. (Laughter) *Give credit where it's due. If she hadn't got those cases I wouldn't be here talking to you today.*

Martha Nierenberg remembered to be herself, to be ordinary, and to present the situation with clarity. A creative life in business is like that, a string of moments in which you make breakthroughs, important decisions, or those small moves that add up in the long run.

Sandra Kurtzig started her company, ASK Computer Systems, in her kitchen (she is fond of pointing out that she didn't even have a garage) because she was at home starting a family. She sums up the kind of ordinary viewpoint we've heard from many of our speakers:

I have never had any long-range plans for creating a company (that I think has gotten too big in my mind right now). I just really did things that I enjoy doing. I enjoy being with people. I enjoy trying to look at problems and figure out ways of solving those problems in the easiest, most direct and simplest way.

I don't think that anything that we do within ASK is particularly creative. I think the only creativity in it, sorry about that, is that we just try to solve some problems in the simplest way possible, instead of trying to do anything unique. We develop software. The whole key to ASK, to our success, and to what we've developed is developing software that is easy to use, that's simple. The person who is using it can understand how to get information in and out of the system, and can do it very quickly.

The creative part of it isn't trying to be creative. It's just solving the problem, and solving it in an easy way. It's just doing what's fun. Jobs, Bushnell, Cook, Zschau—the one thing that all of us do is that we don't try to act out a role that we think we are supposed to be fitting. It is very difficult sometimes to do that.

Lennie Copeland and Lewis Griggs, now married to each other, each earned a Stanford MBA, Lennie getting hers a year before our course was offered and Lewis taking it in his last MBA term. They started their post-Stanford careers in somewhat different ways. Lennie, a dynamic woman, had worked in the movie industry and started her own consulting firm. Lewis was also energetic but liked to work behind the scenes in negotiations that, for instance, helped to start three companies, two in genetic engineering. Then Lewis had a significant failure in negotiating with some potential Japanese partners. This led to Copeland-Griggs Productions, their award-winning training and awareness films, *Going International*, and their book of the same name. As they started working together, they somewhat reversed their roles. It was Lewis who came to our class to explain how they moved beyond the typical feelings of alienation that can sometimes occur at the start of a new project.

I had never produced a film. I had certainly never written a book. Where do I start? I certainly don't know anything about this field. Anything! Well, shouldn't I be the last person on earth to make a film about it or much less to become an international expert about it? Yeah, but I'm kind of cocky and have some confidence that maybe I can do it.

I've discovered that it's true that you can do something that's never been done before, whether it's trivial and small like our work or something gigantic like Steve Jobs' accomplishment. It happens just by doing it. Not much analysis is involved at all. I did a month's worth of market research—just enough to find out that no one had done films like ours and that everybody I talked to wanted them. Then I raised half a million dollars in eight weeks. We found filmmakers who had won awards for cinematography and pulled them together. Lennie, who had grown up overseas, did all the research on the subject and wrote the script. And we launched the films. And the book came out because people in companies and the government who were using the films said they wanted more. So this thing has snowballed, as everything does if you're just aware of yourself.

Lewis has found that he operates best when he is in front of a group or on national television and "out on a limb."

I stand in front of groups and am vulnerable and allow myself to depend on my own sources of energy. If you don't dare to be out there, you'll never feel the success of living and breathing and discovering how to survive. And then you'll continue to wonder about it and still be stuck in your head. I've discovered things about myself, and the more I discover the more fascinated I become as to what else must still be there. I'm losing almost all inhibitions I've ever had that have kept me from doing things. Life just gets more and more thrilling the more you drop those inhibitions and stop worrying about what other people are going to think. Just do it. Do something. Do anything.

Lennie has found a different path. As Lewis says:

There are different ways to be creative, to be successful. I happen to thrive on the challenge of persuading others and communicating, whether to do that through politics or sales or whatever. Lennie Copeland has discovered that, even though she used to be successful in public situations, she didn't like doing that—[the kind of thing] *that I'm beginning to like more and more. What she loves, more than anything, is just being alone in front of her Compaq computer, or whatever vehicle she's using, to distill all of the research she's done and all of the things she's picked up from the outside. She recreates the essence of them in a written or visual form. She is thrilled with writing and being a producer. She wants to do a feature-length film now. And she wants to write more books.*

So there are many styles of creativity. Lennie's is very different. We are complementary to each other, which is why we have been able to work so well together not only as friends, lovers, spouses, and parents, but also professionally.

When he came to our class, Tom Peters was in the process of co-writing *In Search of Excellence*, the first of his best-selling books. He sees the early development of this work in a very nonassuming way:

The thing that I've done that has the highest impact in my short tenure at McKinsey [consulting company] *of seven or eight years has been this material that has dealt with the excellent company. It has had little to do with an act of genius.*

We started on an analysis of excellent companies at McKinsey because we were doing a screen of acquisition areas for Dart Industries about four years ago, and the team that was doing the job was using a bunch of GE software financial models. About a week before their first presentation, which was to be to Justin Dart, the whole GE system crashed, and so the team couldn't produce its report. But we already had Justin Dart's calendar filled for a Good Friday in April 1977. So my boss in San Francisco said, "You've been fooling around with this organization stuff for about two years now. Can you go down and talk to Justin Dart and say something interesting?" I said, "Well, I doubt it." And he said, "Why don't we talk about, you know, what makes for good management."

He and I went down on Good Friday. I had put together a ten-page report, and I titled the thing "Excellence." I'd done no research whatsoever. Dart loved it. Because no one ever talked about excellence or good news in the world. So he said, "Jeez, it's kind of interesting. Must be good stuff, this stuff called excellence."

This led to some research funded by some of the consulting firm's clients. A large report and an impressive slide presentation was developed.

And then a fellow at Pepsi-Cola asked me to come and give a speech to their top hundred managers down in the Bahamas. Since it was cold and wet in San Francisco, it seemed to me like a great opportunity, so I said, "You bet!" And I knew that we couldn't give them four hundred slides. We would have to give them about ten.

So one morning I walked into the office, and it was time to write the speech, because there was only one more day's worth of production time in the office. So I wrote down sort of eight points that seemed to be the major summary statements in my mind. And they are the eight points that have become the McKinsey basics of putting excellence into management and all of that kind of nonsense. But they never changed from that day. And they were just done because they had to be done, because there was a deadline. The deadline was given by the production staff at McKinsey, and so I wrote these eight statements down. And they were not mutually exclusive. They weren't collectively exhaustive. They were totally goddam random.

The speech in the Bahamas was, in Peters' words, "a bomb...awful." But an editor at *Business Week* saw a copy of it and asked Peters to do what at that time was the magazine's only by-lined article by an outsider. This led to an invitation for Peters and his colleagues to give about two-hundred seventy-five speeches on the McKinsey "Eight Basics of Putting Excellence into Management."

They are nothing more than straightforward common sense, except that they are counterintuitive and that common sense has been such a low-value species in the business world for so many years.

And then on top of all that, we hit the right timing. I mean, absolutely! You know, just blind luck. If it hadn't been for the Japanese thing with the automobile industry and in several other industries, if it hadn't been for the criticism of the MBA's and over-analytical methods, if it hadn't been for the fact that the economy went sour—for all those coincidences, starting with Justin Dart and going through Lou Young [the Business Week editor], going through Pepsi-Cola speeches, and going through the right time, and there are sort of twenty-five to a hundred and fifty screens which you pass this thing through. And in any one of those screens, the odds of coming up with something that was a major success had to be terribly low.

So when an innovation occurs, I would argue that it is almost always, as is true with all forms of heroism, a post hoc phenomenon, where suddenly, after the fact, you say, "Goodness gracious, you know Tom Peters sat down and came up with these eight ideas for putting excellence in management, wasn't that a stroke of genius?" There had to be thirty-five thousand people in the world who had said smarter things. Maybe three hundred fifty thousand, or three hundred fifty million, I don't know. But for a whole bunch of random reasons, we got lucky within the context of the business world relative to this set of ideas, and suddenly after the fact, somebody said, "Gee, that was really a creative act." Well, bullshit! It was a lot of data collected, and a bunch of ideas, and seventy-five things all going in a supportive direction. And then we ended up after the fact being identified as heroes.

Modesty like Tom Peters' is not unusual among our speakers; in fact, it is the norm. We think honest modesty is an expression of being ordinary, and is the healthiest frame of mind possible. Desires for and expectation of media recognition interfere with creativity. To be ordinary is to recognize that your dominion unfolds from within.

FINDING YOURSELF IN BUSINESS

As you learn to value your own ordinariness—contentment with your daily tasks, excellence in their execution, modest pleasure over fine results—alienation in its many forms begins to disappear. You begin to realize that there is a way of living that is far higher than the inflation of public success. In *Dr. Sheehan on Running*, George Sheehan speaks of this higher state:

Our lack of heroes is an indication of the maturity of our age—realization that every man has come into his own and has the capability of making a success out of his life. Success rests with the courage, endurance, and, above all, the will to become the person you are, however peculiar that may be.... Then you will be able to say, "I have found my hero and he is me."

Unfortunately, most of us find the challenge to know ourselves quite ominous. As psychologist Carol Hwoschinsky puts it:

When someone asks, "What's your purpose in life?" there is an immediate feeling of fear and a little bit of tension in your throat area. You think, "Oh my God! How do I know what my purpose is?" It is a rather overwhelming thought.

Actually, our purpose isn't that evasive. Just keep in mind that we're all energy. Ask yourself. "What are the qualities that I'm representing by being myself?" What makes you somewhat different from another individual and at the same time very similar? We're all expressing perhaps the same qualities but each in a unique way. It's kind of like having a lens against a beam of light and each one of us is a different way of taking that energy and expressing it. And maybe that's what purpose is. That's what I look at as our life purpose. Ask yourself more specifically what the qualities are that you uniquely express in your life that would be missing if you weren't willing to express those or if you weren't here.

Each one of us contributes something very special and very unique to the greater whole. So what is that? There are signs all around for you. If you begin to look at yourself, at what has value for you, at what, as they say, turns you on, what it is that you're connecting with energetically, you begin to experience yourself naturally.

What is it that you get excited about? When does the juice really begin to run? That is what has a lot of meaning for you, and that is aligned with your purpose. You must be true to that.

Hwoschinsky is emphasizing nothing more than the four tools of creativity: faith in its existence, absence of judgment, observation, and questioning. Her husband Paul echoes her advice about self-observation and questioning:

There's also a test that you can apply. A very simple test. Do you have a sense of peace, a sense of inner well-being when you are doing a particular activity? (Did Howard Hughes have inner peace? He was enormously rich. Did Martin Luther King have inner peace? He certainly didn't pass along an awful lot of physical wealth.) You know that inside. You know when you have that inner peace, that sense of well-being. It's just a knowing that you possess.

Perhaps you already have a solid, unshakable sense of your own self-worth. If so, the following suggestions and exercises will help to confirm it. And for most of us, there is always work to do on finding ourselves. As Jim Benham of Capital Preservation Fund says:

I'm constantly trying to figure out what I am, who I am, and where I'm going with myself. I find that a very provocative thing to be doing, and I always feel like I'm getting closer to where I belong, although I never quite get there.

Come to Grips with Your Approach to Money

We are often surprised that many people who deal adeptly with money in their professional lives avoid the issue in their personal ones. When Rochelle asked approximately a hundred people individually to talk about money in their lives, she found that it was more difficult for them to discuss than sexual relations, personal problems, or death.

Why? We think it's because money is so deeply connected to one's sense of identity. Therefore, analyzing your own feelings about money can give you insight on how you feel about yourself.

Michael Phillips—one of our speakers who, as a bank vice-president, invented among other things the interbank charge card and consumer certificates of deposit—has much to say on the subject of money and self-worth. He sees people's main problem with money as an overconcern with financial security, to the detriment of personal development.

If there's a choice between putting two thousand dollars in an IRA versus two thousand dollars in a trip to the North Pole to see if Admiral Perry's footprints are still there, I'd say "Go to the North Pole," because that will awaken the world around you, and their interest in you, and you'll learn a lot more from it.

In his view, social networks are "infinitely more important than dollars in the bank." His personal priorities, in order: physical health; a broad range of stimulating friends; and a diversity of skills and interests to exercise in a wide variety of circumstances.

In his book, *The Seven Laws of Money*, he discusses these seven precepts:

- *Money will come when you are doing the right thing for you.*
- *Money has its own rules.*
- *Money is a dream—a fantasy alluring as the Pied Piper.*
- *Money is a nightmare.*
- *You can never give money away as a gift.*
- *You can never receive money as a gift.*
- *There are worlds without money.*

It is a provocative book on a provocative subject, and can serve as an outline for your own investigation of your relationship to money.

Go Back to Your Roots

Many of our speakers—including Charles Schwab, Vicky Hardy, Don Prentice, Sandra Kurtzig, Phil Lipetz, Ted Nierenberg, Michael Phillips, Anne Robinson, Wayne Van Dyck, and Steve DeVore—told us about critical incidents in their childhoods, the nature of their early life, or the values they received directly from their parents. And when our students wrote about any of the five challenges, and especially about money and self-worth, they very often went back to their early life for the genesis of their attitudes. If you want to know yourself, look at your history.

Jim Benham, founder of one of the first money market funds, was the sixth of ten children of a minister and his wife. Part of Jim's education was in a one-room schoolhouse with a row for each grade and a teacher whose own schooling stopped before high school. Some very clear messages came to Jim from that upbringing.

I was a very competitive kid. Being from a large family makes you competitive by nature. We would have to say things like, "please pass the potatoes, no stops on the way," because if they stopped along the way, there wouldn't be any potatoes by the time the plate got to you. So you learn to grab....(Laughter) That's the truth! I'm just trying to impress upon you that I came from a very low-income background, where there wasn't a lot of money.

But I learned to compete. I was very good at Monopoly, rarely lost at Monopoly. In different ways I am still playing it, but it's still paper money, isn't it?

Now another thing that I think might be important is the fact that my father played the cornet, and his father played the cornet, and his father played the cornet. Well in fact, I started to play the cornet. I took lessons from a lot of heavyweights in the Washington area like the principal trumpet player of the National Symphony Orchestra. My mother would take money, unknown to my father, from the weekly food and provide money for me to take lessons. My father didn't know that was happening.

I received two college scholarship offers. I wasn't getting any encouragement from my parents to go to school, because they had no money to give to me. I went to Michigan State on a band scholarship, because you didn't have to major in music there. I eventually decided to major in business, so as to have some money someday. I had been without money, and I had seen how our family had evolved without money. And yet I had been aware of this nebulous idea that some people get it.

I want to impress upon you about my background, its competitive nature and somewhat the fact that there's a belief in God going on with me. Also there was a purpose behind playing the trumpet: to continue the tradition that had been going on.

We get a very clear picture of Jim Benham's nature from these few paragraphs about his background. If you heard his whole story, you would also see how his background affected his career as he matured.

The same can be true for you. If you are having difficulty knowing yourself, try reviewing your background and the contributions made to your beliefs and qualities by your parents in particular. Note both the negative and the positive aspects, and consider how they have affected you thus far. Try writing them down and studying them. Recall critical incidents in your childhood, reexperiencing them as vividly as possible. Appreciate the richness of your heritage.

You aren't doomed to follow your parents' negative traits and failures, nor are you entitled to their successes. But by examining and questioning your background, you give yourself a degree of self-knowledge that allows you to make choices.

Go Beyond Desire

You sometimes read or hear stories about people who have tried everything, accomplished everything, and still find themselves in a state of despair and emptiness. Such stories should warn us all about the folly of following false stars.

Of course it is hard to resist the lure of worldly acclaim. You might say, "If only....then everything will be alright," not realizing that the next contract or promotion or raise will only lead you to another "if only." You forget that everything is already all right, that you just have to express the inner gifts you already possess.

To break this vicious cycle you can simulate the experience of already having attained your desires. You can do this in a meditative way as Michael Phillips does with his clients. They meditatively imagine themselves in the most pleasant circumstances they can—with a Cadillac, a Mercedes, a big house, a summer cottage; on a vacation in southern France. Visualize such things until you're sated—that's the point.

One woman who worked with Phillips started out wanting chocolate candy. So she pretended she owned a chocolate store, and ate her way through it. When she'd had enough, she could ask herself some very basic questions about herself.

Of course you don't have to meditate to consider what would happen if your desires came true. In class we ask our students to write down what they would do if they received tax-free inheritances of various amounts: ten thousand dollars; fifty thousand; two hundred fifty thousand; seven hundred fifty thousand; a million and a half; five million. You might try writing down your own answers now before reading about our class findings. Just section off some paper with the various levels of inheritance and write briefly about what you'd do with each windfall. Start with the smallest.

* * *

In class, most people playing this inheritance game find it easy to dispose of the smaller amounts by paying off loans and making overdue purchases. Some, however, imagine that they would continue to pay off loans and buy essentials from their regular income and use even a small inheritance to splurge on fanciful and self-expressive things, like Phillips's trip to the North Pole.

When people are faced with the much larger inheritances, they make some really tough decisions. About half of them, on paper, drastically change their career path, admitting to themselves that what they are doing with their lives now is not expressive of themselves—discovering, when money is no obstacle, what they really want to do. Many spend up to a certain amount and invest the rest for living expenses. They then have to face the question: How can I achieve deep feelings of usefulness and self-worth?

Let Your Self Look at Yourself

With the following exercise—which you might want to tape—you are asked a series of questions as you pay attention to yourself in meditation. In order to answer the questions, you have to put yourself in the position of your Essence or true self. It is from that position that you can begin to know yourself. We are indebted to Carol Hwoschinsky for the general idea.

With writing materials nearby, sit in a chair with your feet flat on the floor and your hands in your lap. Close your eyes. Get into the state between relaxation and sleep. Notice your breath and begin to balance the inhalations and exhalations. That may take time, but let that be easy. Really relax.

Now ask yourself: Who is breathing? As you move through life with attention to millions of other things, who is continuing to breathe? Even when you're not concentrating on your breath, who breathes?

Now turn your attention to your body. Feel your body sitting in the chair. Be aware of the places where your body touches and makes contact with the chair. Feel those places. Feel your feet on the floor. Where do they touch? What does it feel like? These are sensations that go on all the time when you are attending to other things. And ask yourself these questions: Who is feeling my body right now? Who is feeling these sensations?

Now take a moment to pay attention to the sounds that you hear. There are immediate sounds and there are sounds in the distance. And ask yourself: Who is hearing the sounds? And as these sounds change, who is it that holds that awareness?

And as the sensations change, ask yourself: Who is it that is aware of the sensations? Who is it that remains constant, when all these things are changing?

Now ask yourself: Who am I? The sensations change, the sounds change, the awareness of the breathing changes, the sensations of the body are constantly changing. What is it that does not change? Who is it that I am?

Now experience yourself as a deep center of energy that might be called Essence. From this deep sense of knowing, ask yourself: What is my individual contribution in terms of this energy? How do I contribute uniquely as an individual? What's my individual expression of this energy that is called me? What pulls me to life? What pulls me to expression?

You might let an image of this energy, which is your own unique expression, come into your mind's eye. What image or symbol represents this energy that is you?

Now just be aware of what would be missing if you weren't here or if you weren't expressing who you are. What would be missing from the whole? What would be felt by others if you were missing? By the world? By the universe?

Begin to open your eyes and jot down some of the thoughts and symbols that come to you as a representation of your unique qualities.

Dive Within to Find Yourself

The real you is inside, waiting to come forth as your ideas, your decisions, your creative breakthroughs. Here are some more approaches to finding and expressing your inner resource.

Clustering. This is a word and visual game that engages your inner mind in the discovery of yourself. The technique is used by writers to get unstuck about a topic and gain new insights. Play some relaxing music and get comfortable so that you can concentrate and become absorbed in exploration.

In the middle of a piece of paper write a key or nucleus word or phrase—such as "money" or "being ordinary" or "myself"—and draw a heavy circle around it. Then free associate another word that comes off that first word. Write it down, circle it, and draw a line between the two circles. Let your mind go free on the topic and continue to write words, circling, and connecting, stimulated by either the nucleus word or any of the others.

Work quickly and easily, almost impulsively. Don't let your analytical mind get too involved. If you get stuck, try doodling; connect the circles with lines; draw in arrowheads; touch up or go over your circles. Then see if there is anything more coming out.

Be playful. Just let it flow at random. Be ordinary. Allow the words and connections to happen. Have faith that they are within you and you are merely allowing them to come out.

At some point you will sense that you are done. Stop the clustering and start writing a vignette, a paragraph that relates to the cluster on the topic of the nucleus word.

The cluster on the next page is the work of one of our students. Here's his vignette.

Money is complex. It is associated with so much that is good, and so much that is bad. Given the kind of life I want to have, money will always be something to be dealt with. Money is both the key and the lock. Opening up opportunities, freeing for other fun. Shutting, closing off others, self. Fear of letting pursuit get out of hand, losing perspective.

Clustering sample as done by one of our students.

The things, *or more accurately, states of mind can be acquired but need to be appreciated to have meaning. Appreciation requires a mental balance.*

If you want to learn more about clustering, see Gabrielle Rico's book, *Writing the Natural Way*.

The money-talks game. For this dialogue with money, close your eyes and hold a dollar bill in your hand. Feel its particular energy and qualities. What qualities do you attribute to this money? You might want to write down the qualities you sense from it. Then hold it a bit longer, asking yourself, ''What symbol or image do I relate to this money? Write down a description or draw the symbol that best represents money for you. Then after holding the bill a bit longer, answer the question, ''What am I willing to do for money, for that paper I am holding in my hand?'' Write your answers down quickly, without thinking, then hold the bill a bit longer and answer the question, ''What am I *not* willing to do for money?'' Write the answer down, hold the bill some more and then ask yourself, ''What am I willing to do with money? Write down your answer, hold the bill, and ask yourself, ''What am I *not* willing to do with money? Again write that answer down.

Now take some time to look at your answers. What do they tell you about your relation to money and about yourself?

A nonfinancial balance sheet. A financial balance sheet has one column for assets and another for liabilities. The totals balance so that the dollar value of all the assets is equal to that of all the liabilities. You can do the same kind of balance sheet, listing your personal qualities as assets and liabilities.

Take your time and think deeply about your nonfinancial assets and liabilities. Write them down in a balance sheet form. Now look at the liabilities and see how they also can be looked at in a positive light.

You can find your potential in the interaction of your assets and liabilities. The ancient Chinese called these assets and liabilities the Yang and the Yin, and said that their dynamic relationship creates everything, including the individual human from within that human. The Yang/Yin qualities listed on the next page exemplify a nonfinancial balance sheet— one that could represent you. The familiar symbol at the bottom of the page represents the interaction of opposites in the universe and in individuals. The white dot in the black and the black in the white suggest the always-present potential for change and creation. Every positive asset is related to a negative liability, which in turn has positive characteristics. With this in mind, consolidate your balance sheet into a sense of the worthy person you are.

Trance dance. In many traditions dancing is a celebration of inner strength. These people often use strong, rhythmical music and chanting to keep dancers moving; repetitive body movement can obliterate the chatter

YIN	YANG
negative	positive
passive	active
female	male
dark	light
night	day
cold	heat
soft	hard
wet	dry
winter	summer
shadow	sun

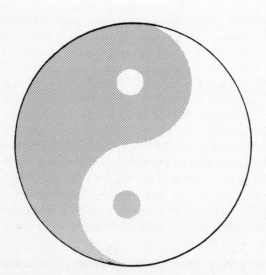

The symbol of Yin and Yang is in the form of a mandala. It represents the interaction of opposites in the universe and in individuals.

of the mind and feelings of alienation. This kind of movement or dancing gives the dancers a sense of their true selves.

You can make up your own movements—completely from within—to achieve the same effect. Americans usually don't express themselves in free-form dance, so it might be something you've never considered doing. When we do trance dancing in our class, everyone puts on blindfolds to give each other complete privacy. You certainly would not try this at the office, but you might wish to try it at home where no one will see you.

Get some music that has interesting and repetitive rhythms, something that will keep you moving. It is best to choose something exotic from another culture; not only will you have fewer associations with it, but you will find that its mysterious quality allows you to move more easily into a trancelike movement. No lyrics, please, unless they are in another language. Some chants might be appropriate, but usually they are a bit too slow to produce the trance-dance effect. Pop music is inappropriate and doesn't really work; some classical music does. We've found that Middle Eastern music is best. We especially like *Dream Dancer* by an American group called Light Rain. Some of the music on it has been used by the Joffrey Ballet, but you can make it your own.

You might want to blindfold yourself, or at least keep your eyes closed in order to keep your attention inside. Select some music that will play for something close to ten minutes. That is long enough to really get into the music and not so long that you will be totally exhausted. Start the music and just move with it in any way you want. Express yourself. Pay attention to the feelings in your body. Keep moving. Be fluid and flexible. Be yourself. There is no one to please or to embarrass you. Dance away the VOJ, negative emotions, and little pains and kinks in your body. Become one with the music. Every time the chatter of the mind comes up, move even more into the music and your body movement.

Then, when the music stops, lie on your back on the floor. Collapse into the corpse pose with your hands open, arms at your sides, and feet apart and relaxed. Close your eyes and meditate in any way you wish. Feel your own energy and joy.

Our students get everything from rushes of energy and tremendous confidence to out-of-body experiences. Some find it is the only way they can really meditate and get into that blank but energizing state between sleep and wakefulness. They very often have spontaneous insights of what they consider to be a higher order. But it is best not to have expectations when you do it. Just enjoy your Self. Be an ordinary dancer.

The I Ching. This is a five-thousand-year-old Chinese method of self-exploration and prophecy. It is called the *Book of Change* and is considered to be a book of wisdom, reflecting the interaction of the Yin and Yang forces in the universe.

"Throwing the I Ching" relates coincidentally to issues of money and self-worth because it consists of dropping three coins and looking up answers related to the fall of the coins. You've already seen how Yang and Yin relate to a dynamic balance sheet. Wall Street people consult the I Ching; psychologist Carl Jung persuaded members of the Mellon family to underwrite the publication of the American edition.

Whatever the source of the insights you get from the I Ching, it is clear that they are valuable. We believe that the coin-throwing and looking up of answers can serve as a projective device that allows your inner creative resource to express itself. But many students feel that the striking answers are unexplainable by such logic. One, for instance, threw the I Ching twice on the same question; the answer on the second throw reminded him that an answer had already been given.

There are computer programs available for using the I Ching without coins, but we recommend *The I Ching Workbook* by R. L. Wing as a guide. In it Wing says:

> *This ritual of stopping time (or "change," if you will) with a particular question in mind is a way of aligning your Self and your circumstances within the background of all that is unfolding in the universe. You can then use this perspective to gain an insight into your own destiny. When you use* The Book of Change *to peer into your future, when you experience the immediateness of your situation through divination, it is like unwrapping, unfolding, and discovering yourself—and, in the process, discovering this intricate and perplexing world to be something that you have intimately understood all along.*

Lucid dreaming is falling asleep, recognizing that you are dreaming and then taking charge, like a movie script writer and producer, by making the dream go in any direction you wish. It has been scientifically verified in hundreds of cases by Dr. Stephen LaBerge at Stanford University's Sleep Research Center. He and his subjects are connected to several physiological measuring devices while they sleep; when they are in a dream and aware of it, they make a prearranged signal with their eyes. Their experiences are collected and reported in LaBerge's book, *Lucid Dreaming: The Power of Being Awake and Aware in Your Dreams*.

If you're interested in trying lucid dreaming, LaBerge has a successful technique called MILD (for Mnemonic Induction of Lucid Dreams). You first use the approaches in Chapter Two for having and remembering dreams. Then LaBerge's technique has four steps.

1. During the early morning, when you awaken spontaneously from a dream, go over the dream several times until you have memorized it.

2. Then, while lying in bed and returning to sleep, say to yourself, "Next time I'm dreaming, I want to remember to recognize I'm dreaming."

3. Visualize yourself as being back in the dream just rehearsed; only this time, see yourself realizing that you are, in fact, dreaming.

4. Repeat steps two and three until you feel your intention is clearly fixed, or until you fall asleep.

If all goes well, in a short time you will find yourself lucid in another dream (which need not closely resemble the one you have just rehearsed).

As with any new skill, you have to really want to do it in order to succeed.

It is intriguing that some lucid dreamers, too, get satiated with having everything they want in their dreams. LaBerge says:

Such lucid dreamers no longer know what they want, only that it is not what they used to want. So they give up deciding what to do, and resign from deliberate dream control.

He shares this dream as an example:

Late one summer morning several years ago, I was lying quietly in bed, reviewing the dream I had just awakened from. A vivid image of a road appeared, and by focusing my attention on it, I was able to enter the scene. At this point, I was no longer able to feel my body, from which I concluded I was, in fact, asleep. I found myself driving in my sports car down the dream road, perfectly aware that I was dreaming. I was delighted by the vibrantly beautiful scenery my lucid dream was presenting. After driving a short distance farther, I was confronted with a very attractive, I might say a dream *of a hitchhiker beside me on the road just ahead. I need hardly say that I felt strongly inclined to stop and pick her up. But I said to myself, "I've had* that *dream before. How about something new?" So I passed her by, resolving to seek "The Highest" instead. As soon as I opened myself to guidance, my car took off into the air, flying rapidly upward, until it fell behind me like the first stage of a rocket. I continued to fly higher into the clouds, where I passed a cross on a steeple, a star of David, and other religious symbols. As I rose still higher, beyond the clouds, I entered a space that seemed a space that seemed a vast mystical realm: a vast emptiness that was yet full of love: an unbounded space that somehow felt like home. My mood had lifted to corresponding heights, and I began to sing with ecstatic inspiration. The quality of my voice was truly amazing—it spanned the entire range from deepest bass to highest soprano—and I felt as if I were embracing the entire cosmos in the resonance of my voice. As I improvised a melody that seemed more sublime than any I had heard before, the meaning of my song revealed itself and I sang the words, "I praise Thee, O Lord!"*

When I tried to understand the words that had somehow contained the full significance of the experience—"I praise Thee, O Lord!"—I realized that, in contrast to my understanding while in the dream, I only now understood the phrase in the sense it would have in our realm. It seemed the esoteric sense that I comprehended while I dreamed was beyond my cloudy understanding while awake. About what the praise did not mean, I can say this: in that transcendent state of unity, there was no "I" and "Thee." It was a place that had no room for "I" and "Thee," but for one only.

Ultimately, as the sages have told us through the millennia, when we go beyond the outer desires and turn toward our inner nature, we discover something far greater. Finding ourselves is discovering our true potential for creativity.

10

BE IN THE WORLD BUT NOT OF IT

We begin by touching our own essential natures, and then we open ourselves to friends, parents, and family. Eventually, we expand this feeling and share it with every living being, extending this openness to all of nature.... When we feel open to all existence, our relationships naturally become harmonious.

Tarthang Tulku
Gesture of Balance

That which was not, came.
That which came must go.
Muktananda, remain calm and steady
in the midst of all that comes and goes

Swami Muktananda

When I relate to the best part of a person and ignore all the other parts of that person, he starts presenting more and more of the best part of himself to me and the problem sort of goes away.

Philip Lipetz
Founder and CEO
General Molecular Applications, Inc.

Essence is in the world like gold in the rock. It is not the rock. It is in the rock.

A. H. Almaas

With each heuristic, we are asking our Stanford business students (and you) the same leading-on question: Why not try a new way? Now in this chapter the sum of the heuristics makes a more compelling demand—that you not only *do* something different, or do something in a new way, but that you also *be* something different: A full-time expression of your creative Essence.

But that's not all. As Rochelle puts it:

We're not suggesting that you redecorate the apartment you're currently living in, but that you move to another town.

So what's wrong with the old apartment—your daily life? The answer to that depends upon how you view your work in the business world.

Most people see business as warfare, a series of minor skirmishes and major battles waged for the sake of personal or company dominance. Terms such as "marketing warfare," "the cola wars," "taking the high ground," "target market," "getting the troops in line," and "product champion" are common and accurate descriptions of the way business people operate. It is taken for granted that one man's success is another's failure.

"Sure," you might say. "That's what competition is all about."

Is it?

Venture capitalist Paul Hwoschinsky says this about the competitive warfare of running:

I was in a foot race. For four mornings a bunch of us had to run a mile, and we had to do our best, whatever that meant. Well, on the final day I was clearly in the lead at the half-mile point, but my energy looked like it just wasn't going to be there for the whole mile. This fellow began to pass me, and as he did he put his hand on my shoulder, and we ran together. Then he passed me. But what we both experienced was the acknowledgement that we were putting out everything we had—that this was the very best that both of us could do, and that we were joined. Out of that experience we both won. It was an incredible connection.

Wouldn't it be more valuable to your company, and more fun for you, if you considered your working world a celebratory arena rather than a bloody one? Almost automatically, such an approach accomplishes several things:

It stimulates the best of your analytic skills. Like a dancer or a quarterback, you fit your movements into an overall plan, with fluidity, precision, accuracy, and grace.

It deepens your intuition. Like an actor, a shortstop, or a golfer, you listen with interest and respect to your own inner voice as well as to your director or coach.

It eliminates destructive competition. The string section of an orchestra knows that the goal is not to kill off the percussion section. The goal is to establish synchronization and to make harmonic contributions to an intricate whole.

It develops skills serially and painlessly. Professional athletes, musicians, and actors consider each performance a rehearsal for the next one, knowing that perfection comes only with persistent practice. As Lama Sogyal Rinpoche said in our class, "Slowly, slowly—is fast."

It develops concentration, efficiency, accuracy, and humor. Painters, writers, skiers, cooks—artists of every kind—discover early that good things move in when fear moves out.

It is far more inspiring to play to the gallery than to shoot to kill or run for your life. Even better: Don't play to anyone. Just continually manifest the best of yourself and bring out the best in others too.

And this mental framework is the "town" that can be your destination. It is also what we mean by "Be in the world but not of it"—not getting caught up in the negative aspects of a situation, not considering each success as someone else's failure, not doing something in a certain way solely because that's the way it has been done before.

AIKIDO: A METAPHOR FOR BEING IN-NOT-OF THE BUSINESS WORLD

As you began this book you might have asked whether the kind of noncombative grace we just described is possible in the midst of a business career. By now you should have some glimmer of how you can deal with the chaos of business through the peace and strength of your inner creativity. But you might still have questions about implementing it in business.

If this is so, consider the nonmartial martial art of *aikido*—not necessarily as a practice but rather as a metaphor for manifesting your creativity. When you find implementation difficult in business, aikido can remind you of your Essence, of how it can be manifested and how, when you are seemingly under attack from others, you can create a situation in which everyone can win.

Sports psychologist Joel Kirsch, who uses aikido as his main approach in his work with business organizations, introduced aikido to our class:

Aikido is a soft martial art. Martial arts like tae kwon do, *a form of Korean karate, are hard martial arts—lots of strikes, offensive reactions, things like that. In aikido, everything is defensive.*

You do not initiate any kind of attack. There is no competition or any reason to hurt anybody. The principle is a loving attack and a peaceful reconciliation.

When you're practicing with your partner, the attacker is called the oke *and the person who receives the attack is called the* nage. *Interestingly enough,* oke *actually translates to mean "He who attacks falls." So the person who breaks harmony by attacking or being aggressive in some way—falls. This is true in aikido, psychology, education, and business.*

You need not actually do any of the following exercises to get the implications for bringing your personal creativity into business. But for most people the exercises are so much fun and the results are so startling that we recommend you try them at some point. When you do, you will need a partner to read the instructions to you and to work with you physically.

Breathing from Center

Kirsch starts with a good way to experience inner balance.

Just stand with your feet comfortably apart, about shoulders' width. Take your left hand and place it on your abdomen an inch or two below your navel.

That spot is the level of your physical center of gravity. Now, your center is really in the middle of your body, in the middle of the abdominal cavity, but it's at a height of an inch or two below your navel. The Japanese call this the hara. *(The best reference for this is a book by Karlfried Dürckheim called* Hara: The Vital Center of Man.*)*

Now, instead of breathing up in your chest, simply breathe from your belly. As you inhale, your belly expands; as you exhale, it contracts. There's a reason for centering your breathing down there. Whenever people get scared or tense, they gasp; they hold breath in their mouth, throat, and chest area. If you have tight shoulders, you have some tension there, fear of some sort, some stress. But when you breathe from the belly or the hara center, you cannot help but relax. Your body will not let you be tense when you breathe from down there.

Soft Eyes

Now Kirsch shares a trick that helps you resonate with the outer world without losing your center.

Stand as you were before, but with both hands to your sides. I'd like you to get used to what's called "soft eyes." Soft eyes means that your eyes are open, but you're not focusing on any one thing in particular. For example, I see the door over there with as much emphasis as I see the woman with the sweatshirt here or the man with his glasses over there. Soft eyes means your eyes are open, that you're not focused on any one thing in particular. But your vision's not blurry, it's not fuzzy.

In soft eyes you allow your right brain to gain dominance over the left brain. That brings out your intuition, your creativity, your athletic ability, whatever you want to call it.

Now try breathing from center and holding soft eyes for a moment.

Kirsch points out that these techniques stop thinking and start concentration. Baseball players he works with find that when they think too much on the field, they lose their natural athletic ability. When they go into a fog, they perform outstandingly. They can't explain it; a soft-eyes, right-brain condition isn't amenable to logical explanation.

Balancing from Within

The next exercise has broad implications for bringing creativity into business.

Please stand with your feet about twelve inches apart and with your hands at your sides. Breathe normally and look straight ahead with regular eyes. Concentrate all your attention up in your head. To help you do that, ask a partner to touch you lightly on the forehead, chin, and neck five or six times in rapid succession. Keep focusing all your attention up there. Then ask your partner to give you a little push on your back between the shoulder blades. You shouldn't know when the push is coming, and, although gentle, it should be strong enough to make you fall a step forward.

After that you should stand up straight as before, but this time go into soft eyes and breathe from your center. Take your left hand and touch your center. Breathe from your belly and use soft eyes. Whenever you're totally focused on your center (and remember it's in the middle of your abdominal cavity), drop your hand to your side. Stay focused on your center. Just stay focused on your center.

At this point your partner should push you from behind in the same way with the same force as the first time.

Simply observe the difference between the first and the second pushes. What happened? Was there a difference in your balance?

Most people find a big difference. The first push moves them forward even when they are skeptical or actually resisting; the second does not. (If you've tried it and this doesn't jibe with your results, you might not yet have mastered the aikido concentration techniques. Practice!)

You can see how aikido provides a metaphor for creativity in business. If you're concentrating wholly in your head you are top heavy, unbalanced. And if some problem comes out of nowhere and hits you from behind, you fall on your face. You flop. The system breaks down. You're a pushover.

But what happens if you're focused on your center? You are balanced. And if a problem appears, you stay put. You have what Kirsch calls grounding.

The parallel—in business as in aikido, in art as in Essence—is balance: a balanced budget, balanced body, balanced design, balanced Essence. The strong grounding provided by a mission, expressed in qualities of Essence or in the principles of art, gives you an unshakable center of gravity. You will keep your balance against both the physically and the psychologically stressful forces of the business environment. You will be in the world but not of it.

Your Own Beam of Force

This aikido exercise, in addition to illustrating the balance you can develop from concentration and centering, can give you a sense of inner creative power.

For this next demonstration, I would like you to stand facing the wall. If you are right-handed, put your right foot slightly in front of your left and stick out your right arm directly in front of you with your thumb up and your fingers straight ahead. If you are left-handed, put your left foot forward and stick out your left arm.

Now your partner will attempt to bend your arm by pushing down with his elbow on top of your elbow joint while pulling up on your wrist with his other hand. Your job is to resist this with as much muscular effort as possible. Your partner will probably be able to bend your arm; that's not the issue here. What is important is that you'll be doing this two different times. Your partner should apply the same amount of pressure each time. The first time, I want you to tense your muscles as hard as you can. Do you feel any stress or strain in your elbow? Okay, tense them harder. Really hard, as tight as you can. Notice where you feel the tension and stress as your partner attempts to bend your arm at the elbow. Now shake out your arm.

For the second trial, stand as before with your arms at your sides and with one foot slightly forward. This time get in soft eyes and breathe from center. Be aware of your feet on the floor and put the hand you use less often (the left hand for right handers or vice versa) behind in the middle of your back. Take your time. Whenever you have soft eyes and are breathing from center, raise your arm just as it was in the first trial with your thumb pointed up and the fingers out forward. Stay in soft eyes, breathing from center. Now we're not going to deny that your arm is made out of flesh and blood and bones and tissue and things like that, but just for a moment, I'd like you to perceive, not think, but feel or experience your arm as part of a beam that is called ki *in Japanese,* chi *in Chinese,* prana *in Sanskrit,* elan vitale *in French, or for lack of a better English word, energy.*

It's like a beam of light that comes from behind through your shoulder, through your arm, your elbow, your forearm, your hand, your fingers, and it's passing from your fingers right into the wall in front of you. It's just shooting through there. Directly through and right out your fingers. You're not shooting it out. It's like water passing through a hose. The beam of light or energy is moving above and below your arm also. Your partner will use his hands to simply pack that energy into your arm, making it unbendable. It's like a cast of energy, a hard cast of energy, and your arm is unbendable. And all you have to do is allow this beam of energy or light to pass through your arm, through your fingers, into the wall, into the next wall, and then through the outer wall of the building, which is brick, and then out across the horizon.

And it's just shooting out there. Your arm is simply unbendable. You don't have to tense any muscles or anything. You just let it keep shooting out of your arm. And you just keep it shooting out there. Okay? Let it shoot out there. Let it shoot through your arm. That's it—let it shoot right through your arm. Good. Now your partner, with the same amount of force he used before, will try to bend your elbow.

The results in the second trial will probably amaze you: unbendability in total relaxation. The difference between the two trials is the difference between striving and surrendering to your inner energy.

Freeing Yourself from the Grip of Problems

In another demonstration, Kirsch had one student hold another's forearm with two hands in a firm grip. Then he asked the student being held to try different approaches to getting out of the grip. Pulling and physically striving to muscle the arm out of the grip doesn't work. But relaxing the arm produces an immediate relaxation of the grip. And going for openings in a relaxed way produces almost immediate success.

Kirsch points out that this is the way you can operate when a problem or an antagonistic person has a grip on you. Rather than getting caught up in a situation of force against force, you can simply use your inner intelligence to move to a new level.

Aikido, of course, is only a metaphor. There is a limit to the usefulness of soft eyes and breathing from center in business situations. People don't literally push you from behind, twist your arm or physically grab you to prevent you from being yourself in business. For the nonphysically violent arena of business you must operate from center, concentrating with balance, energy, and relaxation in a way that is natural to you.

BRINGING YOUR PERSONAL CREATIVITY INTO THE BUSINESS WORLD

You will find that you go through stages as you bring your creativity to work with you. You experience some success and then you seem to be thrown a bit backward, causing the inevitable frustration. If you keep up the struggle, another breakthrough comes, but this time it is on a higher level of creativity. As this spiral of stages continues, you move through periods of stability and discord, remaining aware of your grounding in Essence while being fully involved in the world. In this way you will find yourself, as Muktananda puts it, "calm and steady in the midst of all that comes and goes."

We've given the best-case scenario, of course. But what can you do when people just don't seem to be cooperating with you, when things seem to be going wrong, when the period of discord lasts longer than you think is reasonable?

Four states of mind will smooth your way.

To Be

If that sounds rather impractical to you, consider the five-thousand-year-old Chinese philosophy called Taoism (pronounced "Dowism" as in Dow Chemical Company). The word *Tao* translates roughly to "The Way." It is a state of being that defies definition, beyond that it constitutes your most positive imagination of what it would be like to be consistently creative. Living in tune with your environment is another way of expressing it. Close to the balance and harmony of the Essence qualities of joy and compassion, Taoism is more concerned with being than with doing.

In Benjamin Hoff's delightful and highly informative guide to Taoism, *The Tao of Pooh*, Winnie the Pooh is the perfect representation of the Tao. He just *is*; he solves problems gracefully and imaginatively, and lives life to the fullest. In contrast, his friend Rabbit runs around frantically, never stopping to tune in to the nature of things in an appreciative or productive way.

The classic reference to the Taoist approach is Lao Tsu's sixth-century-B.C. work, *Tao Te Ching*. It gives directions for achieving the Taoist state of being. Here's one from Chapter Sixty-six:

Why is the sea king of a hundred streams?
Because it lies below them.
Therefore it is the king of a hundred streams.

If the sage would guide the people, he must serve with humility.
If he would lead them, he must follow behind
In this way when the sage rules, the people will not feel oppressed:
When he stands before them, they will not be harmed.
The whole world will support him and will not tire of him.

Because he does not compete,
He does not meet competition.

Taoism also contributes the idea of the cycles of the universe, which always follow the sequence be, do, and have. In order to accomplish anything in the world, says Taoism, you must first *be*. Then and only then can you do and have.

If you are having trouble with the business environment, perhaps you have forgotten that message. You might revise the question, "How can I bring my personal creativity into the practical business world?" to "What do I have to *be*, *do*, and *have* in order to bring my personal creativity into the practical business world?" This can push you to such fundamental questions as these:

What do I need to BE?
I need to be myself.
Who is that?

What do I need to DO?
I need to observe and question
What specifically?

What do I need to HAVE?
I need to have understanding.
What is it that I do not yet understand?

Seriously attempting to answer any of the fruitful italicized questions can move you beyond barriers and lead you into implementation of your creativity in the business world. These questions stimulate the four tools of creativity: faith in your own Essence, absence of judgment, precise observation, and penetrating questions.

Taoism will also save you from what Joseph Chilton Pearce calls the "error-correction error" where, in trying to correct supposed errors, you get farther and farther from your real self. Rabbit, in exemplifying this state of mind, has much to teach us on how not to be.

To See

A second attitude that can keep you on the track of bringing your personal creativity into business is that of seeing, in the sense of both observing and understanding. When you see from Essence, you often see things in a new way, unlike the way others have seen.

Some people have experiences that force them to see themselves—their drives, their functions, their best contributions—in a pure way. Steve DeVore's bout with polio led him to create a business, SyberVision Systems, that increases athletic and business performance through observation. A childhood bout with double pneumonia led John Waldroup to his lifelong interest in improving early educational practices, particularly those having to do with reading instruction. Years later, a job in an alien culture—as manager of the Japanese office of a large accounting firm—spawned his creative observation of the American economy. Waldroup began buying rural land in North Carolina that is now the basis of several of his development projects.

Some of our speakers—such as Nolan Bushnell, Paul Hwoschinsky, Hap Klopp, Bob Medearis, Ted Nierenberg, and Michael Phillips—have stimulated their powers of observation by travel. Others, such as M. Scott Fitzgerald, Charles Schwab, and Jim Treybig, were awakened by their wide variety of jobs. Still others learned to see through their deep interest in people from all walks of life.

The practice of almost any of the heuristics will sharpen your powers of perception. Once you see clearly, you implement and operate in organizations with creativity instead of difficulty.

To Detach

It is virtually impossible to live with any heuristic and bring your creativity into business if you are attached to your role or to particular outcomes. You can be sure that almost every discord has some roots in attachment.

Swami Muktananda, in his *I Am That*, tells this story:

Once there was a Guru who told his disciple, "Don't become anything. Live in this world without becoming anything. If you become something, then something else will happen to torture you." One day this Guru and his disciple set out on a pilgrimage. Now, a Guru usually will not teach a disciple in a systematic way. He will not sit him down and say to him, "It is like this," or "It is like that." Instead, he will teach the disciple through a situation or through another person.

While the Guru and the disciple were on their pilgrimage, they came to the palace of a king. Outside the palace was the king's garden, where there was a beautiful cottage in which the king used to stay. The Guru went into one of the rooms and lay down. The disciple asked the Guru, "May I go to sleep in the next room?"

"Yes, you can sleep," the Guru said, "but don't become anything."

The disciple said, "Of course I won't become anything."

The two of them went to sleep. When they had been sleeping for half an hour, the king arrived at the cottage with his entourage. When he saw the mendicants sleeping there, he became furious. "Who are you and what are you doing here?" he cried.

This woke the disciple. "Who am I? I am a swami," he answered.

"What is a swami doing in the cottage of the king?" the king shouted. He took a whip from his guard and began to beat the disciple. He gave him thirty or forty blows and then kicked him out of the cottage.

The king went into the next room and found the Guru on the bed, fast asleep and snoring. "Who are you?" the king cried.

"Hmm," said the Guru Maharaj.

"Who are you?" shouted the king again. Again, the Guru just said, "Hmm."

"He's obviously a half-wit," the king said. "Take the old idiot outside."

The guards carried the Guru outside and laid him down next to the disciple. The disciple was moaning and groaning. "Oh, Guruji," he said. "Look at me. Look at my predicament. I received so many blows. My back is almost broken."

"It was your own fault," the Guru said. "Why did you have to become a swami while you were sleeping on the king's bed? You received that prasad [gift] from the king because you became something. I did not become anything, so I did not receive the king's prasad."

Muktananda goes on to say that *any* kind of role-playing can get you into trouble:

It is when you become a man or a woman, a swami or a professor, a doctor or an engineer that the pure "I" becomes the ego....Because of ego, attachment, and delusion, people are blinded by their senses. They think that they are men or women, that they are five or six feet tall, and that this is their identity. With this understanding they perform their actions. They forget the truth. They forget that they were born in the city of the body to do some great work.

People who can take the approach of nonattachment are amazingly efficient and reap rewards of great satisfaction as well as monetary success. Yet the man on the street never hears of them, sometimes not even of their companies.

Paul Cook, for instance, made sure that his Raychem Corporation was almost unknown and did no advertising or public relations for it, even after the company reached the Fortune 500 and was cited for its corporate style in popular management books. Publicity, felt Cook, would attract unnecessary competition and impair the company's ability to grow. The same can be said for individuals attempting to manifest their creativity.

And the Greatest of These Is to Love

At the outset of your creative quest, it's necessary to diligently apply concepts like surrender, pay attention, destroy judgment, ask dumb questions, make decisions, don't think about it, be ordinary. Later, these purposeful practices transform themselves into a spontaneous way of life as faith gives birth to compassion and love.

A yogic story illustrates the effect that compassion can have in your life. It seems that a good man died and, because he had done a few things wrong, he was required to spend a short time in hell. While he was there, he found that one main torture was that everyone was forced to try to eat with spoons that were longer than their arms. The food kept dropping over their shoulders. The condemned were in the constant torment of hunger in the midst of good food they couldn't eat. Then the man was transferred to heaven. To his surprise, he found that they had the same spoons there—but they never went hungry because they fed each other.

This simple story tells much about the experiences of compassion in business that we've heard both from our speakers and students.

First, true compassion for others can come only after you develop true compassion for yourself. It is only when you have experienced the best of yourself that you can experience the best in others and truly serve them.

Second, true compassion in business is just plain practical. Just as the people in heaven discovered godliness in themselves and were receiving by giving, so can business people on earth reap tremendous benefits—by giving others participation in their business, by spreading responsibility, by allowing others also to live from the best of themselves.

If business has discovered the importance of intuition in this decade, we predict that it will next discover the importance of compassion. And in both cases, it is a discovery of something that has always been prevalent in good business—and is in fact a necessity.

Benjamin Hoff, in his book, *The Tao of Pooh,* has this to say about compassion:

> ...*one of the most important terms of Taoism,* Tz'u, ...*can be translated as "caring" or "compassion" and ... is based upon the character for* heart.

> *In the sixty-seventh chapter of the* Tao Te Ching, *Lao-tse named it as his "first treasure," and then wrote, "From caring comes courage." We might add that from it also comes wisdom. It's rather significant, we think, that those who have no compassion have no wisdom. Knowledge, yes; cleverness, maybe; wisdom, no. A clever mind is not a heart. Knowledge doesn't really care. Wisdom does. We also consider it significant that cor, the latin word for "heart," is the basis for the word,* courage.

The kind of love we're talking about comes in many packages.

Steve Jobs said that Apple Computer was "an opportunity to express some deep feeling about wanting to contribute something to society."

Venture capitalist Wayne Van Dyck's Windfarms, Ltd., was as much motivated by his concern about the energy and environmental crises as by anything else. As he says, "My motivation is to make a contribution."

Jim Benham, while undergoing evaluation on his ability to sell stock, urged his clients, for their own good, to sell rather than to buy.

Michael Bilich says:

> *I personally take the tack that I have absolute responsibility to make sure that my opposite in signing a lease is getting some benefit from it. Otherwise it's going to come back to haunt me. I've even talked certain companies out of leasing with us simply because it did not benefit them, even though they thought it did. Even though you are throwing business away, these things come back to you a thousandfold, because people recognize your honesty in your approach to business.*

Compassion in business comes in the form of being concerned about your co-workers. Ted Nierenberg gave large parts of Dansk Designs to key employees, because "those are the people who helped me be worth what I am." Hap Klopp of North Face allows people to try out ideas he knows won't work, because he feels they should have the same learning experience he has had. Like Rene McPherson of Dana Corporation, he set up classes so that employees could grow within the company at no financial expense. More often than not, business leaders seem to want to share the creative experience with others. That is probably why we have almost never been refused when we ask these people to visit our class.

This kind of love goes beyond business and personal relations to the community at large. The desire to make a contribution to others and to the world moves from a vague itch into concrete expression.

Almost without exception our speakers show a concern for the world outside of themselves and their business, from small acts (Will Ackerman eschewed shrink wrap on his record albums because of the health hazard) to larger efforts: John Waldroup's educational systems; Ed Zschau and Steve Westley's political work; and the efforts of many in such areas as world peace, the elderly, and underdeveloped nations.

These people are expressing themselves and relating to other people in a compassionate and realistic way. We aren't saying that they are saints, but we do see them as truly productive leaders. And we are also saying that you can have that experience too. Complete compassion, for yourself and for others, is your birthright and your responsibility in business.

PRACTICE, PRACTICE, PRACTICE

This book is meant to open you to a new way of life rather than to add a few techniques to the way you live your life now. Our recommendations relate to techniques in the same way that altering the automotive industry relates to repairing a Chevy. Not only are the changes more profound and pervasive than you expect, but they require more stamina and bestow greater benefits.

If you are diligent in applying the heuristics, you will begin to meet challenges in a positive and successful way. You will pass the greatest test, that of being creative even when the conditions aren't exactly right. A student asked Buddhist monk Lama Sogyal Rinpoche this question:

There is a contradiction for me, because the more I need the peace and restfulness that I would get from meditation, the less time I have to do it and the harder it is to do. How can you help me resolve this conflict?

Rinpoche responded:

It is for that reason [the difficult times] *that I have been using a word called practice. The purpose of practice is to gain the perfection. So for example, you practice when you have time, like on Sunday morning or Sunday afternoon. You do that, you integrate, you know how to do that. So that when you are in a hurry you can do it efficiently and quickly, because you know how to do it.*

So you learn the practice when you have time. And you have an experience inside you. Then when you don't have time you can evoke that experience, the memory of that.

Sometimes I find also that reading just a line of poetry, a very calm saying, just a line, opens you. Inspires you. Just a line. And then just enjoy that. Or walk in a favorite park or enjoy a sunrise or a sunset. Find something that opens you, connects you with your Self.

To live a creative life in business you must find your own way and practice it so that it is available instantaneously, without thinking, in even the most difficult circumstances. Then you get into an upward spiral of experiences and tests and more experiences and more tests that gives more than just creativity in business. You become your Self in business. It becomes an enlightening experience for you.

Let's step back for a bit and see how you can get into this upward spiral. Here's one student's experience:

Because of a long weekend, I was involved in more social situations than usual. This gave me the opportunity to try a series of experiments. I would begin each session by meditating. As my breaths went in and out, I saw myself as a trap door, swinging one way and then the other. I was merely a conduit between inner world and outer world. There was no difference between what was in me and what was outside.

Then I would go out among people. Normally I am extremely self-conscious in public, always wondering how I look, anxious to say the right thing. I see the world as emanating outward from me. I am the epicenter of the universe and everything revolves around me.

This week, however, I tried to become detached from my physical presence and imagine how I look from a distance. It's difficult to describe, but it's as if my mind's eye is no longer in me but floating overhead. Rather than observing the world around me, I picture myself in the world. I see that I am just one factor in a panorama of distinct events, all of which come together to form a unified landscape. All of a sudden I am only important in that I am part of the whole. This experience did not lead to any dramatic breakthroughs but did fill me with a sense of belonging, a fraternity with everything in my environment.

His problem is not your problem, maybe. But you can develop your own way of experiencing your own creativity and unity with others and your environment. He goes on:

After awhile I wanted to go a little further. Before, when I talked to people, I always focused on my end of the conversation, how I was coming across, what I was thinking. Now I am experimenting with picturing denying my distinct physical presence. Instead I picture myself as other people and, when I talk to someone else, as the person I am talking to. I imagine that I take on the appearance of my neighbors, blending in with those around me. (This is how I interpret "Be ordinary.") The effect is that I break down the barrier between myself and the world around me. I am more relaxed and conversation flows more easily. The most surprising thing is that, despite denying that my being is removed from the world around me, I retain my individuality.

What can you do to develop your own creative approach to business? Be your own person. Use this book as a springboard, not as a rulebook. Go for the experience of creativity, because every time you experience it, you increase the probability that it will happen again. Really observe what is happening to you so that you experience everything fully. Take responsibility. Don't shy away from anything the world presents to you. Develop your own heuristics that are right for you. Live by them because they have been successful for you. Nurture your Self. Have compassion for yourself and others. Be determined about experiencing a creative life. Become totally absorbed in the moment, in whatever is in front of you to do. Be light and joyous and curious. Give yourself times of peace and silence, even within the business day, even if they are of very short duration. Acknowledge, continuously and joyfully, your Essence, your creativity, your power.

Then you will develop your own way in business and life without having to think anymore about being creative or not. You won't have to read anything more about it. You won't have to learn any new techniques. You won't have to worry about success or failure. You will simply *be* creative.

SUPPLEMENTARY READING

We consider Benjamin Hoff's *The Tao of Pooh*, to be an excellent introduction to the theme of our course and this book. In the first four weeks of our course students are required to read one of these three:

Russell Ackoff's *The Art of Problem Solving*
Edward de Bono's *Lateral Thinking*
Francis Vaughan's *Awakening Intuition*

Ackoff's book is a delightful departure for one of the founders of operations research. It is loaded with actual consulting experiences and the cartoon art of Ackoff's daughter. De Bono's book is a classic introduction to creativity complete with some interesting exercises and a fine point of view. Vaughan brings the prospective of a transpersonal psychologist to the issue of stimulating your own intuition. It is perhaps the best book on the topic.

Toward the end of our course we require students to read from three books. Our students are allowed to choose from:

Shunryu Suzuki's *Zen Mind, Beginner's Mind*
Swami Muktananda's *I Am That*
Tarthang Tulku's *Skillful Means*

Each of these small books is an introduction to a particular tradition for bringing out one's creativity. Suzuki's is the Zen approach. Muktananda gives instructions in an ancient meditation technique and delves into the Self, mantra, and Siddha Yoga. Tulku is a Tibetan Bhuddist who concentrates primarily on how to use work to create an enlightened life. If you're looking for inspiration, you'll find it in these three books.

You will find other books recommended throughout our chapters. Among them:

Gayle Delaney's *Living Your Dreams*
José and Miriam Argüellos's *Mandala*
R. L. Wings's *The I Ching Workbook*

If you're interested in a particular speaker, you might discover that he has written a book or two. Check the Laughter, Tears, and Applause listing to find out. For example there are:

Harold Leavitt's *The Corporate Pathfinders*
Regis McKenna's *The Regis Touch*
Robert McKim's *Experiences in Visual Thinking*
Michael Phillip's *Honest Business*
Charles Schwab's *How to Be Your Own Stockbroker*

Finally we ourselves have two more books in the works — one devoted completely to exercises and techniques for bringing personal creativity into business, and one that goes into greater depth on our speakers' personal expression of creativity in business.

GUIDE TO EXERCISES

INDEX